Theology on the Way to Emmaus

Also by Nicholas Lash

His Presence in the World: A Study of Eucharistic Worship and
Theology (1968)
Change in Focus: A Study of Doctrinal Change and Continuity (1973)
Newman on Development: The Search for an Explanation in
History (1975)
Voices of Authority (1976)
Theology on Dover Beach (1979)
A Matter of Hope: A Theologian's Reflections on the Thoughts of
Karl Marx (1981)

NICHOLAS LASH

Theology on the Way to Emmaus

SCM PRESS LTD

British Library Cataloguing in Publication Data

Lash, Nicholas
   Theology on the way to Emmaus.
   1. Theology
   I. Title
   230   BR118

   ISBN 0–334–02352–1

First published 1986
by SCM Press Ltd
26–30 Tottenham Road, London N1

Phototypeset by Input Typesetting Ltd, London
and printed in Great Britain by
Richard Clay (The Chaucer Press) Ltd
Bungay, Suffolk

Contents

Preface   vii

Introduction   ix

Part I

1   Criticism or Construction? The Task of the Theologian   3

2   Theologies at the Service of a Common Tradition   18

Part II

3   Performing the Scriptures   37

4   What Authority Has Our Past?   47

5   How Do We Know Where We Are?   62

6   What Might Martyrdom Mean?   75

Part III

7   Ideology, Metaphor and Analogy   95

8   Theory, Theology and Ideology   120

Part IV

9   Human Experience and the Knowledge of God   141

10   'Son of God': Reflections on a Metaphor   158

11   Easter Meaning   167

12   The Church's Responsibility for the Future of Humanity   186

13   All Shall Be Well: Christian and Marxist Hope   202

Notes   216

Index   237

Preface

Most of these papers and lectures were written or delivered between 1982 and 1984 (details of when they first saw the light of day are given in the notes). I am grateful to the following for permission to reprint: Stichting Concilium and T. & T. Clark for 'Theologies in the Service of a Common Tradition' and ' "Son of God": Reflections on a Metaphor'; Cambridge University Press for 'What Might Martyrdom Mean?' and 'Ideology, Metaphor and Analogy'; the Board of Management of the Foster and Wills Scholarships for 'Theory, Theology and Ideology'; Professor Ronan Drury for 'Performing the Scriptures'. I am also indebted to the editors of *The Furrow*, *The Heythrop Journal* and *New Blackfriars*.

Dr John Bowden and the staff at SCM Press have been models of painstaking encouragement. My wife has, as usual, been a most kindly and discerning critic: but we were, in a manner of speaking, married on the way to Emmaus.

Cambridge   Nicholas Lash
September 1985

Introduction

Because the original audiences and intended readerships of these essays were very varied, there is some variety in both scope and level of treatment. In view of the fact, however, that they exemplify a common concern or obsession, I hope that the more accessible pieces (such as the little essay on 'Performing the Scriptures') may help to illuminate the more complex and technical items (such as the reflections on 'Ideology, Metaphor and Analogy').

Perhaps the best way to indicate this unifying concern is to be unashamedly personal. I am always unhappy, for two reasons, when people describe me as a 'philosopher of religion'. In the first place, while not (I hope) quite tone-deaf or illiterate philosophically, I simply do not possess the technical expertise that would qualify me as a philosopher. In the second place, and more importantly, what I am trying to do, even when discussing (for example) issues in hermeneutics, or questions concerning the 'grammar' of religious and theological discourse, is to make a specifically *theological* contribution to the discussion.[1]

Are these, then, perhaps essays in 'systematic' theology? I would resist this description also and (again) for two reasons. In the first place, the concept of 'systematics', which 'came into theology in the seventeenth century',[2] reflects the particular problems and perspectives of the circumstances in which it arose. It is far from obvious that 'systematic' usefully describes the way in which it would be best for us, in the late twentieth century, to try to meet certain (perennial) requirements which, three centuries ago, the term may appropriately have named.

In the second place, while it is (I think) incumbent upon any Christian theologian to indicate how the different elements of Christian doctrine 'hang together', and thus to attempt 'a rational and orderly account of the content of Christian belief',[3] preoccupation with the 'systematic' may mislead us into supposing that the provision of such an account is, or can be, a more or less 'self-contained' enterprise. Theologians thus sometimes write and speak as if their subject-matter could be explored in almost total abstraction from any informed consideration of our vastly diverse, confusing, fractured and conflictual human world. It then rapidly becomes unclear what, if anything, theology is *about*. (It is not a complete coincidence that the adjective 'theological' is now used, by journalists and politicians, as a way of criticizing patterns of argument that simply freewheel, unchecked and uncontrolled by fact, reference or circumstance.)

I have some sympathy with the suspicion that 'systematic', insofar as it betokens 'tidiness', order and elegance, is a most improbable quality for a theology that would truthfully interpret the presence and action of God in our most disordered and inelegant world. I do not deny that God elegantly orders our world, but we lose all truthful purchase on this claim if we forget that the manner of his action disrupts our easy use of all such concepts, for the focus of his 'ordering' is the disorder of Calvary; the appearance of his beauty the disfigurement of the crucified.

The academic theologian is often asked: 'But why do you have to make it all so *difficult*?' I can only reply that the theologian does not *invent* either the complexity and illegibility of our history or the pain and confusion of contemporary circumstance. I would go further: part of the theologian's responsibility, I suggest, is to discipline the propensity of the pious imagination to simplify facts, texts, demands and requirements that are resistant to any such simplicity.

This resistance to premature simplification works in two ways: diachronically (in the relation of present to past) and synchronically (in the relationship of 'religion' to 'life', theology to culture, or 'church' to 'world'). Where the diachronic axis is concerned, I am appalled at the ease with which theologians often refer to 'traditional' doctrine, or what other people 'once believed', without any apparent sense of the unremitting, patient and unending labour that is required if we would catch some sense of what it was that people once actually felt, thought, meant and imagined and of the manner in which they did so. My colleague Eamon Duffy has said that 'the theological task of every age is not simply the proclamation, but the *recognition* of the truth it has received'.[4] One of the things I am trying to do in these essays is to indicate why I believe this task of 'recognition' to be much more difficult than is commonly supposed. In a catch-phrase: Christian discourse is autobiographical, and it is no easy matter to produce a truthful autobiography.[5]

What of the problems along the synchronic axis, problems (in other words) concerning the context in which such recognition occurs, if it occurs at all? Here, my complaint would be that too much theological writing restricts that context to matters of 'religion' or (abstractly handled) matters of 'meaning'. But any such restriction implicitly denies that the God of whose ways, word, and deed, it seeks to speak is the creator and redeemer, not of 'religion', but of the world. There are, in other words, no permissible limiting boundaries to the context of Christian interpretation. This does not mean that the theologian should dissipate energy in acquiring an amateur smattering of information about economics, physics, meteorology, psychology, literary criticism, and everything else. It simply means that it is incumbent upon him to discipline our propensity so to confine the horizon of the Christian imagination as to overlook the fact that it is *all* facts and circumstances which require interpretation in the light of the mystery of Christ crucified and risen. The catch-phrase, along this axis, might be that Christian truth is not 'religious' truth, but truth sacramentally displayed and exhibited. (This, perhaps, is why I often find myself quoting one little sentence from the Second Vatican Council's *Constitution on the Church*: the church is 'the sacrament of intimate union with God and of unity for the whole human race'.[6])

The story of the disciples on the way to Emmaus can serve as a parable for the task of Christian interpretation along both axes, and I have taken it as such in one of these essays.[7] Those disciples, like the rest of us, had some difficulty in 'reading' their history, and the context of 'recognition', the occasion on which things began to make sense was, not some 'religious' event in a sacred space, but an act of human hospitality.

The first two of these essays treat of problems which confront all current theology: the tension between the constructive and critical responsibilities of the theologian, and the relationship between theological diversity and the unity of faith. There then follows a group of four essays dealing with aspects of the relationship between scripture, theology and Christian living: problems, that is to say, of 'hermeneutics' or 'fundamental theology'. The next pair, which complement each other, are rather more 'philosophical' or theoretical in character, and the final group considers more directly doctrinal questions concerning (respectively) religious experience and the doctrine of God, christology, resurrection, ecclesiology, and Christian hope.

Somebody is bound to ask me how far Emmaus is from Dover. I do not know the answer, but I have the impression that the *way* to Emmaus lies along that shingle strip (notwithstanding the fact that, since I first suggested Dover as an appropriate place for doing theology, a friend has visited the same beach and seen a rather different prospect).

PART I

1

Criticism or Construction?
The Task of the Theologian

Titles are dangerous things: they are too easily chosen. Once chosen, I began to have doubts: was it really appropriate to discuss what seemed, the more I looked at it, a rather naive or *childish* question?

Not that I have anything against childish questions. Small children are neither experts nor are they wise. They are not experts, because they lack the opportunity to amass specialist stocks of information and skill. And they have neither experienced enough nor suffered enough to be wise.

Nevertheless, small children do often ask fundamental questions as a matter of personal concern.

Theologians are usually elderly, or at least middle-aged. The theologian's audience, therefore, has a right to expect of him a measure of scholarly expertise: they are entitled to assume that he knows a number of things that other people either do not know or have forgotten. Moreover, the theologian's audience also has a right to expect of him a measure of that wisdom which is the fruit of experience and suffering. (The fact that, on both counts, the audience will often be disappointed does not render their expectations the less legitimate.)

It is, I believe, part of the theologian's responsibility, a function of his expertise and his measure of wisdom, to try to ask, and to help other people to ask, fundamental questions as a matter of personal concern. There is a sense in which the theologian who is not in his second childhood is not doing his job properly. (And I consoled myself with the thought that many of the questions to which even Thomas Aquinas most profoundly addressed himself were, quite properly, childish questions.)

As I continued to rationalize my original decision, I was further reassured by the thought that the question I had chosen to discuss does at least seem to be one which is raised by many intelligent and responsible people when they complain that too many academic theologians, instead of building up the faith and strengthening the hope of the ordinary Christian, spend their time, at best, wrapped in cocoons of academic abstraction and technicality and, at worst, 'knocking' or undermining the beliefs of the person in the pew.

In other words, because of all the talk that goes on about the 'gap' between academic theology and the life, language and experience of ordinary Christians, my childish question seemed worth considering.

Moreover, much of the talk about the 'gap' between theology and Christian living seems to presuppose that 'doing theology' is the exclusive responsibility of those on one side of the 'gap': those whom we usually describe as 'theologians'. And yet this seems to me to be, from a Christian standpoint, a rather odd presupposition. I would, therefore, like to begin by considering the question: who *counts* as 'a theologian'?

Who counts as a theologian?

According to Professor Johann-Baptist Metz, 'The important questions to be asked by theology are. . . Who should do theology and where, in whose interest and for whom?'[1]

Who should do theology? Or, as I put it just now, who counts as a theologian? Why should a young, sickly, self-important, snobbish Freemason who composed innumerable pieces of music to entertain wealthy Austrians, count as a theologian? Why indeed? And yet Karl Barth would not be wrong to protest indignantly from his grave at any suggestion that Mozart was *not* a theologian.

Why should someone who read few books, and who could perhaps hardly read at all; someone who spent his life clambering up and down scaffolding giving instructions to a gang of stonemasons and wood-carvers, count as a theologian? Why indeed? And yet I, for one, would protest indignantly at any suggestion that the master-builder of Chartres was *not* a theologian.

Would not someone count as a theologian who, throughout his life, struggled accurately to depict the complexity and tragedy of human experience as a tale most truthfully told in the light of the mystery of Christ? It would seem so, and yet, most textbooks of theology contain few references to Dostoevsky.

Would not someone count as a theologian who regularly sought to express in suitable words his trust in God's love and care? Again, it would seem so, and yet, when people talk about 'theologians', they are not usually talking about children at prayer.

Human beings, like other animals, struggle to meet their needs: the need for food and shelter, for companionship and survival. Unlike the other animals, human beings are never satisfied: they seek ever to transcend present boundaries of knowledge, freedom and fragile identity. Patterns of human action embody particular conceptions, not only of what it *is*, but of what it *might be*, to be human: they simultaneously express both fact and possibility, actuality and hope. Patterns of human action – whether individual, domestic, social or political – thus symbolically express both what is and what might be meant by 'humanity'.

If, however, the meanings that our actions express and embody are to be consciously appropriated and responsibly assessed, they demand – over and above the 'language' of action – *explicit* formulation in the languages of music and story, art and ritual, politics and philosophy. The function of these symbolic constructs is to contribute to the construction of humanity.

Let me make the same point, and draw the same distinction, from the standpoint of Christian belief. If human existence, as it is and as it might be made to be, is the contingent expression of the creative and transformative action of God, then patterns of human action are not merely symbolic but are, in principle, sacramental – expressive of the mystery of grace. If, however, the sacramentality of human action is to be consciously appropriated and responsibly assessed, it demands explicit expression in the structure and consciousness of a community which declares human existence to have *this* significance and *this* destiny: to be, in fact, the history of grace.

Thus it is that the second Vatican Council described the church as 'the sacrament of intimate union with God and of unity for the whole human race'.[2] The function of this sacrament or, if you prefer, the mission of the church, is to contribute, by its declaration – in word and deed – of the mystery of grace, to the construction of a redeemed humanity, to the realization of that imperishable human fulfilment and freedom which will be the kingdom of God. The theological responsibility of the church, as sacrament of the kingdom, is – indubitably – constructive.

The works of Mozart and Dostoevsky, of the master-builder of Chartres and the child at prayer, are random examples of the sacramentality of Christian action, a sacramentality which is brought into sharpest focus, given its most explicit 'definition', in the '*opus Dei*': the public confession or proclamation of the Creed and the celebration of the sacraments of faith. Indeed, to describe the 'human work' of Christian worship as the '*opus Dei*', the work of *God*, is to declare one's trust in its sacramentality.

I began by asking: Who counts as 'a theologian'? If, by 'doing theology', we mean giving symbolic expression to that meaning of 'humanity', that account of human identity, significance and destiny, which Christian faith declares, then *all* Christian existence is, in varying degrees of explicitness, 'theological' in character. It follows that theological *responsibility* is ineluctably borne by every Christian individual and by all Christian groups and institutions. (And non-Christians, whether they are attracted or repelled by Christianity, often grasp this elementary truth more clearly than do those Christians who seek to 'pass the buck' by supposing that 'doing theology' is always *somebody else's* business.)

We have already gone some way to answering Metz's second

question, concerning where theology is to be done. Without prejudice to the particular responsibilities of teachers, parents, church leaders and academics, it seems necessary to say that if theological responsibility is borne by every Christian individual, and by every Christian institution, then theology is to be done *wherever* Christians live, work, speak, act and suffer.

I should perhaps point out that it is not my intention ingeniously to understate the particular responsibilities of the *academic* theologian. In the first place, the academic is a scholar, and it is no *easier* to be a good New Testament exegete, church historian or philosopher of religion than it is to be a good interpreter of Shakespeare, historian of the Napoleonic wars, or philosopher of mathematics. In the second place, if the Christian community is really concerned with truth, rather than with reassurance, then it should demand of its academics that they be fearless in enquiry and quite uncompromisingly rigorous in their standards of exploration and argument. (It should also, I might add, be therefore tolerant of the technicality that is frequently inseparable from such rigour.) In the third place, I believe that the academic theologian, if he or she is also a Christian believer, must accept a share of responsibility for the primary task of *articulating* Christian faith in our culture. The academic theologian is a technician, a 'boffin', but is not merely a technician. He shares the responsibility, common to *all* Christians, for continually attempting to see the wood for the trees, to grasp 'the heart of the matter', and thus to be brought himself, and to bring his hearers or readers, into ever closer contact with the single mystery of God and his grace.

My purpose, in laying the emphasis so far on the fact that *every* Christian, and not only the academic, 'counts' as a theologian, bears theological responsibility, and hence on the fact that theology is to be done, and responsibly done, *wherever* Christians are, and not only in universities or seminaries, has been two-fold.

On the one hand, I wanted to suggest that if there is, as there seems to be, considerable confusion and uncertainty as to what Christianity might *mean*, this crisis of meaning is both misdescribed and trivialized when it is presented as a failure on the part of academic theologians constructively to expound a system of beliefs which can then, as it were, be simply 'adopted' or appropriated, without effort, by other Christians.

If Christian action and Christian confession is to exhibit the 'sacramentality' that I have ascribed to it; if the church is, in *fact*, to be 'the sacrament of intimate union with God and of unity for the whole human race', then there is no field of human endeavour and human enquiry – be it domestic, artistic, literary, social, scientific, economic or political – which lies *outside* the scope of the Christian project. The contribution of the academic theologian to the common task may, indeed, be irreplaceable, but it is far more modest than many theologians (and others!) seem to suppose.

On the other hand, I wanted to undermine the widespread assumption that the academic theologian is the 'expert', the 'professional', in comparison with whom other Christians are mere 'amateurs'. I am not denying that the academic theologian has responsibility for particular areas of expertise – in New Testament studies, in church history, in the philosophy of religion, or whatever. I only want to insist, as strongly as possible, not only that, in a situation such as ours, in which problems and perspectives, data and discoveries, languages and criteria, multiply exponentially in irreducible diversity, even the 'expert' is necessarily an 'amateur', but also – and this is the really important point – that there are not, nor can there ever be, 'experts' in the knowledge of God: not even the saints, let alone the scholars.

If someone were to react: 'what a splendid liberal Protestant this Roman Catholic is! He is saying that each of us is our own expert', they would have missed the point. And the point is not that all of us are equally expert, but that *nobody* is or can be an 'expert' in the knowledge of God, because the knowledge of God is not like the knowledge of sub-atomic particles, Egyptian hieroglyphs, cost-benefit analysis or the mating habits of the great white whale.

The knowledge of God is knowledge of incomprehensible mystery, of that which is not *less* unknown the more deeply it is understood; it is a knowledge which thus bears all the hallmarks of ignorance; it is knowledge of him whose presence is felt as absence; whose touch is perceived as torture; whose approach is experienced less as the rising of light than as the gathering darkness of our dying. And if this seems a curious description of our knowledge of God, then I would refer you to the gospel accounts of Gethsemane and Calvary.

I suggested earlier that the theological task is *constructive* inasmuch as the theologian shares responsibility for the mission of the church, which I described as contributing to the construction of a redeemed humanity. My remarks in the last few paragraphs were intended to suggest that the *critical* dimension of the theological task is to be sought in the direction of the critique of idolatry – the stripping away of the veils of self-assurance by which we seek to protect our faces from exposure to the mystery of God.

In order to develop this suggestion a little, I now want briefly to consider the question: Is the quest for *truth* a 'critical' or a 'constructive' enterprise?

The quest for truth

There are many things which, as human beings, we build. We build relationships and cities, economic systems and dishwashers, laws and aeroplanes, patterns of meaning in ritual and narrative. And the strength of our constructions is a function of their truth. The relationships that founder, the cities that malfunction and degenerate, the economic systems that produce not wealth but poverty, the aeroplanes that crash, the narratives that don't ring true, the dreams that turn to ashes, are failures in the quest for truth. The fragility of our constructions is a function of their *un*truth or irreality.

Our often bitter experience of this fragility – our experience, in other words, of the contingency and mortality of the human world and all its constituents – generates at least three strategies for coping with this circumstance.

In the first place, there is the strategy of nihilism. For the nihilist, the crumbling of our constructions holds no surprises because he knows that 'truth' is a fiction, and that all our projects are laden with illusion – are temporary windbreaks against the onrush of chaos. The nihilist correctly appreciates that all our constructions are, indeed, but card-houses if their 'truth' resides *only* in our attempts to make them true; if the goal of our quest is only 'internal' to our striving. And he is convinced that there is no *other* 'truth' than that which we illusorily create; and that the object of our striving exists only in imagination.

In the second place, there is the strategy of absolutism. The absolutist seeks to ensure the permanence of our constructions by ascribing *absolute* status to whatever patterns of relationship, language and self-interpreting narrative, of economic, legal or political order, we have so far succeeded in fashioning. The absolutist correctly appreciates that, if there is truth, it resides in how things are, not in how we would have them be; that the ultimate ground of truth lies not in human judgments, but in that which makes it possible for true judgments to occur. But the absolutist *incorrectly* supposes that the ways in which we have succeeded in making things to be *is* how they ultimately and appropriately are. The absolutist construes truth as reality *grasped*, as possession to be preserved against the ravages of time and change. The absolutist is an idolater.

Both nihilism and absolutism are strategies of fear. If there is a third strategy, a strategy of trustfulness and not of terror, it will insist, against the nihilist, that truth is not reducible to illusion: that there *is* imperishable truth in our constructions, truth that has its ground beyond all human endeavour in immunity from human folly and self-deception; in reality that infinitely transcends our projects and imaginings. This strategy recognizes the legitimacy of the nihilist's question concerning the reality of truth, or the truthfulness of reality, but answers 'Yes', whereas the nihilist answers 'No'. And that 'Yes' is the fundamental form of faith in the mystery of God. Faith is the practical acknowledgment that we have *only illusion* to fear.

But we *do* have to be permanently fearful of illusion. This third strategy acknowledges the legitimacy of the absolutist's conviction that the stability of our constructions – of patterns of language, relationship and organization – is indispensable for human life and freedom; it agrees with the absolutist that truth is grounded, not in human judgment, but in that which makes it possible for true judgments to occur; it agrees with the absolutist that our constructions are not lacking in truth. *But*, this third strategy refuses to *identify* 'truth' with its particular expressions and achievements. Fearful of illusion, and perceiving any such identification, any such absolutization of particular constructions, to be idolatrous, it pursues the quest for truth along the path of dispossession. Faith in God, and in God *alone*, is inherently iconoclastic.

Before summarizing the argument so far, I would like briefly to consider one objection to the account that I am offering. Surely my emphasis on faith as *quest* is misplaced? Do we not suppose, as Christians, that we have no need to *seek* God, having already found him?

Christians do, indeed, often talk this way, but they are – I believe – ill-advised to do so. It is, of course, true that our quest never *starts from scratch*. Except we had some experience of truth, or freedom, we would not know what it meant to characterize our human existence as *quest* for truth and freedom. But it would be odd to say that, *because* we have experience of truth, *therefore* our existence ceases to consist in exploration. Similarly, except we have experience of God, we would not know what it might mean to characterize our existence as quest for God. But it would be odd to say that, *because* we have experience of God, *therefore* our quest is at an end.

It seems better to say, not that we have found God, but that we acknowledge him to have found us. In the strength of this acknowledgment, we are enabled to continue the quest – to move in the dark without terror of the dark. To put the point technically, to speak of God finding us has the merit of respecting the primacy of grace, whereas to speak as if we had found God is not only Pelagian but, by encouraging us to suppose that, having 'found' him, we now have only to 'hang on to' him, it reduces the 'God' whom we have found to a 'possession' that we have acquired – and this is just another form of idolatry.

I began by suggesting that if the life of the church is to exhibit that sacramentality which constitutes its specific identity and mission, then each and every aspect of Christian existence will be 'theological' in the sense that it will, in varying degrees of explicitness, give symbolic expression to that account of the identity, significance and destiny of the human which is the gospel message.

Theological responsibility, therefore, is borne by every Christian individual and by all Christian groups and institutions. This is a constructive responsibility inasmuch as its task is to contribute to the building-up of a redeemed humanity. It is a responsibility exercised in personal relations, in art and literature, in science and politics.

That all these bewilderingly diverse and demanding enterprises, each of which has its own absorbing urgency and irreducible autonomy, are nevertheless aspects of a common quest, a single project, is dramatically expressed and declared in the celebration of the liturgy, in which the sacramentality of human existence receives explicit, concentrated, symbolic expression. And one of the tasks of academic theology is to seek, at the level of reflection, for that *connectedness* which the liturgy enacts and exhibits dramatically. Or so at least Thomas Aquinas believed when he affirmed that the 'subject-matter' of 'holy teaching' is *all things* in their relationship to God, their origin and end.[3]

However, in all human affairs, policies of what we might call 'uncritical constructivism' result only in disaster. Except our projects are tested and purified, they atrophy – in the collapse of marriages and skyscrapers, in the failure of economic policies and the fading of dreams. Thus it is that, with an eye to the critical dimension of theological responsibility, I described 'faith' as the practical acknowledgment that we have only illusion to fear; as that trust in the reality of truth, or the truthfulness of reality, which is inherently iconoclastic in its steadfast refusal to *identify* 'truth' with its particular expressions and achievements – whether in language, art, religion or social order.

It may not have escaped your notice that the account which I am offering of the relationship between construction and criticism is really no more than an attempt to give contemporary expression to that dialectic of celebration and silence, endorsement and protest, affirmation and negation, which, for two thousand years, has been one of the hallmarks of serious Christian theology.

It is as easy to *say* 'I believe in God' as it is to say that 'all we need is love'. But if we attend, calmly and fearlessly, to the actual complexity, obscurity and intractability of our circumstances, it is not easy to give specific, appropriate, intelligible, practical *content* to either assertion. If the 'ordinary Christian' has a complaint against academic theology, it should be, I suggest, not that theologians make it too *difficult*, but that they frequently appear to find it too *easy*, appropriately to speak of the mystery of God and his grace.

You may feel, however, that my apparently casual equation of the quest for truth with the quest for God has unnecessarily confused things. Surely the specifically *religious* quest, the quest for *God*, is not to be identified with the execution of domestic, literary, scientific and political projects?

If this objection is intended as a reminder that the quest for God is not reducible to the sum total of our particular human projects, then it is legitimate. Any such reduction implicitly identifies 'God' with the aggregate of actual or possible particular realities and aspects of reality. It identifies 'God' with the world. And this is pantheism.

We are, nevertheless, gravely mistaken if, in our attempts to sustain our awareness of the *difference* between 'God' and 'the world', we construe the quest for God as one particular quest upon which we may (if we have the taste or inclination for it) be sometimes engaged 'alongside' the quest for domestic happiness, unified field theory, social justice, a cure for cancer, or whatever.

All attempts thus to construe the difference between God and the world fall into the trap of supposing 'God' to be one of a number of actual or possible objects of experience, expectation and discourse. But *such* a 'God' would be merely a 'feature' of reality, a part of the world, not the incomprehensible mystery of its origin, significance and destiny.

If God were one of a number of actual or possible objects of experience and discourse, then the concept of God would have immeasurably more restricted range than the concept of 'truth'. And such a God, such a *tiny* God, could be no more than a figment of our imagination, a child's comforter clung to against terror of the dark.

If, however, the God whom we seek, the God whose truth sustains and infinitely transcends all projects and all imaginings is, in fact, the incomprehensible ground and goal of all reality and all significance, the creator and redeemer of nature and history, then each and every aspect of the human quest – in all its bewildering, uncontrollable and often conflictual diversity – is an aspect of the quest for God, even when it is not so named or characterized. There is no truth, no reality, 'outside' the truth and reality of God and his grace.

Therefore, whatever the particular project upon which we are engaged, we are, in fact, in quest of God, or in flight from his presence. Correlatively, there is no one particular area of human experience and human endeavour that can be fenced off and labelled: Here, and not elsewhere, is God to be sought and found.

Not being one of a number of particular objects of action and enquiry, God has no proper name. 'Naming' is always 'the naming of parts', the classification of items and categories. Hence the insistence, in the Jewish and Christian traditions, that God, who eludes our imaginative and classificatory grasp, can only be described in negative terms.

This is not, it is true, the end of the story. Theological language also carries a positive freight: it declares God to be he who creates, he who saves, he who sets his people free. And the nuclear form of this positive expression of our faith, our trust, is – in the Christian tradition – the declaration that the mystery of which we seek to speak, the mystery that has become part of the truth and texture of our history, in the form of a servant, is least inappropriately addressed as 'Father'. However, before we take this name and use it to weave comforting patterns of speculation concerning the 'domestic' character of the relationship between human beings and the mystery of God, we need to remind ourselves of the context which is paradigmatic for all description of ourselves as 'sons' and 'daughters' of him whom we call 'Father'. That context, once again, is Gethsemane and Calvary. That is where we learn what it is truthfully to stand in filial relation to the mystery of God.

I suggested earlier that the academic theologian shares the responsibility, common to all Christians, for continually attempting to grasp the 'heart of the matter', to concentrate attention on the single mystery of God and his grace. And the heart of the matter is that all theological construction, all positive expression of faith in God, which cannot stand the strain of exposure to negativity, is suspect of illusion.

'Negativity' is an ugly word: I intend it to embrace, at one and the same time, experience of mortality, of loneliness and the loss of meaning; of all forms of physical and mental suffering; and of the recognition of the sheer finitude, impermanence and ambiguity of all particular human achievement.

This is, I think, a terrifying suggestion. But it does at least seem consonant with the claim that the transformative power of the *creator spiritus* is at work – not 'even' here, but *above all* here, in particularity and tragedy. I do not see what belief in the incarnation of the Word, in the divinity of the crucified, can mean if it does *not* mean this.

If we have nothing to fear but illusion and if, nevertheless, in all contexts and circumstances, we *do* have illusion to fear, then it seems clear that the appropriate exercise of the task of the theologian will, in all times and places, he critical in character, and *thus* – and only thus – will be truthfully constructive, contributive to the work of our redemption.

I would, however, like to make it clear that, in thus describing the relationship between 'construction' and 'criticism', I am not, for example, endorsing the views of one of Rudolf Bultmann's teachers who saw the task of theology as being that of imperilling souls, leading men into doubt, shattering all naive credulity.[4] That account seems to me as arrogant as it is sadistic. But I *am* saying that it is part of our theological responsibility prophetically to expose the peril of those who imperil the livelihood, well-being and self-respect of others; to provoke doubt in those whose certainties are, in fact, oppressive of the dignity and freedom of others; to shatter the credulity of those who naively suppose that they can better attend to God by failing to attend to anything else.

Theological criticism will, moreover, only be constructive if it is, and is seen to be, from start to finish, *self*-criticism in the light of the gospel of Christ crucified and risen; self-criticism of our conception of the theological task, and of the language, art, ritual and organization in which that conception, and its relationship to each and every aspect of the human quest for truth, is embodied and enacted. Without such self-criticism, undertaken in the conviction, which only God can give us, that we have only illusion to fear, our constructive efforts will be illusory and our critical activity destructive.

In the last few paragraphs, in fact, I have been commenting indirectly on the third and fourth of the questions singled out by Metz as important for theology: namely, in whose interests and for whom should theology be done? In the light of my remarks about self-criticism, these questions demand sharper expression: in whose interest and for whom is our theology in *fact* being done, and in whose interest is it perceived *by others* to be being done?

If we do theology in *our own* interest, then, whoever 'we' are, we risk putting God to human use. And that is ideological idolatry, not Christian theology. And the risk is even greater when the 'we' in question are, not the 'wretched of the earth', but the secure and the powerful, the educated and the prosperous. I am not, I think, just scoring an easy rhetorical point when I say that it is difficult to imagine the Magnificat being sung with sincerity at a Conservative Party conference.

It is the task of those who bear the burden of theological responsibility to show, quite concretely, in particular situations and circumstances, *how* it is that the question of human identity, significance and destiny may be construed as the question of God; to show how it is that the *coincidence* of these questions, as the content of specifically Christian hope, is clarified, defined and illuminated by the life, teaching, death and resurrection of Jesus the Christ.

That is the scope and character of the constructive dimension of theological responsibility. And the critical dimension arises from our need continually to purify our perception of that single mystery of grace aspects of which are symbolically expressed, sacramentally enacted, in the music of Mozart, the stonework of Chartres, the novels of Dostoevsky and the prayer of a child. Such things as these only exhibit their sacramentality when perceived, from the depth of human need and the heart of human pain, to celebrate – without illusion – our hope and responsibility for the meeting of the need and the healing of the pain.

2

Theologies at the Service of a Common Tradition

Introduction

All human utterances occur in a context. And the contexts in which they occur modify their meaning. Having been invited to reflect on the ways in which an irreducible theological pluralism might contribute to the sustaining, recovering and deepening of unity in faith, it may therefore be useful to indicate certain features of the context in which this essay was written.

The general context is that of a non-denominational Faculty of Theology in a secular university. Most of my colleagues, and most of our students, are Christians. The teachers in the Faculty, all of whom have been appointed for their competence in a particular theological discipline, with no thought given to their denominational allegiance, represent, as it happens, eight different denominations: we include Baptists and Lutherans, Anglicans and Catholics, Methodists and Presbyterians.

In such a context, a number of things soon become apparent. In the first place, the diversity of experience that we bring to our work enriches the 'catholicity' of our conversation.

In the second place, working in a secular university in which no church body has any say in the appointments that we make, our ecclesial responsibilities are less immediately apparent than they would be if we taught in a 'Catholic' or 'Protestant' Faculty. Most of my colleagues are, in fact, very conscious of their ecclesial responsibilities. But we serve less as 'spokesmen' for particular traditions than as 'mediating interpreters' of a common tradition.

In the third place, in so far as we discover (as we often do) that we share a common faith, this discovery occurs not in spite of but because of the diversity of language and experience, memory and thought-form, that we bring to our work. We discover that diversity, far from being necessarily a barrier to common conviction, can be a significant condition of the depth and quality of such conviction.

In the fourth place, however, we also often discover how fragile is our unity, how profound our divisions in faith. But, almost invariably, these divisions are not drawn along denominational lines. They lie deeper than the divisions that appeared in the sixteenth or eighteenth centuries; divisions that are now in process of being healed. They are rooted in fundamental perceptions of the relationships between theology and culture, Christian faith and human striving, the eschatological reign of God and particular patterns of human ordering in culture and politics.

This brings me to a second, more specific context in which this essay was produced. In March 1983, the Pope had just completed a visit to Central America. If there is one lesson for European theologians to learn from the struggles and the suffering of that part of the world, it is surely that questions concerning the relationships between unity in faith and theological diversity are embedded in intractable practical problems of culture and politics, power and economics, suffering and the quest for human dignity and fraternity.

Theology has a part to play, perhaps even an indispensable part, in the clarification and resolution of such problems. But any theologian who loses sight of the *modesty* of this contribution, who supposes that clarification of the theological issues can of itself be a major factor in determining the course of events, has fallen victim to the kind of idealist academic *hubris* from which Christianity in modern times has already suffered quite sufficiently.

It was with considerations such as these in mind that I decided to situate the specific issues to which I have been asked to address myself in a broad context of problems of human and Christian unity. The result, inevitably, is that instead of providing the carefully detailed examination which these specific issues undoubtedly demand, all I can offer is an impressionistic sketch of the wider agenda or framework within which such detailed examination should proceed.

Inadequate models

(a) 'Classicism'

'On classicist assumptions there is just one culture. That one culture is not attained by the simple faithful, the people, the natives, the barbarians. None the less, career is always open to talent. One enters upon such a career by diligent study of the ancient Latin and Greek authors. One pursues such a career by learning Scholastic philosophy and theology. One aims at high office by becoming proficient in canon law. One succeeds by winning the approbation and favor of the right personages. Within this set-up the unity of faith is a matter of everyone subscribing to the correct formulae.'[1]

The classicist, as there described by Bernard Lonergan with unerring irony, can tolerate diversity of expression, for catechetical or apologetic purposes. What he cannot tolerate, or even understand, is the suggestion that a genuine and irreducible diversity of methods and arguments, of discourses that are not mutually translatable one into another 'without remainder', can be other than a threat to common faith.

The 'classical', normative, concept of culture has been super-seded by an 'empirical' notion according to which 'A culture is a set of meanings and values informing a common way of life, and there are as many cultures as there are distinct sets of such meanings and values'.[2] On this account, unity of faith will find expression in a common way of life, not in common subscription to some single set of formulae.

However, to say that classicist notions of culture have been superseded is not to say that they have ceased to exist, but only that the assumptions on which they rest have been historically, sociologically and philosophically undermined. Not everyone recognizes the occurrence of this shift, and hence classicist assumptions survive like beached whales on the shores of contemporary culture. Even beached whales, however, are a force to be reckoned with. No small part of the pain and misunderstanding in contemporary theological debate arises from the fact that we have to deal not simply with the bewildering diversity of contemporary theology, but with the survival (by no means *only* in 'Rome')[3] of the classicist mentality for which the very fact of significant theological diversity is *prima facie* evidence of error and discord, and a threat to common faith.

On non-classicist assumptions, no individual, no group, no institution, stands *outside* that complex and frequently conflictual process of remembrance, interpretation, discrimination, hope and enquiry, within which meanings and values are sought, affirmed and sustained. It does not follow that there are no standards, no criteria of truth and value, but simply that *arbitration* – the reaching of decisions in matters of meaning, truth and value – is a permanent task and process in which a structured community is unceasingly engaged. Such arbitration is not, and cannot any longer be, 'gnostically' conceived as the exclusive prerogative of a group of 'authorities' or 'experts', uniquely 'in the know' and situated outside the process which requires such arbitration.[4]

(b) 'Liberalism'

For the majority of those theologians who work in the universities of the Western world, 'unity of faith' is certainly not a matter of 'everyone subscribing to the correct formulae'. On the contrary, such subscription is suspect. Pluralism is encouraged and diversity fostered. The strength of the 'liberal' tradition derives from its recognition that disagreement and diversity are evidence of the irreducible complexity of patterns of human experience, and hence of the partial and limited nature of all knowledge and understanding.

On liberal assumptions, the life of the church (as of the wider society) is thought to resemble an unending academic seminar.

But those who take part in the seminar, frequently unmindful of the social and economic privilege which makes their performance possible, tend to overlook the extent to which theoretical disagreement is but the abstract expression, in the order of ideas, of conflicts which, outside the seminar room or the 'salon', frequently find harsher and more concrete form. In other words, the weakness of theological, as of political, liberalism lies in its neglect of the calculus of power and in the inadequacy of its analysis of the grounds and sources of conflict and contradiction.

A common tradition, a common way of life, is not sustained by discussion alone. It requires the structuring of common experience, and the pursuit of agreed goals and purposes in common action. Any movement or way of life which is to sustain its identity and vitality, *as* a movement, has to be able to decide and to declare what it stands for. And if a movement or way of life is concerned with meanings and values that are central to human need and human flourishing, then, in the measure that it calls in question the operations and the legitimacy of the 'powers that be', it can expect to meet not merely with 'disagreement' but with more practically enacted forms of resistance.

Neither the 'classicist' nor the 'liberal' model can furnish us with a convincing account of the ways in which a theology acknowledged to be irreducibly pluralist in character can contribute to building up and sustaining the unity of Christian faith. 'Classicism' cannot accommodate genuine diversity, and 'liberalism' construes that diversity in too abstract or 'idealist' a manner. In search of an alternative account, therefore, we must begin by looking further afield.

The unity of mankind

The problem of 'unity of faith' is part of the problem of the unity of the church and this, in turn, is part of the problem of the unity of mankind. It is with this broader notion, with questions concerning the content, scope and criteria of the concept of a 'common human nature', that we must begin.

The unity of mankind may be a biological fact: that is for the scientists to say. But, even if it is a biological fact, even if we appropriately describe some animals (and only those) as 'human' in virtue of their belonging to a single biological species, that fact only provides us with a small part of what is meant by sharing a 'common human nature'. Whatever be the case where other species are concerned, in our case 'genetic fraternity' is not enough to warrant the claim that we share a common nature. The reason for this is that we are curious animals which do not only breed and feed, and make social arrangements (many other animals do as much). We also speak and consider, tell stories, construct policies and make plans. Our cultures, the meanings and values that inform our ways of life, form *part* of our nature. In other words, for all members of the species to share a common *human* nature, they would have to share a common life, a common hope and a common language: that is to say, a common tradition. And this, in significant measure, they fail to do. It follows that there is an ethical and political as well as a biological component to the concept of 'human nature'. The 'unity of mankind', far from being a mere biological datum, remains a permanent task and responsibility.

Moreover, on a Christian account of these matters, human beings have not only a common origin, as creatures of God made in his image; they have also a common destiny, in virtue of the promise of God who is confessed to be not only Creator but Redeemer of the world. The concept of a 'common human nature', of the 'unity of mankind', has, therefore, not only biological, ethical and political components, but also an eschatological component. The redemption of the human race would be the imperishable constitution, for all members of the species – dead, living and as yet unborn – of that common humanity which, in so many ways, we manifestly lack. The unity of mankind is, at one and the same time, a fact, a task, and the object of our hope.

The church and the unity of mankind

The church, according to Vatican II, is called to be the 'sacrament of intimate union with God and of unity for the whole human race.'[5] But the church does not realize its vocation simply by *declaring* that this is its nature and destiny. It has unceasingly to seek to become, in fact, that which it purports to be.

The practical and political implications of the church's vocation to sacramentality will be different in different circumstances. There is no single set of such implications which can be timelessly, ahistorically inferred from the doctrine of *Lumen Gentium*.[6] Nevertheless, there are some very general or formal considerations which are worth bearing in mind. The most important of these concern what we might call the 'positive' and 'negative' aspects of the church's sacramental vocation and responsibility. The positive aspect arises from the fact that it is the vocation of the church to be the sacrament, in this world, of God's kingdom. The negative aspect arises from the fact that God's kingdom is not to be *identified* with any past, present or future state of affairs in this world. Let us consider each of these aspects in turn.

Sacraments, like all symbols, must be 'legible'. An illegible symbol, like an unintelligible language, is a contradiction in terms. If only Christians are able to 'read' the church as symbolizing the unity of all mankind, then the church is not yet the adequate symbol of that unity. The church, in any particular place and time, has at its disposal an inherited symbolic vocabulary: artistic and architectural, musical and poetic, narrative and theoretical. By drawing on the resources of this vocabulary, Christians seek to show what it is that faith declares to be mankind's origins, task and destiny.

In so far as what Christians *do* contradicts what, in the language they construct from their symbol-stock, they declare themselves to be about, the 'legibility' (and hence the sacramentality) of the church is threatened. But, for all its importance and urgency, my primary concern in this essay is not with this ethical dimension of the problem of sacramentality.

Even when deeds and words, action and discourse, closely correspond, it may still be the case that the symbols used are (by and large) expressive only of the history and experience of some one class or interest-group, some one race, culture, sex or nation. In this case also, a church which drew upon so restricted a range of resources could only be an impoverished symbol, an attenuated and 'one-sided' sacramental expression, of the unity of all mankind in the mystery of God.

In the world as it is and has ever been, there is no such thing as 'universal' memory or 'universal' language. There are only particular memories and particular languages. Therefore, in speaking only 'from' some particular circumstances, places and times, the church does not succeed in speaking intelligibly or accessibly *to* those whose circumstance and experience, language and memory, are 'other' than those that it has made its own. And a church which employs a 'language' or symbol-stock that is, in fact, not appropriable as its own by other than a portion of the human race (whether that portion be Indo-European or masculine, rural or industrialized, rich or poor) can only be an impoverished sacrament of the unity of *all* mankind.

(It should hardly need emphasizing that what is at issue here is not whether the message of the gospel, as 'encoded' in particular languages and symbol-systems, is universally 'agreeable', but whether or not it is universally accessible. We have to ask, of each particular human group, in each particular set of circumstances: what is the message that can actually be 'heard' *from here*, when Christians speak and act in whatever ways they do, in fact, act and speak?)

From the very beginning, from Peter's vision at Joppa and the Council of Jerusalem,[7] Christianity has acknowledged *in principle* its vocation to catholicity. But the shift from 'classicist' to contemporary concepts of culture carries with it a qualitative shift in our perception of the implications of that vocation. 'Catholic' is what the church is under obligation to seek to become, and the quest for catholicity is frustrated by the exclusion from its symbol-stock, whether by accident or by design, of any of the irreducibly diverse languages that constitute the memory and interpret the experience of mankind. This is the positive aspect of the church's vocation: its responsibility to become, in fact, the sacrament in this world, throughout this varied world, of God's kingdom.

The negative dimension arises from the fact that the unity which we seek, that 'common human nature' whose realization will be the fullness of the kingdom of God's grace, is not attainable within the confines of historical process. There is no past, present or future state of affairs in this world that could be declared *identical* with the kingdom of God. The vocation to catholicity therefore carries with it the responsibility prophetically to resist all absolutization of historical particulars: of particular persons, circumstances, languages, images and institutions. The God who acts, appears and speaks in history remains the hidden God, the God who may never be identified with particular forms of his appearance.[8] Totalitarianism, whether from the 'right' or from the 'left', whether secular or ecclesiastical, whether of language or of organization, is always idolatrous.

In circumstances in which some such idolatry prevails or threatens, the sacramental expression or eschatological hope for the unity of *all* mankind must take the negative form of resistance on behalf of those whose particular experience and identity is being obliterated and suppressed, forgotten and excised from the definition, narrative and memory of mankind.

Unity of faith and unity of the church

(a) Aspects of unity

Having commented briefly on the concept of the 'unity of mankind', and on the church's responsibility unceasingly to seek to become that which it is called and constituted by God's grace to be: namely, the sacrament of human unity in the mystery of God, we now turn to the problem of what might be meant by 'unity of faith'. (Thus, at each stage of the enquiry, we are narrowing the area of concern.)

Here, the first thing that needs to be said is that the Christian confession that there is but *one* Lord and *one* faith, far from being an expression of sectarian arrogance or ethnocentric imperialism ('we are right and the rest of the world is wrong'), is a confession of trust in the singleness or consistency of God's grace. A Christian doctrine of God, a doctrine of God's grace as our salvation, seeks to tell the tale of *all* human experience, *all* human striving, not only as the story of our irreducibly diverse approaches to God but also, and more fundamentally, as the story of the diverse expressions of God's consistent approach to us, to human beings. Central to the Christian perception of the mystery of God is the conviction that the story of all nature and all history is, ultimately, the story of a *single* process of divine self-bestowal, a single 'economy' of creation and salvation. The unity of saving faith is the unity of God's single constitutive and transformative self-gift.

How is the unity of God's gift to appear, to find expression, in the diversity of human experience, perception and response? We distinguish, traditionally, three aspects of that single gift: the aspects named as the 'theological' virtues of faith, hope and charity.

Where charity, or love, is concerned, the unity of God's gift finds expression, or fails to do so, in reconciliation and the making of peace. Not the illusory peace that comes from exhaustion, fear, or the imposition of order, but the peace that the world cannot give and which, within the history of sin, and striving, and suffering, it never unsurpassably attains: there is an incompleteness in the peace 'made through his blood, on the cross', so long as blood continues to be shed.

God's gift is already and always one in the singleness, the consistency, of divine action. Man's self-constituting[9] acceptance of that gift is her permanent task and responsibility, the achievement of which is eschatological. Because unity in love, the peace of Christ, is God's gift, therefore failure in love, the rupture of relationship between individuals and between groups, may never simply be *accepted* (though it may have to be *endured*), with resignation, as insuperable tragic fact, as the end of the matter. Thus to accept the finality of failure would be to despair.[10] Because the unsurpassable achievement of unity in love is eschatological therefore, within history, all talk of 'complete' or 'full' unity is dangerously misleading.

Everything that we have said about unity in love as God's gift, man's task and responsibility, and as the object of eschatological hope, can also be said of unity in faith (except that, in the kingdom, faith becomes unclouded vision, whereas love, purified, endures). Unity in faith, like unity in love, admits of infinite gradations: it waxes and wanes, is stronger or weaker and may, from time to time, be ruptured and broken. Within history, all talk of 'complete' or 'full' unity in faith is dangerously misleading.

This symmetry between unity in faith and unity in love is obscured from view by the influence of the classicist assumption that 'unity of faith is a matter of everyone subscribing to the correct formulae'. Once abandon classicist assumptions, however, and the problem of how unity in faith might be discerned, sustained, sought and recovered, demands altogether different description.

Before outlining such a description, there is one further point to be made, for the sake of completeness. I have said nothing about 'unity in hope'. What is the relationship between common hope, common faith and common love? I suggest that unity in hope, sharing a common hope, *mediates* between unity in faith and unity in love. Thus, on the one hand, sharing a common hope helps those who share a common faith, a common conviction, to grow together in love, common life and responsibility. Conversely, sharing a common hope helps those who share a common life and responsibility to grow together in common conviction. Where unity in hope is absent, the quest for solidarity, for unity in life and love, degenerates into activism and pragmatism, and the quest for common faith degenerates into an intellectualist quest for formulae of concord.

(b) Mutual recognition

I remarked earlier that, on non-classicist assumptions, unity of faith will find expression in a common way of life, not in common subscription to a single set of formulae. But, since it is a common way of *human* life that is in question, it certainly does not follow that 'words do not matter'. Unity of *confession* of faith, the unity of the Creed, is integral to unity of faith, because common life that cannot find expression in common language is less than human unity. Agreement, which means agreement that finds expression in *language*, is a necessary though not a sufficient condition of the unity of any human movement or way of life.

But, if such agreement does not necessarily consist in subscription to a single set of formulae, in what might it consist, and what are the criteria of its achievement? We can approach these questions by observing, first, that the paradigm or 'focal' forms of Christian (as of Jewish) religious discourse are narrative in character. More specifically, they are 'autobiographical' both in the sense that they are 'self-involving' (which will be shown in their performance, or use, and not necessarily in their grammatical form) and in the sense that, as self-involving, they situate the speaker (or the group for which he or she is a spokesman) in a particular cultural, historical tradition: 'My father was a wandering Aramean.' Christians are tellers of a tale, narrators of a story which we tell as *our* story, as a story in which we acknowledge ourselves to be participants. The Christian creeds are abbreviated statements of a story which, as the autobiography of the narrators and of the Christ 'in whom' they seek to tell their story, is a *particular* story and which yet, as the story of the origin, course and destiny of the world, purports to express what is *universally* the case.

Abandon the unity of the Creed, and its universal import is threatened or implicitly denied. Evacuate it of its particularity, and it ceases to be capable of truly expressing any particular history.

In a culture that is, or is presumed to be, more or less homogeneous, the tension between these two aspects of the function of the Creed may not become apparent. But, once the irreducible diversity of culture and memory, history and experience, language and thought-form, is taken seriously then, as Karl Rahner remarked, 'There will no longer be any one single and universal basic formula of the Christian faith applicable to the whole Church'.[11]

In these circumstances, the unity of the Creed, no longer maintained by subscription to a single formula, will be maintained by continual quest for *mutual recognition*.[12] The stories that differently express different experiences will not be verbally identical. But, if each creed, each 'abbreviated statement' of faith, containing what are taken to be the essential elements of the Christian narrative, is to be a *Christian* creed, a 'catholic' and 'orthodox' creed, and not a narcissistic celebration of nationalist, sectarian or particularist egotism and self-interest, then it must be offered as, and be capable of being accepted by others as, a different version of the same story, not a different story.

The temptation is to suppose that such mutual recognition can only occur if there is, somewhere, some neutral 'standard of measurement' by which the adequacy of particular creeds could be assessed. But, on non-classical assumptions, there is not, nor could there be, any such standard. Not even the scriptures can fulfil this function, because it is precisely the adequacy of each creed as a 'reading' of the scriptures, through particular experience, which is in question.

However difficult it may be, from a theoretical point of view, to reconcile the unity of the creed with the diversity of its 'versions', to differentiate between different stories and different versions of the same story, a simple analogy may indicate how such mutual recognition could occur in practice. I am a native English speaker who is reasonably fluent in French. It is not at all far-fetched to imagine that, in conversation with a native French speaker who was reasonably fluent in English, we might find ourselves not only understanding each other but reaching *agreement*, while yet acknowledging that what it was that we were agreed about could not be put in quite the same way in each of our two languages.

It is important to notice that, in such situations, maintained linguistic diversity is *necessary* in order for agreement to occur and to find expression (unless, of course, one of us brought pressure to bear to force the other to abandon his native tongue); it is by no means evidence of imperfection or incompleteness in the agreement arrived at. Moreover, the process of 'dialogue' which issued in the agreement would, if conscientiously under-taken, purify the self-understanding, and render more precise the language, of each of the participants. With the introduction of this analogy, however, I have begun to touch on questions concerning the tasks of theology in contributing to, sustaining and deepening unity in faith.

The tasks of theology

The relationship between theology and the practice of faith has taken, we might say, three primary forms in the history of Christianity.

Until the seventeenth century theology was, first and foremost, 'faithful enquiry': *fides quaerens intellectum*. In these circumstances, so long as unity in faith was sustained in social practice – in a relatively homogeneous culture drawing upon a common stock of symbols – theological diversity and disagreement (often acute) posed no direct threat to unity in faith. (It was when the unity in culture or social practice was eroded that theologies – Eastern and Western, for example – became mutually unintelligible.)

From the late seventeenth century,[13] as the church became 'citadel' rather than 'sacrament', the tasks of theology shifted from enquiry to *defence*, demonstration and 'proof'. The theologian became a propagandist for church doctrines, and theological pluralism was perceived as a threat to the foundations of the single, well-ordered citadel.

From the early nineteenth century (in Protestant theology) and the mid-twentieth century (in Catholic theology), as the church began to recover a sense of its sacramentality, the task of theology increasingly became that of *mediating* between the practice of faith and the irreducibly diverse languages and social practices – in work, art, narrative and organization – in which human self-understanding finds primary expression.[14]

In these circumstances, a multiplicity of theologies becomes a necessary, but not sufficient, condition of the achievement, recovery and deepening of unity in faith. Today, it is no small part of the theologian's task, as 'mediating interpreter', to help different groups of Christians to attain and sustain that agreement, that 'mutual recognition', in which unity in faith is realized and strengthened.

To that general account, there are four comments to be

added. In the first place, theologians must exercise their responsibilities, as mediating interpreters, not only between our
diverse human 'presents', but also between the present and the
past. They must be 'recoverers of memory', using the resources
of historical scholarship to criticize the selective stereotypes by
which we shape the past to suit our present preferences.

In the second place, it is not the theologian's business, as
mediating interpreter, to foster agreement 'at any price'. The
divisions, the painful conflicts, that exist between Christians
(as between all other human beings) are not healed or reconciled
by 'papering over the cracks'. Nevertheless, the theologian, as
mediating interpreter, as the servant of unity, will seek *critically*
to reflect on the ideological distortions of his *own* group, class,
national or cultural consciousness.

In the third place, there is not, nor can there be, any grand
synthesis, any 'global theology'. Pseudo-universalist theologies
often, in their excessive abstractness and generality of
expression, serve unity in faith less well than those which
seek accurately to reflect cultural particularities depicted in
narrative and poetry. (It is no accident that the Psalms, the
Gospel narratives and, come to that, the plays of Shakespeare,
are more 'universally accessible' than any abstract conceptual
system.)

In the fourth place, the emphasis on the irreducible diversity
of culture and context, memory and experience, must not
encourage the illusion that different contexts and cultures are,
in principle, mutually 'impermeable' or illegible. Not only are
there constants of human experience – of suffering and joy,
labour and hope – however diverse their specific form and
expression. But the 'shrinking of the planet' – economically
and politically, through travel and the mass media – offers
opportunities as well as threats to the sustaining of a common
tradition, a common service of sacramentality.

Finally, what are the conditions that must be fulfilled in order
for any particular theology to assist the church in its quest for
catholicity? We might mention two. In the first place, each
theology must genuinely *be* a 'particular' theology, expressive
of some particular context and circumstance, seeking to mediate

between that context and some other particular 'place' or places
of experience, meaning and value. This necessary specificity of
the contexts of dialogue affords another reason for individual
theologians, or 'schools' of theology, to be exceedingly modest
in their ambitions.

In the second place, theological modesty has a further
aspect inasmuch as the theologian, the facilitator of mutual
recognition, works *at the service* of the church's quest for catholicity. It is not the theologian's business to tell other people
what to believe or how to believe it, but simply to facilitate that
growth in mutual understanding which may enable theologians
and their sisters and brothers 'near' or 'far off', to discover,
sustain, and deepen, common life, common work, common
conviction and a common hope. The many theologies exist at
the service of a common tradition.

All human utterances occur in a context. And the contexts
in which they occur modify their meaning.

PART II

3

Performing the Scriptures

Open a copy of the New Testament, leaf through its pages. What do we see? A letter from Paul to his friends in Corinth? Matthew's account of the passion of Jesus? John's reflections on the significance of this one man whose words and fate, whose particular flesh, 'speak' from beyond all time and circumstance? No, we don't see anything of the kind. All that we *see* is a set of black marks on white paper.

What does one do with a set of black marks on white paper? One could decide that they make so pleasing a pattern that their best use would be to frame them and hang them on the wall. (That is not a completely far-fetched suggestion: a friend of mine, an expert in Hebrew calligraphy, once wrote a letter in Hebrew to my wife; it hangs in the hall, not for its message, but for its appearance. Family Bibles are sometimes like that, decorative rather than functional.) But, confronted with a pattern of black marks that we recognize as a form of notation, what we usually do is to try to make sense of it, to read it, to interpret it.

How does one 'read' or interpret a text? The activity is so familiar that the question may seem foolish. And yet a moment's reflection suggests that, for different kinds of text, different kinds of activity count as what we might call the primary or fundamental form of their interpretation.

Two random examples. A group of people tramping across the hills, bits of paper in one hand, compasses in the other. What are they doing? They are engaged in what the army calls a 'map-reading exercise'. Another group, in a pub, one speaking, the others listening, are taking part in a poetry reading. (Notice that all of them, not just the speaker, are 'taking part' in the reading.)

There are some texts the interpretation of which seems to be a matter of, first, 'digging' the meaning out of the text and then, subsequently, putting the meaning to use, applying it in practice. That might be a plausible description of what someone was doing who, armed with a circuit diagram, tried to mend his television set. But it would be a most misleading description of what a judge is doing when, in the particular case before him, he interprets the law. In this case, interpretation is a creative act that could not have been predicted by a computer because it is the judge's business to 'make' the law by his interpretation of precedent. What the law means is decided by his application of it.

What it means to read or interpret a text depends in part, then, on the kind of text that is being used. Different kinds of text call for different kinds of reading. And the reader must take responsibility for the reading, for deciding what kind of text it is with which he or she is dealing. This does not mean that it is simply 'up to me' arbitrarily to decide what to do with a text. (It would be silly to sing railway timetables, rather than use them to catch trains.) What it does mean is that it is the *reading* of the text, rather than merely the text itself, the material object, the black marks on white paper, which embodies decisions as to what kinds of reading are appropriate. And the richer the text, the more complex its relationship to the culture which reads and remembers it, the more varied the range of more or less appropriate readings which it evokes.

Thus (briefly to anticipate the discussion of the New Testament which I shall get round to eventually) it is possible, at least in some versions, to read the scriptures for the beauty of their language; it is possible to read them because they speak to our condition; it is possible to read them because they speak of Jesus; it is possible to read them because they speak the mystery of God. And however we decide to take them, the decision to take them one way rather than another is *ours*, at each reading. We cannot pass the buck. It is, therefore, incumbent upon us to read as competently and responsibly as we can.

This raises another set of problems, because not just anybody can read just any text. I am useless at reading circuit diagrams, and I can't read Polish. Confronted by such texts, I have to pass the buck to the appropriate expert.

Open a copy of the New Testament, leaf through its pages. If it happens to be a copy of the Greek text, most of us would be stuck from the start. We would need the help of the expert. But do we also need his help in the case of texts that were written in, or have been translated into, a language with which we are familiar? And, if the answer is 'Yes', what is the relationship between the expert's contribution to the task of interpretation, and that of the 'general reader'?

At the time of the Reformation, the attempt was made to rescue the New Testament from the clutches of the ecclesiastical authorities, who claimed that they alone were competent to interpret the text, and to place it once again in the hands of those for whom it was written. But a lot has happened since the invention of the printing-press helped to bring about that particular revolution in the reading of the New Testament. We have become very conscious of the fact that there is no such thing as what any text 'obviously' means. What a text obviously *seems* to mean, at first sight, on examination may turn out to have little or nothing to do with what it meant to those who produced it or to those for whom it was originally produced. (What did *they* make of the story of Christmas, or the Sermon on the Mount, or the trial before Pilate? And how do we know, without trying to find out?) This is by no means only true of ancient texts, produced in cultural contexts whose patterns of thought and argument, illustration and imagery, memory and expectation, were very different from our own. But it undoubtedly *is* true of such texts. And so, between the New Testament and the ordinary Christian, who seeks so to read these texts as to hear in them the Word of Life, there seem to be set up thickets of expertise, insurmountable barriers of scholarship. And, as everybody knows, there is not a line in the New Testament concerning the interpretation of which the experts are not deeply divided. If the New Testament once needed rescuing from the ecclesiastical authorities (some of whom have still perhaps too tight a grip on it) does it now need rescuing from the professors of theology?

So far, I have only tried to make four simple points. In the first place, 'reading' is always a matter of interpreting a text, of putting it to appropriate use. In the second place, what counts as an appropriate strategy of use or interpretation will depend upon the kind of text with which we are dealing. In the third place, the reader cannot avoid taking personal responsibility for the interpretative strategy which he or she employs. In the fourth place, there are difficulties concerning the relationship between our use of the New Testament, as ordinary Christians, and the responsibilities of 'authoritative' interpreters, whether ecclesiastical authorities or academic experts.

I suggested earlier that, for different kinds of text, different kinds of activity count as the fundamental form of their interpretation. I would now like to illustrate this suggestion and to indicate, at the same time, something of the relationships that exist between such fundamental interpretative activity and the interpretative tasks of the scholar and critic.

There is a set of black marks on white paper which are recognizable as the score of one of Beethoven's late string quartets. Consider four people playing the quartet. What are they doing? They are interpreting the text. Even if the performance is technically faultless (and is, in that sense, a 'correct' interpretation) we might judge it to be lifeless, unimaginative. There is a creativity in interpretation which, far from being arbitrary (the players cannot do whatever they like with the score) is connected in some way with the fidelity, the 'truthfulness' of their performance.

There is, undoubtedly, an expertise which the musicians need. Behind any great performance lie years of disciplined experience. But the particular expertise necessary for good performance is neither the same as, nor in competition with, the academic skills of the textual critics who make the score available through scholarly research and the critics and music-ologists who have their own contribution to make to the continuing history of Beethoven interpretation. The fundamental form of the interpretation of Beethoven consists in the performance of his texts. The academics have an indispensable but subordinate part to play in contributing to the quality and appreciation of the performance.

Since the differences between a Beethoven score and the text of the Gospel according to Matthew are more obvious than the similarities, consider another example: a company of actors and an audience performing *King Lear*. Once again, the activity upon which they are engaged is that of interpreting a text. And, once again, the quality of the interpretation depends partly upon an element of creativity that is essential to the interpretative task. We look to the actors and the producer to enable us in some measure freshly to experience and understand the play.

But, at the end of an outstanding performance of *King Lear*, is it only the *play* that we feel ourselves newly to have understood? If we say, after the performance, 'I'd never *seen* that before', are we referring only to something which we had never previously seen in the text? Or are we also referring to an element of self-discovery which the performance had helped us to achieve? And what is the relationship between these two discoveries? Might it be that, in the performance of a great work of art, a 'classic', self-discovery and the discovery of fresh meaning in the text converge? Might it be that the 'greatness' of a text lies in its inexhaustible capacity to express, to dramatize, fundamental features of the human drama?

Leaving such questions on one side for the time being, *King Lear* does seem to be another example of a text the fundamental form of the interpretation of which consists in its performance. As in the case of the musical analogy, the expertise required by actors and producer in order to perform well is of a different order from that required of the indispensable but subordinate academic interpreters: the textual critics, historians of Elizabethan drama, literary critics and philosophers.

What both these examples suggest is that there are at least some texts that only begin to deliver their meaning in so far as they are 'brought into play' through interpretative performance. This is also true, I suggest, of such other 'works of art' as the poem, the novel and the story.

Now, at last, we are getting to the point. Not all the texts of the New Testament are stories but, taken together, they 'tell the story' of Jesus and the first Christian communities. I want to suggest, first, that, although the texts of the New Testament may be read, and read with profit, by anyone interested in Western culture and concerned for the human predicament, the fundamental form of the *Christian* interpretation of scripture is the life, activity and organization of the believing community. Secondly, that Christian practice, as interpretative action, consists in the *performance* of texts which are construed as 'rendering', bearing witness to, one whose words and deeds, discourse and suffering, 'rendered' the truth of God in human history. The performance of the New Testament enacts the conviction that these texts are most appropriately read as the story of Jesus, the story of everyone else, and the story of God.

In comparison with some other 'models' of the relationship between interpretation and discipleship, Bible and theology, scripture and tradition, this suggestion does at least have the merit of reminding us that the *poles* of Christian interpretation are not, in the last analysis, written texts (the text of the New Testament on the one hand and, on the other, whatever appears today in manuals of theology and catechetics, papal encyclicals, pastoral letters, etc.) but patterns of human action: what was said and done and suffered, then, by Jesus and his disciples, and what is said and done and suffered, now, by those who seek to share his obedience and his hope. We talk of 'holy' scripture, and for good reason. And yet it is not, in fact, the *script* that is 'holy', but the people: the company who perform the script.

Moreover, as my musical and dramatic analogies were intended to indicate, the model has the further advantage of keeping the experts firmly in their place while acknowledging their skills to be indispensable. To say that the fundamental form of the Christian interpretation of scripture is the performance of the biblical text affords no licence to that 'fundamentalism' which is still a depressingly widespread feature of popular preaching and catechesis. In order to do the job

properly, Christian discipleship, the performative interpretation of scripture, needs (just as much as does the interpretation
of Beethoven and Shakespeare) the services of scholarship and
critical reflection.

I have been at pains to emphasize that those who engage in
the activity of reading a text bear personal responsibility for
their reading. But to say that the responsibility is personal is
not to say that it is executed by isolated individuals. Personal
responsibility is not the same thing as 'private judgment'.
Christian living, construed as the interpretative performance
of scripture is, for two reasons, necessarily a collaborative
enterprise.

This is so, first, because (as I have pointed out already) the
performers need the help of the 'experts'. The second reason
arises from the nature of the texts: it takes two to tango and
rather more to perform *King Lear*.

For even the most dedicated musician or actor, the interpretation of Beethoven or Shakespeare is a part-time activity. Off-
stage, the performers relax, go shopping, dig the garden. But
there are some texts the fundamental form of the interpretation
of which is a full-time affair because it consists in their enactment
as the social existence of an entire human community. The
scriptures, I suggest, are such texts. This is what is meant by
saying that the fundamental form of the Christian interpretation
of scripture is the life, activity and organization of the believing
community. The performance of scripture *is* the life of the
church. It is no more possible for an isolated individual to
perform *these* texts than it is for him to perform a Beethoven
quartet or a Shakespeare tragedy.

Another analogy may help. The fundamental form of the
political interpretation of the American Constitution is the life,
activity and organization of American society. That society
exists (not without change, conflict and confusion) as the
enactment of its Constitution. Similarly, we might say that the
scriptures are the 'constitution' of the church.

Even in the case of societies that have a written constitution,
the interpretation of that constitution is an unending enterprise.
Times change, circumstances change. The 'meaning' of the

constitution is never definitively 'captured'; it is, ever and again, sought and constructed. Similarly, each new performance of Beethoven or Shakespeare is a new event in the history of the meaning of the text. There is no such thing as an interpretation that is 'final' and 'definitive' in the sense of bringing that history to an end.

But how can this be true of the New Testament? How can we square the recognition that the history of the meaning of the text continues indefinitely with the ascription of *finality* to God's work of revelation in Jesus the Christ? This is a large question; all I can do is offer a couple of clues.

In the first place, the range of appropriate interpretations of a dramatic or literary text is constrained by what the text 'originally meant'. This is what keeps the historians and textual critics in business. Good Shakespearean production, for example, presupposes an effective and abiding interest in what was originally meant. The author retains his authority if it is *his* text, and not some other, that we seek to interpret.

In the second place, in order to understand a text we have to understand the question to which it is an answer. We may give up the enterprise: there are texts that we no longer bother to read, or which we feel ourselves unable to make sense of. But so long as the enterprise continues, so long as we continue to seek to perform *these* texts, we are continuing to endorse that which we take the texts to have originally meant.

And if the question to which the text sought originally to provide an answer was a question concerning the ultimate and definitive character, outcome and significance of human history: and if the answer (expressed in the text) consisted in the ascription of ultimate, unsurpassable, effective significance to the words and work and death of one man, then, to continue appropriately to perform this text is to continue to ascribe such significance to this man.

To put it very simply: as the history of the meaning of the text continues, we can and must tell the story differently. But we do so under constraint: what we may *not* do, if it is *this* text which we are to continue to perform, is to tell a different story.

There is another objection to the model I am proposing which needs briefly to be considered. *King Lear* is fiction; the Gospels are, in some sense, historical. They therefore carry a built-in reference to particular, completed past events which renders them resistant to the interpretative relativism to which fictional constructions are subject.

Once again, all I can do here is to offer some clues to the resolution of the dilemma. In the first place, we would not bother to continue performing *King Lear* (except as a museum piece) if we no longer believed in it, if we no longer found it 'true to life'. Some people, I think, give up the practice of Christianity for a similar reason.

In the second place, however, the New Testament texts do not simply give symbolic, narrative expression to certain fundamental and pervasive features of the human drama (although Christians are apt to overlook the extent to which the fact that they *do* do this is part of their enduring power and attractiveness). They also express their authors' confidence in one man in whom the mystery of divine action is seen to have been embodied and disclosed.

We can perform *King Lear* even if the central character in the text had no particular prototype. But if we were to read the New Testament on this supposition, or on the supposition that the accuracy of the portrait did not matter, we should have excised a central element from what the text originally meant. We would be telling a different story.

Moreover, the texts of the New Testament not only purport to express the fact and significance of one man but, in doing so, they refer both fact and significance to the mystery of divine action. It follows that, for the practice of Christianity, the performance of the biblical text, to be true, it must be not only 'true to life', but 'true to *his* life'; and not only 'true to his life', but 'true to God'. That it is so, and may be made so, is at once our responsibility, our hope and our prayer.

I have been suggesting that the fundamental form of the Christian interpretation of scripture is the life, activity and organization of the Christian community, construed as perform-ance of the biblical text. The best illustration of what this might mean is, of course, the celebration of the eucharist. Here, that interpretative performance in which all our life consists – all our suffering and care, compassion, celebration, struggle and obedience – is dramatically distilled, focussed, concentrated, rendered explicit. In this context, the principal forms of discourse are 'practical': in praise, confession, petition, they seek to *enact* the meanings which they embody. And if, in the liturgy of the Word, the story is told, it is told not so that it may merely be relished or remembered, but that it may be *performed*, in the following of Christ.

At the end of a performance of *Lear*, the actors leave the stage, remove their costumes, 'return to life'. But, for each Christian actor, the performance of the biblical text ends only at death. The stage on which we enact our performance is that wider human history in which the church exists as the 'sacrament', or dramatic enactment, of history's ultimate meaning and hope. If the texts of the New Testament are to express that which Christian faith declares them capable of expressing, the quality of our *humanity* will be the criterion of the adequacy of the performance. And yet this criterion is, in the last resort, hidden from us in the mystery of God whose meaning for man we are bidden to enact.

4

What Authority Has Our Past?

There is a party game that Christians sometimes play. The company is divided into two groups, labelled 'conservatives' and 'radicals'. The game consists of each group sitting around wondering whether it is any longer worth attempting to communicate with the other and, indeed, whether it is proper to consider the others to be Christians at all. According to one way of playing the game, the 'conservatives' are those who ascribe authority to particular features of our past, whereas the 'radicals' are those whose ultimate authorities are 'contemporary modes of thought' or 'what people can believe today', or whatever.

As a preliminary indication of the pointlessness of the exercise, consider the question: which team does Hans Küng play for? He is often described as a 'radical', and yet the strategy that he proposes is that of 'getting beneath' accumulated layers of Christian imagery, language and organization, in order to rediscover and be guided by what the Christian programme '*originally* meant, before it was covered with the dust and debris of two thousand years'.[1] Küng, we might say, is an archaeologist, scraping away the dust to recover buried treasure. Archaeologists are admirable people but, when the game is played in the way that I have indicated, archaeology does not leap to mind as a paradigm of radicalism. And yet the suggestion that Küng plays for the conservatives would seem, to many members of that team, subversive fantasy.

It is worth noticing that neither side regards the present state of affairs as satisfactory. Both sides agree that change or reformation is desirable. But whereas the 'conservatives' conceive of reformation in terms of the recovery of the past, the 'radicals' conceive it as the construction of the future. There are historical precedents for both conceptions.

Thus, for example, medieval programmes of reform such as those pursued in the sixteenth century were aimed at the recovery of an original purity which had been smothered by the dust of historical process. Pope John XXIII would have been most unpopular, amongst Catholics and Protestants alike, had he proposed, in the sixteenth century, a programme of 'aggiornamento', of 'bringing things up to date'. Medieval reformation was, in an important sense, 'conservative' reformation, but it was hardly the less 'radical' for that.

In contrast, many eighteenth- and nineteenth-century programmes of reform or revolution were aimed, not at the recovery of the past, but at the construction of the future. This shift in direction was partly brought about by a deeper sense of the pervasiveness of change: of the extent to which change, far from being the mere modification of fundamentally invariant reality, was constitutive of the very 'stuff' of human, historical existence. Social institutions, including the institution of language, were perceived, far more deeply than before, to be human, cultural artefacts. As such, they have no features that are immune from mutability. Moreover, the process of historical change was newly perceived to be unidirectional, irreversible. In the nineteenth century, especially, this awareness that irreversible change, rather than immutability, was, as it were, the 'prime matter' of the universe, was perceived as promise rather than as threat. In such a climate of perception, it was hardly surprising that the 'arrow of reform' should be seen to point to the future, rather than to the past.

The twentieth century is not the nineteenth. We are no longer so ready to identify change with improvement, 'process' with 'progress'. Our awareness that all human institutions, including the institution of language, are subject to continual and unidirectional change is, today, perhaps less likely to engender celebration than terror, delight than despair.

Nineteenth-century 'progressivism', or 'liberalism', is as

anachronistic, as out of tune with our predicament, as are the forms of 'conservatism' with which (at least according to the 'received account' caricatured in my opening paragraph) it is locked in combat. If we are to play more profitable games, it is the problem itself which requires reformulation.

As a first step towards this, we need to consider some of the implications of the fact that (as the example of Hans Küng indicates) it is by no means only 'conservative' Christians who insist on ascribing unique authority to particular features of our past on the grounds that, *in* those features as nowhere else, the mystery of God's being and action is acknowledged to have been perceived, found form, taken flesh. I shall therefore offer one or two general observations on the problem of revelation.

Revelation and authority

Why have Christians supposed that unique and unsurpassable authority is to be ascribed to certain past events or sequences of events? One answer (perhaps the most common answer) to this question would be: because they believed that, in these past events, God has revealed himself in a manner, and with a finality, which definitively surpasses the manner of his revelation in all other events or sequences of events. Thus, at the end of the nineteenth century, Martin Kähler affirmed that 'Christianity . . . is *the* historical religion because it originates from a history absolutely normative, from historical revelation'.[2] Kähler was disturbed by a tendency, amongst his contemporaries, to 'extricate [themselves] from all authority of the past', by regarding the Bible as simply the 'source of our knowledge of our origins'.[3]

The tendency which disturbed Kähler is exemplified in the work of Professor Maurice Wiles. 'Of course', says Wiles, discussing the passage I have just quoted, 'Christianity derives from certain past events.'[4] Therefore, 'As Christians, we should seek to understand [our historical heritage] as fully as we can'.[5] In this quest for understanding, the study of scripture is irreplaceable, because it is the record of our origins. But, although it would be irresponsible (on Professor Wiles' account) to *neglect* the scriptures, they can hardly be said to be 'authoritative' for present belief and action any more than Magna Carta could be said to be 'authoritative' for present political belief and action.

Martin Kähler and Maurice Wiles represent sharply contrasting positions in a debate which, continually reshaped by changing circumstances and climates of enquiry, is, nevertheless, as old as Western thought itself. We can call it the debate between 'realism' and 'idealism', or between 'discovery' and 'construction', but such labels are too imprecise to be illuminating.[6] In the present context, something of what is at issue may be indicated by asking what might be meant by speaking of 'revelation' as 'authoritative'.

The 'idealist' knows that if sense is to be made of things, then *we* have to make it. If some circumstance is found to be revelatory of deep truth, then it is *we* who judge it to be so. He insists that we may not evade the requirements of rational responsibility by appealing to some notion of what we might perhaps call 'brute truth'. In his attempt to make some sense of things, however, he is tempted to conceive of God as a factor, perhaps the crucial factor, in the world's coherence; tempted to use the concept of God to ease the burden of the inexplicable. From such a perspective, all talk of the *authority* of revelation is suspect as an attempt to short-circuit the laborious and fragile processes by which we seek to make sense of our predicament.

The 'realist', on the other hand, knows that the world sets limits to our attempts to order it. He acknowledges that the sense of things, if sense there be, is ultimately beyond our control, and that our attempts at 'mastery' by technique and explanation are only too often destructive. He is, we might say, the ecologist of the imagination. He agrees that, if some circumstance is found to be revelatory, then it is we who judge it to be so, but he supposes the *character* of that judgment to be qualified by the fact that we are 'gardeners' rather than 'masters' of the world. From within this less Promethean perspective, to speak of the *authority* of revelation may be not an abdication of our responsibilities, but an acknowledgment of the manner in which they are best exercised.

Perhaps we could say that the 'idealist' sees the attempt at *explanation* as the paradigm of the mind's quest, whereas the 'realist' (as I have characterized him) insists that cognitive responsibility may also be exercised in contemplation, in worship.

In offering that impressionistic sketch of two contrasting intellectual tempers or strategies, I may seem to have wandered some way from the question of what is at issue in the ascription of unique revelatory authority to particular past events. I now want to ask, therefore: whatever the character of our acknowledgment that events and circumstances are revelatory of God, expressive of his reality and purpose, on what grounds do we suppose him to have expressed himself in *some* events more luminously, peremptorily, or with greater finality, than in others?

Here, the first thing that needs to be said (picking up, in a theological context, the insistence that 'brute truth' is an illusion) is that there cannot be any question of pure and unmediated theophany. The 'gods' may appear without mediation, may be im-mediately 'seen', because gods are particular objects or entities. But the creator of the world is not a particular object or entity. God is not 'a god' (although we often hide from his presence by trying to make him so). The God of Christian belief can only 'appear' as the unfathomable and hidden mystery which natural and historical events exemplify and signify. There cannot be any event, any series of events, any person, any institution, which is 'obviously' expressive of the mystery of God. And if we think that Jesus is an exception to this rule, then our christology is docetic or monophysite.

The question stands, with greater urgency. If all events, and sequences of events, and persons, and institutions, are obscurely, and ambiguously, and non-obviously expressive of the mystery of God, on what grounds do we ascribe to *some* events and persons, more than to others, revelatory status and hence revelatory authority?

It is sometimes suggested that we should choose between either attributing revelatory significance to 'history in general', 'history as a whole', or attributing revelatory significance only to some particular events: to the event (for example) of Jesus of Nazareth. This suggestion is misleading. The action of God is *always* 'particular', because the effects of divine action are particular events, and occurrences, and patterns of events. 'History in general', or 'history as a whole', are abstractions of our construction, not effects of divine action. (I suppose that, at the end of history, it might be possible to speak concretely of 'history as a whole', but, *at* the end of history, there will be no one to make the speech.)

All historical events are particular and have particular significance. The answer that we give to the question: 'On what grounds do we ascribe to *these* events, more than to *those*, revelatory significance, and hence revelatory authority?' is not unlike the answer that we would give to the more general question: 'On what grounds do we ascribe to some events and persons, more than to others, historical significance?' In both cases, there is a subtle and complex discrimination involved in making such judgments and in specifying the grounds on which they are made. And, in both cases, the judgments that we make are fragile, fallible, exposed to the risk of error and illusion.

The limits of this analogy begin to become clear, however, when we remember that no competent historian would, *as* an historian, ascribe to any particular event definitive and unsurpassable significance (for 'absolutes' do not lie in the historian's territory). And yet just such significance is ascribed, by many Christians, to the event of Jesus. Such ascription of significance, therefore, is either an unwarranted and improper historical judgment, or it is a complex judgment which is only in part historical. Let us consider the latter possibility.

Individual human beings are not interchangeable instantiations of something called 'human nature'. Each human being is particular, unique. Jesus was not simply 'a man', he was one particular man, who said and did and suffered certain particular things. Definitive and unsurpassable significance can only legitimately be ascribed to Jesus on the grounds, first, that this man said and did and stood for certain things (and this is an historical judgment) and secondly, that this man was *right* in saying and doing what he said and did (and this is a judgment of faith, of personal trust, which we suppose to be warranted, however darkly obscure those warrants may be). It follows that the answer to the questions: 'On what grounds is definitive and unsurpassable significance to be attributed to Jesus?' is to be sought in terms of the specific character and content of Jesus' behaviour and preaching as 'eschatological prophet'. If Jesus was *wrong*, then I may *admire* him, but I may not *follow* him. To decide that he is to be followed is to decide that he was not merely admirable but correct. To sum up: in view of what it was that Jesus said and did and stood for, to ascribe revelatory status and authority to him is to risk affirming him to be the expression, the embodiment, of that which he proclaimed: namely, the eschatological reign of God.

Just two more remarks, before moving on. Jesus of Nazareth lived in the past. Nevertheless, to attribute unique and unsurpassable revelatory authority to God's action in Jesus, to God's action *as* Jesus, is to attribute unique and unsurpassable authority to an aspect of the past not *because* it is past, but because this past event is perceived, even today, to embody God's promise for the future.

Secondly, the revelation of God in Christ is not an event of which an adequate account can be given independently of and prior to an account of the human recognition of that event as revelatory. Christian faith is, as recognition, a constitutive element in the event of revelation. And Christian faith has a history. It follows, first, that it makes no sense to speak of 'preserving' revelation, but only of continuing its history, which is the history of faith. It follows, secondly, that a Christian doctrine of God is a doctrine of God as the unfathomable and hidden mystery expressed in history, of God as the definitive 'appearance' in historical form of that mystery, and of God as the life, the gift, enabling us thus to ascribe such significance to the history of God's appearing. A Christian doctrine of God is a doctrine of God as Father, Son and Spirit.

The impossibility of immobility

It seems not unreasonable to describe as 'conservative' the strategy of those who not only ascribe unique authority to certain particular features of our past but who suppose that, *because* these features of our past are still to be acknowledged to be authoritative, *therefore* the terms in which we express our relationship to that past must be preserved from change. I now want to suggest that such a strategy is, in fact, doomed to failure and, in so far as it apparently succeeds, is radically innovative.

A strategy of 'preservation', of attempted immobility, is doomed to failure because, whether we like it or not, the contexts in which it is pursued are subject to continual changes which are largely beyond our control. Consider a trivial illustration. The founders of most religious orders put the members of their order 'into uniform'. These 'uniforms' were forms of contemporary dress. Fashions change, but the religious orders, in an attempt to preserve their past, preserve their habits, and the 'statement' made by the habit is radically, and unintentionally, altered. If, in thirteenth-century Italy, you wandered around in a coarse brown gown, with a cord round your middle, your 'social location' was clear: your dress said that you were one of the poor. If, in twentieth-century Cambridge, you wander around in a coarse brown gown, with a cord round your middle, your social location is curious: your dress now says, not that you are one of the poor, but that you are some kind of oddity in the business of 'religion'. Your dress now declares, not your solidarity with the poor, but your amiable eccentricity.

I apologize to my Franciscan friends. The same point could be made about much church music, all church vestments and a great deal of church architecture. I am not decrying such music, vestments or architecture. I am merely drawing attention to the fact that the one thing that ecclesiastical 'preservatism' does *not* do is to preserve the past. It obliterates the meaning of the past by transforming it into anachronism. We lose sight of what past forms originally meant and, by failing to change them, invest them with new meanings.

What is true of our sartorial, musical and architectural symbols is also true of our linguistic symbols. If we seek to preserve them – like flies in amber – they become, not symbols that express today what was meant in the past, but symbols *of* the past. It does not follow that all inherited forms, all inherited images, are simply dispensable. It may well be the case that, to allow a particular word or metaphor to die is to contribute to the silencing of the question to which that word or metaphor once formed the response. Nevertheless, the *mere* preservation of the word is no guarantee that the question is kept alive.

Any strategy of attempted linguistic immobility is doubly doomed to failure. It will fail because words and images have a history; they change their meaning. And it will fail because the history of the English language is not under the control of any sub-group of users of that language: words will not mean what we declare them to mean, simply in virtue of our declaration.

I once heard Professor James Barr say that it is not an ancient book that needs to be elucidated for the present day, but the present that needs to be elucidated in the light of an ancient book. I have been suggesting that, in seeking to elucidate the present, we do not have at our disposal any invariant symbols, words and images. Fidelity to tradition, in action and speech, is a risky business because it entails active engagement in a process of continual change. To seek to 'hang on to' the past is to lose the past and to betray the future.

The impossibility of radical novelty

Having suggested that it is through change, rather than immobility, that we achieve our fidelity to the past, I now want to turn the problem round and to suggest that it is more difficult to break with the past than is sometimes supposed.

A desire to break with the past emerges in situations in which our inheritance from the past is experienced not as the authority of a heritage to be fostered, of wisdom to be transmitted, of hope to be sustained, but as a weight on our shoulders, a chain on our legs. The present state of affairs is unsatisfactory, and the present has been shaped by the past. To ascribe authority to the past is to cramp our style and inhibit our creativity and freedom. It is time we grew up, time we liberated ourselves from the tutelage of the past.

These are the accents of a generation confident of its maturity, or restless for its freedom. Such confidence and restlessness was characteristic of the eighteenth-century enlightenment. 'Enlightenment', said Kant, 'is man's emergence from self-incurred immaturity. Immaturity is the inability to use one's own understanding without the guidance of another. This immaturity is self-incurred if its cause is not lack of understanding, but lack of resolution and courage to use it without the guidance of another. The motto of enlightenment is therefore: *Sapere aude*! Have courage to use your own understanding.'[7]

Splendid stuff, admirable in its rejection of all obscurantism and intellectual servility! But has not Kant overlooked something? Has not he overlooked the fact that those whom he encourages to use their own understanding inhabit a context and are the products of some particular history?

I have a hunch that a study of the formation of theologians might show that the 'motor' of theological radicalism is often the rejection of certain rigidities in early training. 'Radicals' are often conservatives 'on the rebound'. The trouble is that rejection does not necessarily flow from discriminating comprehension and, in the measure that it does not, the radicalism which it engenders, for all its appearance of freedom, in fact may be a form of antithetical bondage.

'A human being discovers his finitude', says Paul Ricoeur, 'in the fact that, first of all, he finds himself within a tradition or traditions.'[8] The irony of the rationalist tradition, exemplified by my quotation from Kant, is that it failed to 'discover its finitude'. That failure has been (as Marx knew) amongst the most potent sources of its power. The past never exercises authority more powerfully, and more dangerously, than when its influence is undetected.

The Enlightenment set great store by the autonomy of human reason. It is one thing, however, to *assert* the autonomy of human reason, to *assert* our responsibility to think for ourselves. But such assertion leaves two questions unanswered. First, within what limits is such autonomy in fact attainable (and for whom)? Secondly, within what limits is the pursuit of such autonomy in fact contributive to human freedom (and whose freedom)? I will say a word on each of these.

That the autonomy we assert in having 'the courage to use our own understanding' has definite limits is indicated by the very fact of language. We cannot create new languages, new modes of imagination and discourse, 'new every morning'. The language we inherit shapes our understanding of the world. 'The cultural tradition', says Jürgen Habermas, 'is a complex of symbols that fixes the world-view . . . of a social group, and thus the framework for communication within this group.'[9]

There are two points being made here. The first is that the complex of symbols which we inherit places fairly narrow limits on the range of *alternative* world-views that we can seriously entertain. Our immediate past, the inherited complex of symbols that structures our present understanding, makes it difficult for us imaginatively to grasp either alternative futures that are radically different from our present (except, perhaps, as 'mirror-images'), or those linguistic and symbolic contexts in our more distant past that are significantly different from our own. There are, at any given point in place and time, ways of imagining, of thinking, of acting, that are (for all practical purposes) inconceivable. I say 'for all practical purposes', not 'in principle'. I am not expounding a doctrine of cultural solipsism. I am only saying that, as creatures shaped by inherited language, the range of alternative imaginative and conceptual possibilities available to us is more restricted than the rationalist usually supposes.

The second point made by Habermas was that the inherited complex of symbols fixes the framework for communication within the group. Having had the courage to make use of my own understanding, I may decide that the way in which those around me perceive and describe the world is radically mistaken. I propound an alternative, bend old words to new use, concoct new words and construct new metaphors. If my readers are benign, they will shake their heads in amused bewilderment. If they are less tolerant, they will exclude me from their society (be it academic, ecclesiastical or political) as heretical, subversive or insane. It is not only in the world of the Gulag archipelago that the limits of rationality are set dangerously near the limits of what most people uncritically think. As the white-coated gentlemen hurry me along the corridor, I may console myself with the thought that I have courageously asserted my autonomy, but it is less clear that this commendable behaviour has liberated me from the authority of the past.

This brings me to the second question that I raised a little earlier. Within what limits is the pursuit of rational autonomy in rejection of the past in fact contributive to human freedom? One remembers the admirable parable in the Preface to the *German Ideology*: 'Once upon a time, a valiant fellow had the idea that men were drowned in water only because they were possessed with the *idea of gravity*. If they were to get this notion out of their heads, say by avowing it to be a superstitious, a religious concept, they would be sublimely proof against any danger from water. His whole life long he fought against the illusion of gravity, of whose harmful consequences all statistics brought him new and manifold evidence. This valiant fellow was the type of the new revolutionary philosophers in Germany.'[10]

Are there not ways of proclaiming our freedom from the past which not only leave untouched the forms of bondage that, in fact, have been inherited from the past but, by asserting such bondage to be illusory, actually contribute to our deeper enslavement? And is there not a lesson here, for those who would proclaim the gospel of humanity's freedom in Christ, concerning the manner of that gospel's effective proclamation?

Models of authority

I began by suggesting that the fashionable distinction between 'conservatives' and 'radicals', between those who ascribe authority to particular features of our past and those who refrain from doing so, was most misleading.

In my remarks on revelation, I suggested that those Christians who continue to ascribe unsurpassable authority to one particular feature of our past: namely, to the event of Jesus Christ, need not be supposed to be ascribing authority to the past *because* it is past, but rather to be declaring today their trust in this one past man as the definitive embodiment of God's promise for the future. And because there are those who suppose any such ascription to be intellectually disreputable, I tried to indicate some of the issues at stake in the debates about 'historical revelation' which have played so influential a part in theological discussion for the past two hundred years.

In support of my contention that thus to ascribe unsurpassable authority to one particular feature of our past is by no means necessarily to endorse a non-historical cultural immobilism, I argued that fidelity to the past demands that we continually risk change in the present. And in the last section, in order to keep our feet on the ground, I indicated some of the ways in which the past continues to exercise its authority especially over those who suppose themselves to be free from it.

I now want to suggest, by way of conclusion, a simple model in terms of which we might locate the various ways in which individuals, and social groups, relate to the authority of the past. Like any model, it must not be asked to do too much, but it may help. And the model that I have chosen is that of three stages in the maturation of the individual, from childhood through adolescence to adulthood.

The small child lives in a world in which what it is told is true, and in which the way things are is the way that they have ever been. The child is innocent of the possibility and tragedy of history. It can be said of the child, as has been said of the authors of the first chapters of Genesis, that, for him, 'what is true in principle is true from the beginning'. For the child, the authority of the past – the received wisdom of parents and teachers and stories – provides security of information and guidance, of meaning and value. But childhood is a passing phase, and the adult who seeks to recover this lost world we describe not as childlike but as infantile. Where the authority of the past is concerned, there are questions which the small child cannot ask, but with which it is incumbent upon the adult to come to grips. In the child's world, fidelity to the past demands that we do or say today whatever was done or said yesterday. This assumption, admirable in the small child, is impermissible for the adult. Fundamentalism, then, is a form of infantilism.

The child does not yet know the dignity and agony of personal autonomy. The adolescent is in initial possession of this ambiguous knowledge. And the adolescent, exploring its autonomy, often supposes that autonomy is achieved through the rejection of parental authority. The adolescent is an icono-clast, for whom the authority of the past is an idol to be broken, a bondage from which it would be free. Only subsequent experience will reveal, often in circumstances of considerable suffering, the illusory character of freedom won through indis-criminate rejection of the authority of the past. In a word, Christian rationalism, whether in its eighteenth-century or more recent manifestations, is a form of adolescence.

The child, sheltered by authority, knows that it enjoys security and freedom. The adolescent, conscious of insecurity and bondage, seeks to *possess* security and freedom through personal autonomy. And the adult? Adulthood is a condition which few of us attain, but which, in the measure of its attainment, we know ourselves constrained, in integrity, continually to seek. The adult knows that truth, security and freedom are never *objects possessed*; that in the measure that they are claimed, clung on to, they slip from our grasp as we regress to infantilism or adolescence. The adult knows that the uncritical innocence of the child, its unquestioning acceptance of the authority of the past, is irrecoverable. The adult also knows that individuals and social groups liberate themselves from the oppressive, restrictive features of their past not by ignoring that past, or angrily rejecting it, but by critically appropriating it. And the therapeutic, salvific task of critical appropriation is never complete because it is, at the same time, the task of constructing the future.

Where the following of Christ is concerned, the adult Christ-ian acknowledges the obligation to risk attempting the recovery and reconstruction, in continually changing circumstances, of the fundamental aims and commitments of past generations of Christians and, first and last, of Jesus himself. He knows that *'the'* faith is an abstraction, and that 'faith' is not a possession, but the character of a quest. He knows that (in this quest) a trust, an obedience, patterned on the obedience of Jesus entails having the courage to live, work and die in the darkness in which Jesus himself worked and died.

What authority has our past? For all people, whether or not they are religious believers, the past has the authority of whatever truth and value have been perceived and achieved in the past, truth and value that can only be 'recovered' and sustained to the extent that we risk critically appropriating that past in transformation of the present for the construction of our future. For Christians, for men and women committed to the following of Christ, there speaks today, from the past, a voice that authoritatively declares (and the future tense is of fundamental importance) that 'the truth shall set you free'.

5

How Do We Know Where We Are?

Can we have a 'theology of history'?

According to Butler's *Analogy*, the 'conviction arising from [the] kind of proof' appropriate to the 'evidence' of Christianity 'may be compared to what they call *the effect* in architecture or other works of art; a result from a great number of things so and so disposed, and taken into one view'.[1]

As adopted by Newman and his colleagues at Oriel, the requirement to 'take a view' became a kind of shorthand for an entire educational and intellectual strategy. And if they were impatient of those who potter around, accumulating (often with painstaking precision) ever greater quantities of data, burying themselves in the detritus of their unshaped scholarship, they were equally critical of those who disdain the rigour and discipline of meticulous research in favour of self-indulgent speculative synthesis: this, for Newman, was 'viewiness'.

But, between the poles of 'viewiness' and 'mere learning' there stood the possibility, or at least the requirement, of 'taking a view'. To have a 'view' of some matter is to accept personal responsibility for the perspective opened up by the interplay of data laboriously and dispassionately acquired with the synthesizing power of intellect and imagination. The person who has a view of the matter knows where they stand and why.[2]

'When we have lost our way', wrote Newman in 1845, 'we mount up to some eminence to look about us', we do not plunge 'into the nearest thicket to find [our] bearings.'[3] (It is worth noticing that he is explaining to a correspondent why he had written the *Essay on Development*, a work which is surely in some sense an exercise in the theology of history.)

Twenty years later, in 1867, we find Newman complaining that his friend Ignatius Ryder 'is ever deep in Devonshire lanes – you never know the lie of the country from him – he never takes his readers up to an eminence, whence he could make a map of it'.[4]

That image of the hill-top, or 'eminence', is put to very different use in some lines from Hölderlin which Professor W. B. Gallie set at the start of his study of *Philosophy and the Historical Understanding*:[5]

> Since round us are heaped
> The summits of time,
> And those that are dearest are near yet languishing on
> Most separate mountains,
> So give us innocent water,
> O give us wings of the mind most faithfully
> To cross over and to return.[6]

Is is possible to say anything sensible, today, about the 'philosophy of history'? For some people the impossibility of the project derives primarily from the fact that the mind has not been given wings: that, whether we like it or not, we languish on separate mountains, conscious of our affinity (through membership of a single species) with those who inhabit very different times and circumstances, yet unable to *translate* that affinity into the kind of generalized understanding which would enable us to construct a single narrative of the sense and direction of things. We can say how things seem 'from here', but we cannot lay claim to any larger knowledge of the way of the world. I am suggesting that Hölderlin's 'most separate mountains' might be taken as a pictorial version of some of the difficulties which led Collingwood to elaborate his doctrine of 'absolute presuppositions'[7] and, in so doing, 'to abandon a philosophy of history'.[8]

For other people, the impossibility of constructing a philosophy of history derives primarily from the fact that 'deep in Devonshire lanes' is, quite simply, where we *are*, and that to regret, or to seek to transcend this situation is to be in bondage to illusion. There simply *is* no 'summit' from which we could look down on the world and 'make a map' of its countryside.

This would be one way of characterizing the position of those, such as Nietzsche, Heidegger und Wittgenstein, who sought to unmask as illusory the expectation that it might be possible to 'understand ourselves from some Archimedian standpoint outside the system to which we belong (taking the God's eye view)'.[9] Such thinkers sought to cure us of 'the inveterate idea that we can get outside our world in some more substantial sense than that we talk about our world'.[10] If there is sense to be made, it can only be made *here*, where we are, and not as if we were, or could be, nowhere in particular. And even when we talk about our world, our talk remains a feature of the world of which we speak.

But if the philosophy of history now seems so questionable an enterprise, how much more problematic must be the idea of a *theology* of history. If 'the meaning of history', the idea that history has some single sense or direction, is a will-o'-the-wisp, how much more insubstantial must be any attempt to perceive how such 'meaning' stands in relation to the mystery of God.

Nevertheless, Newman is surely right that, when we have 'lost our way', we would be ill-advised to plunge into the nearest thicket to take our bearings.[11] To do so would be not only foolish, but irresponsible. In Christian terms, it might be tantamount to despair. And, if so, it is incumbent upon us to attempt some formulation of our hope, some account of where we take ourselves and all people to be in relation to the mystery of God.

To put it as baldly as possible: whatever be the case with some other religions, I do not see how a *Christian* theology could fail to be, in some sense, a 'theology of history'. If, therefore, we acknowledge 'theology of history' to be the name of an enterprise that is simply impossible, then it is the possibility of Christian theology itself that is, in such acknowledgment, denied. So, here are some brief reflections on the problem of a 'theology of history', the relationship between the sections of which is not *linear*. Taking my cue from Bishop Butler it is, at best, contributive to an 'effect'.

The middle distance

The options with which we are presented in these matters are often exceedingly stark: either 'all the kingdoms of the world', shown from 'a very high mountain' in 'a moment of time',[12] or the view from the parish pump; either unwarranted metaphysical assertion or unrestrained relativism; either 'absolute knowledge' or 'mere belief'.

We should resist these disjunctions. There are no good reasons for being pressured into choosing *either* the 'distant scene' *or* just 'one step' ahead in the 'encircling gloom'.[13] It is possible to attempt to set one's gaze, in respect of both the past and the future, on what we might call the 'middle distance'.[14]

In respect of the past, such a strategy would entail attempting to 'transcend' present circumstances and preoccupations sufficiently to discover something of where we have come from, and of how we came to be the way we are, without succumbing to the illusion that the continuity and 'sense of direction' that we thereby discern have, or can be claimed to have, 'absolute' validity. We can, without attempting to get 'outside' our world, at least seek to extend its horizons.

The possibility of doing so is grounded in the fact that we are not simply 'on our own'. Each individual, each generation, is shaped by the tradition which precedes and constitutes it. Memory may play tricks, and our attempts truthfully to 'read' the traces of the past are not without difficulty. Nevertheless, 'absolute relativism', elevating such difficulty into a metaphysical principle, is simply loss of nerve disguised as philosophy.

In respect of the future, the situation is somewhat different (because, whereas the past once was, the future does not yet exist) but it is, once again, a matter of keeping one's nerve. The strategy of focussing on the 'middle distance' is a strategy of *hopefulness*, of the refusal to succumb either to optimism or despair. Despair is 'near-sighted', it allows the sharp and painful edges of existing fact to obliterate from view the possibilities inherent in the present situation. Optimism, on the other hand, is 'far-sighted': its vision wanders to distant horizons which appear attractive because they are, in fact, invisible.[15]

To seek to focus both memory and hope on the 'middle distance' is to acknowledge that historical understanding, whether religious or secular, is at once possible, provisional and unstable.

It is unstable because we are always under pressure, from present concerns and predicaments, either to contract our vision, succumbing to the egocentricity of despair or, fearful of the fragility of our finitude, so to expand that vision as to take in invisible 'ultimate' horizons of either memory or expectation, enabling us to 'see' the *principium* and *finis* of things.

Historical understanding is provisional because, as circumstances and perceptions change, so too does the content of both memory and expectation. Is this acknowledgment dangerously or excessively 'relativist'? Dangerously so, perhaps, but there is no escaping the danger. The 'absolutist' does not *avoid* the danger: he merely succumbs to fantasy; and fantasy, allied with power, becomes the imagination of oppression. Excessively? But what are the non-illusory alternatives? The assumption that *all* 'relativism' in these matters is 'absolute' relativism is one that springs from the mistaken assumption that relativism can be 'absolutely' avoided.

Moreover, whatever be the case where *philosophies* of history are concerned, one essential factor in a Christian *theology* of history is the recognition that the 'nerve' that is necessary, if we are to keep our sights set on the 'middle distance', expresses the conviction that we are, in fact, *enabled* to exist and act in a truthful relationship to both past and future. In other words, a theology of history acknowledges that the 'truth' of history is, in the last analysis, truth as grace given, not as artefact constructed or commodity possessed.

All history is history of grace

The Christian, the creature who seeks to be obedient (and, in that obedience, to find freedom and autonomy), the disciple who seeks to be faithful (and, in that fidelity, to find life) confesses all truth to be grace given. A Christian theology of history is, or should be, simply the attempt to indicate the implications of that confession.

If we wanted a slogan, it might be: memory is possible and hope permitted because all history is the history of grace.[16] But, if misunderstanding is to be avoided, there are two directions in which that slogan needs to be spelt out.

On the one hand, to say that all history is the history of grace is not to deny that that which is *constituted* by grace, namely 'nature', has its own intelligibility, regularity and autonomy. Grace is not a colour, sound or number; it cannot feature in any table of the categories. There have been theologies of history that have succumbed to the 'theocratic' temptation of collapsing all secularity into a single, undifferentiated process of salvation or damnation.[17] And, from such short-circuiting, appalling human suffering has ensued (not to mention a great deal of sheer vulgarity).

On the other hand, to say that all history is the history of grace is to insist that distinctions between 'creation' and 'salvation' are not to be drawn in such a way as to suggest that these two concepts refer to two different sets or sequences of events. Concerning this claim there are two points to be made.

In the first place, it is often forgotten that the doctrine of creation is itself an aspect of the doctrine of grace. From this forgetfulness flows the tendency to reduce the range of reference of the concept of grace to questions concerning the fact and scope of redemption, with the result that the natural order is reduced to the status of a (theologically indifferent) 'theatre' on the boards of which the drama of human redemption is enacted.

In the second place, the plausibility of this reduction, this dissociation of 'redemption' from 'creation', is enhanced by our tendency to speak, mythologically, as if God undertook, successively, two different tasks. First, he *established* the world, 'a spatially and temporally extended reality of a profane character',[18] and then, by a second act or fresh initiative, intervened to sort out the mess in which this profane world had landed itself. Within this scheme of things, the 'history of salvation' (which forms the subject-matter of 'theologies of history') is taken to refer to the working-out of the consequences of this second divine act or initiative.

It is often further assumed that once this second and super-vening process, the 'history of salvation', has as it were 'got under way', it proceeds concurrently with the (previously established) history of the secular. From now on, we have two distinct processes or sequences of events, proceeding side-by-side. And, of course, the sensible thing to do is to situate oneself in the 'salvific' sequence as speedily as possible – the leap by which one effects this transfer is called conversion – because the 'profane' sequence (which, *as* 'pro-fanum', goes its way *outside* the 'holy places') is rushing headlong to destruction.

If the 'theocratic' model tends to collapse all distinctions between nature and grace, the tendency of the model I have just been considering is to suppose that, in order to sustain such distinctions, it is necessary to postulate two materially distinct sequences of fact, event, language and institution. What both models have in common, however, is their underestimation of the autonomy, dignity and *theological* significance of 'profane' or secular reality.

Fortunately, we do not have to choose between being either 'theocrats' or 'manichees'. It is possible to treat the necessary distinctions between nature and grace, creation and redemp-tion, secular history and 'history of salvation', as *formal* rather than material in character.

God's single, eternal act (which he is) finds contingent expression in a single process of gracious self-bestowal, a single world, a single history. 'Profane' history and 'salvation-history' are, as Karl Rahner put it, 'materially co-extensive'.[19] The distinction between what we call 'church' and what we call 'world' is not a distinction between two empirically distinct 'places': an oasis of light and a wilderness of darkness. It is a distinction between one single, vastly diverse, bewilderingly complex, frequently conflictual and largely 'illegible' process and, *within* that process, an unexpected language: a discourse of clarification and the promise of peace. The church, and its constituent narratives and relationships, is the *sacrament*, not

the 'place', of God's presence and promise. And it is sacramentally, or 'symbolically', that we use (or should use) that 'single
narrative of the sense and direction of things' which receives
summary expression in our creed or 'symbolum'.

Distance and presence

Does it not, however, become increasingly difficult to display
the sense of the church's sacramentality the further removed
we become from those events which stand at the centre of our
confessional narrative? He 'suffered under Pontius Pilate' a
long time ago, and in a far-away place.

We have all been told, from time to time, that the 'biblical'
view of time was 'linear', whereas the 'Greek' view was 'cyclical'.
It may, indeed, be that 'the emphasis upon the non-repeatability
of events' and, in that sense, upon the 'irreversibility' of time,
is characteristically Christian.[20] But is it true that all notions of
time which carry such emphasis are patent of characterization
in straightforwardly 'linear' terms?

I take it, for example, that on a *simply* 'linear' account, the
greater the quantity of time elapsed between two events the
further apart they would be. It does at least seem to be some
such consideration which troubles those Christians who fear
that, the 'further' we move in time from those events in relation
to which we number, in our culture, the passing of the years,
the more the memory of Jesus may fade until he disappears into
the 'mists of time'.

But perhaps the relevant notions of 'distance' and 'proximity'
are not as straightforward as they at first sight appear to be.
How far is Cambridge from central London? There are (at
present) at least two correct answers to that question: 'just over
fifty miles', and 'just over an hour'. It used to be quite a lot
further. It is not fiction, but fact, that the development of
modern modes of transport has brought 'close' cities, and their
inhabitants, that were formerly very 'distant' from each other.[21]

But what has all this to do with time and memory? Are not
all events that occurred (say) two hundred years ago, equally
distant from us? No: some of these events are, or can be, brought

close through memory and the interpretation of the past, whereas others – that left no traces, or no traces accessible to and decipherable by us – are, perhaps irretrievably, 'out of sight'.

I intend the concept of 'accessibility' to refer to what we might call the 'material conditions' of memory, of the *presence* of the past. These material conditions include the 'storage' of the past through the survival of buildings and artefacts, of social institutions (such as ritual and language) and, on an increasing scale, of such 'storage-tanks' of language as libraries and computer banks.

Accessibility is, in part, a function of social power. No theological theory of the abiding 'presence' of Christ would be of much use to us for very long, if the government, disturbed by the subversive potential of Christian memory, burned all our books and suppressed our ritual practices. However distasteful it may be to those who suppose that 'religion' has nothing to do with 'politics', engagement in the struggle for social power can be a necessary condition for the survival of memory. In our case: a necessary condition for the recognition of the enduring presence of Christ and, hence, of the promise of God.

If 'accessibility' refers to the material conditions of memory, 'decipherability' refers to its *formal* conditions. Here, of course, we touch once again upon the whole question of hermeneutics, concerning which I wish to make only one point, namely, that physical proximity in space or time is not a sufficient condition of what we might call 'human' or 'personal' proximity.

We sometimes notice this, as when we say of two people who live in the same house at the same time: 'he and she have grown terribly *far apart* these days'. We can put the point more generally: the 'shrinking' of the planet through economic inter-dependence, air travel, telex and television, is not a sufficient condition of 'personal proximity' between the planet's inhabitants. If it were, the threat of nuclear war would be receding.

In other words, to speak of 'proximity' between *human beings* is to speak not only of physical factors but also of growth in relationship, understanding and reconciliation. And if we tend, as we do, to dissociate the material and formal conditions of proximity, this is only further evidence of how deeply our imagination is distorted by the dominant dualisms between 'spirit' and 'matter', 'persons' and 'things'.

Events and persons are not necessarily 'near' because they are recent or geographically proximate, nor necessarily 'far' because they occurred or existed a long time ago or many miles away. And events and persons that once seemed very 'distant', or even disappeared from view, can, with changes in conditions, circumstances and patterns of perception, come 'close' again. Who is my neighbour? There are no fixed patterns of attainable proximity.

A Christian theology of history, an account of the process whereby the eternal mystery of God, temporally transcribed in particular events, brings 'near' to him and to each other those who were once 'far off', must, it seems to me, attempt to take into consideration (practically, as well as theoretically) the entire exceedingly complex range of factors and conditions that constitute the problem of 'distance' and 'proximity', of 'absence' and 'presence', in social and historical existence. All these factors and conditions, on only a few of which I have touched in this chapter, are at least germane to the question of the 'real presence' of the eternal in time.

Matter, spirit and 'narratability'

I suggested earlier that distinctions between 'secular' history and 'salvation-history' should be taken to be formal rather than empirical in character. I now want to suggest, more generally and much more tentatively, that we might consider similarly construing the distinction between 'matter' and 'spirit'. The history of concepts of matter and spirit, and of the relationship between them, is far too varied and (often) obscure for this proposal to serve as more than a general indicator as to how we might *begin* to consider the question. It does, however, have this great merit: it enables us to acknowledge the indispensability of the distinction without jumping to the quite unwarranted conclusion that the items which constitute the framework and furniture of the world are of two and only two kinds: 'material' and 'spiritual' events and things.

The distinction is indispensable, but to take it 'grammatically' is to take it (initially at least) as a distinction between types of discourse rather than between kinds of thing. We need to 'take' things (to treat them, and to consider them) in many different ways, but the recognition that (for example) the language of 'spirit' is as indispensable as the language of 'stuff', or the language of 'mind' as indispensable as the language of 'body', does not justify the inference that to each type of discourse or practice there corresponds a distinct class of entities or events.

But, it might be objected, is not God a spirit, and is it not *because* God is a spirit that we need to draw the distinction between spirit and matter, empirically, as a distinction between different kinds of things? God is certainly not a lump of matter but, on the other hand, there is *no* kind of thing that God is. God is not an entity of *any* kind. (That, too, is a grammatical observation: I am not an atheist.)

But how else, other than empirically, other than as a distinction between 'kinds of thing', might the distinction be drawn? We might begin by remembering that the distinction between matter and 'form' used to be drawn as a distinction, not between kinds of thing, but between that which was organized and the pattern, or character, or 'shape' of its organization: what was sometimes called its 'soul'.

Next, in order to feed in the dimension of temporality (which those admirable Aristotelean abstractions too easily leave out of account), we might try restating the distinction in terms of the 'narrated' and its 'narratability'. There is nothing of which a tale cannot be told, but the more complex the organization, the greater the narrative potential. Rabbits are richer narrative material than rocks.

In the third place, the difference between *human* beings and the other kinds of thing that there are might be indicated by having recourse to a distinction between 'having' and 'telling' a story. Everything has a story, but only human beings also tell stories. They tell all kinds of stories, and some of them are true. But the important thing to notice is that the limits of narratability are not set by the narrators but by the matter of which they seek to speak. Stories that overstep these limits are not fiction but fantasy.

We tell stories, set things in order, make plans, formulate policies, not in order to *escape* from the world but to render it, so far as may be, 'legible', inhabitable. The 'life of the spirit' is a labour of 'form-ation' and transformation. The antithesis of spirit is not 'matter' but destructiveness, 'de-formation', deadliness and chaos.

My notion of narratability is close cousin to the concept of 'followability' which Professor Frank Kermode uses to describe that property which history, like story, has to have if it is to be patterned into a single narrative.[22] In Kermode's judgment, the world lacks this property: it is 'unfollowable'. 'The world', he says, 'is our beloved codex. We may not see it, as Dante did, in perfect order, gathered by love into one volume; but we do, living as reading, like to think of it as a place where we can travel back and forth . . . diving consequences . . . extracting secrets from its secrecy. . . This is the way we satisfy ourselves with explanations of the unfollowable world. . . . World and book, it may be, are hopelessly plural, endlessly disappointing; we stand alone before them . . . knowing that they may be narratives only because of our impudent intervention, and susceptible of interpretation only by our hermetic tricks'.[23] (The 'book' that he has especially in mind is the Gospel according to Mark, and there is much that he has to say, especially concerning 'character', 'agency' and 'plot', which theologians would be imprudent to ignore.)

The judgment that the world is 'unfollowable', that such overall narrative pattern as we impose on it is, in the last analysis, invention and not discovery, is the judgment of sober and clear-sighted atheism. As such, it seems to me both more persuasive and more responsible than many versions of theistic 'optimism', which make to override vast tracts of darkness and savagery merely by the telling of a tale. Kermode's judgment, then, expresses one form of the conviction, cumulatively and painstakingly arrived at, which results from 'a great number of things so and so disposed'; a form which acknowledges that these things can only be 'taken into one view' in the measure that *we* do so, and which knows that, in so doing, we are unprotected from arbitrariness, illusion and destructive fantasy.

Perhaps so. But it is also possible that such 'followability' as we are enabled to discern *is* grounded in what is in fact the case, and is not simply the product of imaginative invention. To confess God as 'spirit' is not to say what kind of thing God is, but to confess the followability of the world that he freely forms, inhabits and transforms into his likeness. If the discipline of that confession checks our propensity to self-indulgent despair, it *also* checks our propensity to 'far-sighted' optimism, because the focus of that narrative in which our confession of followability finds paradigmatic expression is the darkness of Gethsemane and the brokenness of the cross.

Conclusion

Deep as we are in Devonshire lanes, how do we know where we are? Only, I think, by continually attempting to reorientate ourselves in relation to such understanding as we discover ourselves to have of the story of Jesus the Christ. (It would not be mere word-play if we said that the following of Christ is the praxis of the world's followability.)

According to Professor Walter Kasper, the 'three basic attitudes' to which such orientation gives rise are, first, the faith that acknowledges that, in the light of Christ, 'history cannot now be basically a nightmare'; secondly, the hope that is able to yield to, and to live and work with, 'the ever-changing newness of history'; and, thirdly the 'love and solidarity' that continues to co-operate, 'in word, life and suffering', in the 'humanizing and pacification of the world'.[24] No 'theology of history', as I see it, can hope to do more than to give to these attitudes provisional and unstable narrative expression, acknowledging the while that any such expression is threatened with illusion. But, if Bishop Butler is right, no *other* 'kind of proof' would be appropriate to the 'evidence' of Christianity.

6

What Might Martyrdom Mean?

All Christians, and not only New Testament scholars, seek to understand the New Testament. But the standpoints from which understanding is sought are manifold. The individual Christian, meditating on the text, the preacher, the textual critic, the systematic theologian and the exegete, are all concerned with understanding the New Testament. And yet they are clearly not engaged in identical enterprises. How might these different enterprises be characterized, and what relationships obtain, or should obtain, between them?

There is a received account, in this country, both of the character of these enterprises, and of the relationship between them, which goes something like this. Christian hermeneutics is principally concerned with negotiating the 'gap' between what was once said and what might appropriately be said today. The biblical scholar, and the historian of doctrine, are expected to recover, today, what the text meant; the systematic theologian is supposed to transpose the recovered meanings into contemporary idiom; and Christian living is conceived as the practical application or implementation of meanings thus recovered and transposed.

In this essay I propose to indicate some of the reasons why I regard this hermeneutical model as profoundly unsatisfactory. The relationships between exegesis and preaching, on the one hand, and between exegesis and critical or systematic theology, on the other, that are inscribed in this model, are often expressed in terms of a distinction between what the text 'meant' and what it 'means', or might mean, today. I shall, therefore, discuss

Professor Krister Stendahl's use of this distinction and Professor Dennis Nineham's variation on the theme. From this discussion it will, I hope, emerge that the model is defective both in its neglect of questions of interpretative truth and in its failure to locate problems concerning the relationship between theory and practice *within* the description of the interpretative process. The essay is thus an invitation to my New Testament colleagues to reconsider, on the one hand, their view of the relationship between their activity and other aspects of theological inquiry and, on the other hand, their view of the relationship between the 'obedience of faith' and critical, scholarly reflection. Whether or not it thereby also constitutes an invitation to them to reconsider some features of their own exegetical activity is for them rather than for me to say.

'*Meaning*', past and present

According to the article on 'Exegesis' in the Supplementary Volume to the *Interpreter's Dictionary of the Bible*, 'the distinction between what the text meant and what it means is fundamental, even though it should not be pressed'.[1] The article also tells us that 'when exegesis is distinguished from exposition, the former refers to the process of ascertaining the original meaning, and the latter, the meaning for today'.[2] This formulation, so slipshod as not to merit detailed commentary, at least reminds us of the abiding influence of Krister Stendahl's article on 'Contemporary Biblical Theology' in the original edition of the dictionary.[3] In that article, Stendahl observed that 'the *religionsgeschichtliche Schule* had drastically widened the hiatus between our time and that of the Bible . . . The question of meaning was split up in two tenses: "What *did* it mean?" and "What *does* it mean?".[4]

According to Stendahl, attention to the first of these questions is the responsibility of 'the descriptive task', while the movement from the first to the second is a matter of 'hermeneutics'. In undertaking the 'descriptive' task, 'our only concern', he tells us, 'is to find out what these words meant when uttered or written by the prophet, the priest, the evangelist, or the apostle

– and regardless of their meaning in later stages of religious history, our own included. . . . The meaning for the present . . . is not involved'.[5] Later, commenting on the relationships between what the text originally meant, and what it subsequently came to mean or might mean today, he insists that this is 'a relation between two highly developed types of theology',[6] and he describes 'the task of systematic theology' as being 'by its very nature one of translation from one pattern of thought into another'.[7]

The importance of the point upon which the article was concerned centrally to insist is beyond question. The exegete is an historian, and any historian, whatever the motives that lead him to undertake his inquiry, seeks to understand and to exhibit some aspect of the past 'in its pastness'.[8] Christians are not alone in being tempted to 'read' the past anachronistically, to find in it what they expect or hope to find, but they are peculiarly exposed to this temptation because of their conviction that certain words spoken and deeds enacted in the past are of unique and enduring significance. Nevertheless, the framework within which Stendahl expresses this concern is, for a number of reasons, highly questionable.

In the first place, his characterization of the respective tasks of the historian and the systematic theologian, in terms of a distinction between 'description' and 'hermeneutics' comes dangerously close to endorsing the positivist myth that exegesis is not yet interpretation. Let us suppose that the textual critic has done his work, and provided the exegete with the materials for his task.[9] What are these materials? They are 'just a series of signs'[10] or notations. And 'anything over and above a reissue of the same signs in the same order will be mediated by the experience, intelligence, and judgement of the interpreter'.[11] Moreover, the perspective within which the exegete works, and the language he employs, have been shaped by the history of the culture to which he belongs. To insist on this self-evident truth is by no means necessarily to subscribe to some form of radical hermeneutical relativism, nor to espouse the strange view that different cultural contexts are always mutually 'impermeable', rendering good historical interpretation impossible.

It is merely to issue a reminder that the notions of 'objectivity' and 'scientificity' presupposed by some New Testament scholars betray the influence of a discredited positivism all the more insidious for being unrecognized.

In the second place, the concept of 'meaning' with which Stendahl works is dangerously imprecise. If we say that the exegete, as historian, is concerned to understand and exhibit what the text 'originally meant', to what are we referring? Do we have in mind some notion of 'authorial intention', such that what we are after is what Luke, or Paul, was 'trying to get at'? Or, bearing in mind that what people intend to say, or suppose themselves to be saying, is often by no means identical with what they succeed in saying, do we read the text, as a cultural artefact, in the light of the cultural conditions in which it was produced? Or do we have in mind that which the text was 'heard' to say by its original audience – and, if so, is not the idea of some single, uniform, 'original audience' itself highly problematic? If these considerations seem unhelpfully abstract, consider the following question: what was the 'original meaning' of *King Lear*, or of Mr Whitelaw's speech, at the 1979 Conservative Party Conference, announcing the government's intention to set up detention centres to administer 'short, sharp shocks' to juvenile offenders?

In the third place, we have seen that Stendahl describes 'the task of systematic theology' as being 'by its very nature one of *translation* from one pattern of thought into another'.[12] That description distracts attention from the fact that, as I have already insisted, the exegete's task, the historian's task, is itself already an interpretative enterprise. This being so, if the metaphor of 'translation' is to be used, it should be used, not only of the task of systematics, but also, as Bultmann claimed, of 'the task of historical science'.[13] Stendahl admits that the model of 'original' and 'translation' is only an analogy,[14] but he seems to suppose that the analogy is appropriate. Whereas I should wish to argue, following Professor David Kelsey, that from many points of view the analogy is singularly *in*appropriate. 'The metaphorical use of "translation" ', says Kelsey, 'stretches the concept into unintelligibility';[15] it 'obscures the fact that there may be a *conceptual discontinuity* between what the biblical texts say and what the theological proposals say';[16] and, for all its apparent methodological neutrality, it is in fact parasitic upon certain *theological* decisions concerning the nature of revelation.[17]

In the fourth place, the metaphor of 'translation' and, more generally, the assumption that the task of the systematic theologian is that of transposing meaning recovered by the New Testament scholar into contemporary idiom presupposes what we might call the 'relay-race' model of the relationship between the two enterprises. When the New Testament scholar has done his job, produced his completed package of 'original meanings', he hands this over to the systematic theologian, whose responsibility it is to transpose the meanings received into forms intelligible within the conditions of our contemporary culture. Systematic theologians who subscribe to this model are sometimes irritated by the fact that, because the work of New Testament interpretation is never finished, the baton never reaches them. The New Testament scholar appears to be 'running on the spot'; he never arrives at the point at which the baton could be handed over. The New Testament scholar, for his part, either ignores what the systematic theologian is doing (it is not his business: he is only running the *first* leg of the race) or disapproves of the fact that the baton is continually being wrenched prematurely from his hands.

It is, however, the model that is defective and, especially, the assumption that there is a one-way dependence between New Testament scholarship and systematic theology. I should wish to argue that the relationship between the two enterprises is, or should be, dialectical: that it is, or should be, a relationship of mutual dependence.

As I have put it elsewhere:

If it is true for us, as creatures of history, that some understanding of our past is a necessary condition of an accurate grasp of our present predicament and of our responsibilities for the future, it is also true that a measure of critical self-understanding of our present predicament is a necessary condition of an accurate 'reading' of our past. We do not *first* understand the past and *then* proceed to understand the present. The relationship between these two dimensions of our quest for meaning and truth is dialectical: they mutually inform, enable, correct and enlighten each other.[18]

The more peripheral that aspect of the past with which the historian is concerned, the more fragile the validity of this claim. In order to decide whether it was a cloak or an overcoat that Paul left at Troas and, if a cloak, what kind of cloak it was likely to have been, no very profound existential and cultural self-awareness is demanded of the historian. But most of the New Testament is concerned with weightier matters. Let us suppose that Professor Lindars is correct in saying that, according to the Fourth Gospel, 'The works of Jesus reveal not only his identity as the Father's agent, but also his unity with the Father'.[19] Or let us suppose that Mr Beck is justified in proposing 'a martyrological interpretation of Luke's Passion narrative'[20] as at least one strand in what the narrative 'originally meant'. In both these cases, is there not a sense in which it is a necessary condition for understanding, with any depth and sensitivity, what either of the texts in question 'originally meant', that we have some articulated grasp of those fundamental features of the human predicament to which those texts were constructed as elements of a response? (This would only not be the case on the supposition that the affirmation of Jesus' unity with the Father, or the construal of his Passion in martyrological terms, 'meant nothing' for the hope and self-understanding of those who thus interpreted his fact and significance.) I am not saying that this condition is always, or even frequently, capable of being fulfilled. It may be the case that the culture, the 'structure of feeling', that we inhabit is such as to render us incapable of seriously entertaining those questions to which the authors of the New Testament sought to respond. It may be the case that the world of the New Testament is, at least for the time being, so different from ours as to be quite opaque, illegible. I am only saying that, when we have to do with texts which treat of, and embody particular responses to, fundamental aspects of the human predicament: questions of life and death, innocence and freedom, hope and suffering, then, in order to 'understand' those texts, the technical skills of the historian, although indispensable, are inadequate for the task.

If the questions to which ancient authors sought to respond in terms available to them within their cultural horizons are to be 'heard' today with something like their original force and urgency, they have first to be 'heard' as questions that challenge us with comparable seriousness. And if they are to be thus heard, they must first be articulated in terms available to us within *our* cultural horizons. There is thus a sense in which the articulation of what the text might 'mean' today, is a necessary condition of hearing what that text 'originally meant'. And, once again, there can be no *a priori* guarantees that this condition is or can be fulfilled. Just as certain features of the past may be rendered quite opaque or illegible by the differences between past and present contexts of meaning, so also certain features of the present may be rendered quite opaque or illegible by the circumstances of contemporary existence. It is no part of my argument that we should suppose it to be a straightforward matter to 'make sense' either of the past or of the present, let alone to make a sense that would be recognizably Christian. Moreover, it is no part of my argument to suggest that the distinction between our attempts, in the present, to understand the past on its own terms, and our attempts, in the present, to articulate self-understanding and hope, and thus to formulate coherent and responsible policies for future action and attitude, is not fundamental and irreducible. I am only concerned to insist, as a matter of general hermeneutical principle, that understanding what an ancient text 'originally meant', in the circumstances in which it was originally produced, and understanding what that text might mean today, are mutually interdependent and not merely successive enterprises.

It is not, I think, irrelevant to point out that exegetical practice frequently neglects its own theoretical stipulation consistently to distinguish what the text 'meant' from what it might 'mean'. As a matter of fact, New Testament scholars frequently conduct their discussion in the present rather than the past tense. They insist that 'this is not what Paul is saying', or 'this is what the text means', and so on. It seems likely that certain awkward questions concerning the adequacy of the theory of meaning presupposed by the distinction are thereby obscured from view. It would be interesting to discover what modifications of exegetical practice resulted from a rigorous adherence to the 'past tense' rule.

Consumers and tourists

So far, I have taken Professor Stendahl's influential and controversial article as the background to my remarks. A somewhat different approach to the distinction between past and present meaning is to be found in the work of Professor Dennis Nineham. 'What', asks Nineham, 'is an interpreter of the new Testament . . . seeking to do? So far as he aims to go beyond the satisfaction of simple antiquarian curiosity and bring his readers contemporary enlightenment of some sort, how should he conceive and set about his task?'[21] An historian would, I suspect, find Nineham's distinction doubly puzzling. It is puzzling, first, in its apparent depreciation of the historian's craft. 'Antiquarian' has overtones of cobwebbed eccentricity; the implication is that historical study is a harmless and slightly self-indulgent hobby: its goal is the 'satisfaction' of 'curiosity'. It is puzzling, secondly, because when an historian publishes a piece of work, he presumably does so in the expectation, or at least the hope, that his readers will find it 'enlightening'. And I fail to see how such 'enlightenment' as the reader receives could be other than 'contemporary': it is, after all, *today* that I am reading the historian's text, not yesterday or tomorrow.

It could be objected that I am obscuring the perfectly straightforward distinction that Nineham is drawing between information or 'enlightenment' concerning the past and the 'enlightenment' of present perplexity. The trouble is that I do not find that distinction, thus drawn, at all straightforward. Self-understanding, whether of an individual or of a group, is a matter of producing, or being able to produce, an autobiography. And in so far as historical research concerning some aspect of my past, or the past of some group to which I belong, or of some tradition within which I seek to stand, results in 'the discovery of new knowledge, the connection of previously unrelated facts, the development of new theory, or the revision of older views',[22] it constitutes a challenge to reassess some features of my autobiography and hence of my self-understanding.

In other words, someone who acknowledges the origins of Christianity to be an aspect of *his* past, and not merely of 'the past of mankind' in general, is thereby precluded, in logic, if not necessarily in psychological fact, from regarding the historical study of Christian origins as being 'simply' a matter of 'satisfying antiquarian curiosity'. The contrast drawn by Professor Nineham, and the manner in which he draws it, could be the expression of a particular *theological* judgment of a kind with which students of Bultmann are familiar. Not that Nineham, I think, regards himself as a Lutheran. And yet it seems to be being suggested that the human work of the antiquarian profiteth nothing unto salvation or, should we say, unto 'contemporary enlightenment'.

Nearer the surface of his text, Nineham's question concerning the interpreter's task reflects his dissatisfaction with certain ways of drawing distinctions between what the text 'meant' and what it 'means' or might mean today. And he answers his own question as follows:

> We ask the New Testament exegete to help us to pass over into the beliefs and relationships with God witnessed to in the New Testament, not in the belief that they were necessarily better than our own, but in the faith that they will prove complementary to our own, revealing to us new insights, new dimensions of relationship with God . . . which, once they are revealed, must, and can, be dealt with in our own terms.[23]

What particularly interests me in that passage (aside from problems concerning the force of 'better', the grounds of that 'faith', the sense of 'complementary', and the legitimacy of the shift from 'must' to 'can') is the enthusiasm with which here, as in other places in his recent writing, he appropriates Professor

John Dunne's metaphor of 'passing over'. Dunne himself defines 'passing over' as 'a shifting of standpoint, a going over to the standpoint of another culture, another way of life, another religion. It is followed by an equal and opposite process we might call "coming back" '.[24]

Dunne's allusive and evocative study makes no pretence to be a work of disciplined theoretical rigour. Even so, I confess that I find his repeated use of this favoured metaphor under-developed, uninformative and not particularly illuminating (were I seeking for a sign, I would take comfort from the fact that the first reference to 'passing over', in the index to the edition of *The Way of All the Earth* that I consulted, is to a page that, on examination, turns out to be blank). And yet, passing over (!) decades of sustained and often rigorous debate on problems of interpretation-theory – in historiography, literary criticism and the philosophy of the social sciences – this metaphor is served up to us as a description of the interpreter's task.

Professor Raymond Williams has complained that

> nearly all forms of contemporary critical theory are theories of *consumption*. That is to say, they are concerned with understanding an object in such a way that it can profitably or correctly be consumed. The earliest stage of consumption theory was the theory of 'taste', where the link between the practice and the theory was direct in the metaphor.[25]

Not the least serious deficiency of 'consumption theories' is their mistaken assumption that a literary text is, as an embodiment of meaning, a kind of 'material object'. If this were the case, then 'reading' a text would be a process similar to that whereby we seek to 'understand', say, a piece of rock or a plate of food, by isolating its constituent components. There is undoubtedly a sense in which some cultural artefacts – a building, for example, or a painting – do have 'specific material existence'. But the same is not true of literary, dramatic and musical works.

There is no *Hamlet*, no *Brothers Karamazov*, no *Wuthering*

Heights, in the sense that there is a particular great painting. There is no *Fifth Symphony* . . . which is an object in any way comparable to those works in the visual arts which have survived. . . . In literature, especially in drama, in music and in a very wide area of the performing arts, what we have are not objects but *notations*. These notations have to be reinterpreted in an active way, according to particular conventions.[26]

A performance of *Hamlet* is an interpretation of the text. The history of performances of *Hamlet* is the history of successive interpretations of the text. An historian of Tudor drama, exploring the circumstances of that text's 'original production', is engaged in the second-order activity of constructing an 'interpretation' of that original 'interpretation'. That way of putting the matter may seem cumbersome, but it serves to remind us not only that there are irreducibly distinct aspects of the hermeneutic process, but also that there is a sense in which a text, any text, becomes an expression of meaning only in so far as it becomes an element in the human activity that is its production, use or interpretation. Williams' criticism of 'consumption' theories of interpretation thus helps us to see what is wrong with a statement such as the following: 'Exegesis is a process by which one enables *the text's own meaning* to come forth in its own terms.'[27] Here we are clearly confronted with the mistaken belief that texts 'have meaning' in somewhat the same way that material objects 'have mass'. (It should perhaps be added that considerations of this generality concerning the relationship between sign and signified, text and meaning, are equally applicable to texts – such as many New Testament passages – interpretative of particular historical events and persons, and texts – such as those mentioned by Professor Williams – which lack such particularity of concrete reference.)

Taking our cue from Raymond Williams, we might describe that received account of the relationships between New Testament study, systematic theology and Christian living, which I sketched at the beginning of this paper, as the 'consumption' model of Christian hermeneutics. According to some versions of this model, the historian of Christian origins provides the 'raw materials', and the systematic theologian 'cooks' them, according to taste, for contemporary consumption. According to others, such as Professor Stendahl, with his insistence that the relation between past and present meanings is 'a relation between two highly developed types of theology',[28] the historian is an importer of foreign manufactured goods, while the systematic theologian's task is that of repackaging ('translating') them for local use.

If I understand Professor Nineham, he is unhappy with sharp distinctions between the provision of goods and their adaptation. His disapproval of 'antiquarianism' seems to spring from a suspicion that the importer may be insufficiently concerned about the usefulness of, or likely demand for, his goods on the home market. I confess that I do sometimes have the impression that some biblical scholars, in their apparent lack of interest in questions concerning the disproportion between energy expended and results achieved, and in questions concerning the wider implications and significance of their work, do exhibit a tendency towards the dilettantism against which Nineham is protesting. (It will, I hope, nevertheless be clear from remarks I made earlier that I believe Nineham's criticism, with its implied blanket disapproval of historical study 'for its own sake', to be far too indiscriminate.)

Be that as it may, we can perhaps suggest that, in recommending a unified account of the interpretative process, Nineham turns for his hermeneutical model to another aspect of modern life: tourism. There are, of course, some tourists who derive little benefit from the experience of foreign travel, because they insist on ascribing normative status to the customs, language and eating-habits of their domestic context. Foreign countries are experienced as defective forms of England. There is an analogy between such tourists and those whose 'reading' of ancient texts is vitiated by the 'eisegetical' tendencies that Nineham rightly deplores.

There are also more open-minded and less ethnocentric travellers who allow the experience of foreign travel to modify and enlarge their domestic horizons of experience. These are the tourists whom Nineham would propose to us as paradigms of Christian interpretation (even though it must be admitted that his insistence that ancient texts 'must, and can, be dealt with in our own terms',[29] is not lacking in traces of ethnocentricity: within what limits are 'our own terms' sacrosanct?).

There are, however, at least two reasons why the model of 'tourism' is hardly more satisfactory than that of 'consumption' as a characterization of the process of the Christian interpretation of the New Testament. In the first place, both models focus on considerations of 'meaning' to the neglect of questions of truth. In the second place, both models assume that the poles of the interpretative enterprise are expressions of 'meaning' rather than patterns of human action. Let us briefly consider these two issues in turn.

Meaning and truth

Dr John O'Neill has argued for an affirmative answer to the question: 'Did Jesus think that his death would do for mankind what no one else could do?'[30] Other New Testament scholars may contest O'Neill's interpretation of 'the Cross sayings and the servant sayings'.[31] But let us suppose that his interpretation is broadly correct and can be shown to be correct. This still leaves untouched the far more interesting question: was Jesus right?

The authors of the New Testament offer a variety of responses to this question, and contemporary exegetes interpret these responses in different ways. But, notwithstanding this twofold pluralism, it appears to be agreed that the authors of the New Testament shared a common conviction that, in the death and vindication of Jesus, that was done for mankind which was uniquely and unrepeatably done.

We now have two questions, rather than one: Was Jesus right? Were the authors of the New Testament right? If we addressed these questions to a representative group of contemporary New Testament scholars we would, I think, be told by most of them that it is beyond the competence of the exegete, as an historian, to answer either question and, especially, the former.

To what extent is this modesty becoming, and on what grounds does it rest? It sometimes seems to be grounded on the conviction that exegesis, as historical interpretation, is concerned not with questions of 'truth' but only with questions of 'meaning'. But this distinction, thus employed, is less than satisfactory. A history of the Peninsular War, or of the October Revolution, in which the author systematically refrained from all judgments of appropriateness, correctness or truth concerning Wellington's conduct of the campaign and his estimation of the chances of success, or concerning Lenin's analysis of a turning-point in Russian history, which restricted itself to exhibiting what Wellington's diaries or Lenin's letters 'originally meant', would be a very queer kind of history. Historicism, in the sense of a refusal to risk judgments of truth or appropriateness, has its limits.

The exegete, as an historian, cannot, it would seem, legitimately evade responsibility for assessing, however tentatively, the truth, correctness or appropriateness of those interpretative judgments concerning the fact and significance of Jesus that are expressed or implied in the writings of the New Testament. And yet there are considerations that may help to explain, and that in some measure justify, the exegete's hesitation. The most important of these considerations arise from the fact that the truth-conditions of the proposition, 'In Jesus' death that was done for mankind which was uniquely and unrepeatably done', are hidden in the mystery of divine action and do not lie open for historical scrutiny. To put it very simply, oversimply: the exegete is correct in supposing that the question 'Was Jesus right?' is not one that he is competent, as an historian, to answer.

And yet the question remains, shall we say, interesting. If the New Testament scholar cannot answer it, who can? Should we turn to some other field of expertise or professional competence: to philosophy, perhaps, or to systematic theology? No. It is not that kind of question. It is at once more general, more personal and more particular. To refrain from answering it, or to answer it in the negative, is to refrain from giving, or to refuse to give – not to a 'meaning', but to a man – the kind of trust that the authors of the New Testament gave and, in giving it, exhibited their intention to maintain 'the testimony of Jesus'.[32]

It appears to be the case, therefore, that recognition of the fact that the interpretative process is concerned not only with 'meaning' but also with 'truth' obliges us to consider questions concerning the relationship between the practice of faith and the goal and function of academic reflection and inquiry as constitutive features of the hermeneutical problem. I submit that any model of Christian hermeneutics that ignores such questions, or treats them as marginal or merely consequential, is *theoretically* deficient. And I suggest that the two models that I earlier considered – the 'consumption' and 'tourism' models – are deficient on precisely this score.

Locating the 'gap'

This conclusion can be reinforced by considering the second charge that I brought against the two models of interpretation previously considered: namely, that they both mistakenly assume the poles of the interpretative process to be expressions of 'meaning' rather than patterns of human action. (That formulation may be misleading. 'Action' and 'speech', 'deeds' and 'words', are not to be contrasted dualistically. All human actions 'speak', and all uses of language are aspects of human action and behaviour. The contrast that I wish to draw is between the abstract and the concrete: between expressions of meaning and judgments of truth considered, on the one hand, 'in themselves' and, on the other hand, as aspects of concrete, historical, human practice and behaviour.)

W. F. Flemington does not share this mistaken assumption. He expresses the worry that 'Pauline theology may seem utterly remote and unreal'[33] to many people today. And he attempts to meet this difficulty, not by producing some fresh abstract description, in contemporary concepts and images, of what it was that he supposes Pauline theology to have 'originally meant', but by offering us the pattern of Maximilian Kolbe's action, the manner of his witness, as a correct or faithful *interpretation of Pauline theology*.

Following up a suggestion at which I hinted in my discussion of Raymond Williams, I would wish to argue that the fundamental form of the Christian interpretation of scripture is, in the concrete, the life, activity and organization of the Christian community, and that Christian practice consists (by analogy with the practical interpretation of dramatic, legal and musical texts) in the performance or enactment of the biblical text: in its 'active reinterpretation'. The elucidation of this suggestion would demand another study,[34] but Mr Flemington's evocation of the example of Maximilian Kolbe may perhaps serve as a parable. Flemington does not suggest, nor am I suggesting, that the attribution of primacy to interpretative performance dispenses those ancillary interpreters, the textual critics, exegetes and theologians, from the need to pursue their enterprises with relentless scholarly and intellectual rigour (any more than the attribution of primacy to dramatic, legal or musical interpretative performance dispenses with the need for submitting scripts, statutes and scores to continual historical and theoretical scrutiny and assessment). We are, however, reminded of the need to situate academic tasks appropriately in that broader context of interpretative practice of which they form an indispensable part.

Moreover, it is not only the contemporary pole of the interpretative process that demands description in concrete, rather than abstract, terms: the same is true of the *interpretandum*. The practice of Christian faith is not, in the last resort, a matter of interpreting, in our time and place, an ancient text. It is, or seeks to be, the faithful 'rendering' of those events, of those patterns of human action, decision and suffering, to which the texts bear original witness. To acknowledge that the criteria of fidelity are hard to establish and are frequently problematic is to admit that there is, indeed, a hermeneutical 'gap'. But this 'gap' does not lie, in the last resort, between what was once 'meant' and what might be 'meant' today. It lies, rather, between what was once achieved, intended, or 'shown', and what might be achieved, intended, or 'shown' today. The poles of Christian interpretation are, on the one hand, 'the testimony of Jesus' in his own time and in the time of those who first sought to share that testimony and, on the other hand, such continued sharing in that testimony as may be demanded of us today.

There are, as any reader of Gadamer's *Truth and Method* will appreciate, general considerations of hermeneutical theory that point in the direction that I am indicating. But, in addition to such methodological or philosophical considerations, there are also theological considerations that can be adduced. Only an incorrigible idealist (in Marx's sense) could suppose that Christianity's primary concern is to 'make sense' of suffering – whether the suffering of Jesus or of anybody else. That would be to 'leave everything as it is'. It was not thus that Jesus – by his words and deeds and death – bore witness to God, interpreted the divine in his historical particularity. Nor was it thus that those who first interpreted him as God's self-interpretation sought to share his testimony. Nor was it thus (to put it theologically) that God 'interpreted himself' in those historical persons and events.

God's self-witness, the 'martyrdom' of God, is not the provision of a more or less satisfactory account of the human condition, but is rather the transformation of that condition: divine utterance is 'performative'. Similarly, the transformative power of Christian 'martyrdom', of 'sharing the testimony of Jesus', is a condition of its truthfulness.

What might 'witness' or 'martyrdom' mean, today? The form of the question, derived from models of interpretation the inadequacy of which I have tried to indicate, is unsatisfactory. It should rather be: What form might contemporary fidelity to 'the testimony of Jesus' appropriately take? And this is a practical and not merely a theoretical question. It is a question that will continue, often in darkness, strenuously to engage all those resources of integrity and discernment without which patterns of human action are not responsibly undertaken or pursued. And it will also continue to engage all those resources of textual, historical and literary criticism without which the

New Testament scholar cannot competently perform his indispensable function. That function, I have suggested, is an aspect, but only an aspect, of the broader task of Christian interpretative practice, of the attempt to bear witness faithfully and effectively to God's transformative purpose and meaning for mankind.

PART III

7

Ideology, Metaphor and Analogy

Introduction

Theologians are more frequently charged with flight from reality than with strenuous engagement in its obdurate complexity. If 'it is the fault of the idealist always to seek escape from the authority of the tragic',[1] then it must be admitted that much Christian preaching and theological writing, appealing as it does to 'ultimate reality', or to a 'higher truth', in a manner that depreciates or trivializes the urgency and agony of particular choice and particular circumstance, provides ample warrant for Donald MacKinnon's contention that 'idealism remains a besetting temptation of the theological understanding'.[2] 'Idealism' he wrote twenty-five years earlier, 'is always in the end the acceptance of the realm of ideas as somehow self-justifying, of man's spiritual experience as the real motor force of historical change.'[3] It is hardly surprising that one who thus characterized idealism should insist that 'There are deep lessons to be learnt by the contemporary theologian from serious engagement with the Marxist rejection of idealism'.[4] And if, for Marx and for most Marxists, religious discourse is presumed to be inescapably idealist in character, MacKinnon himself is one of many contemporary Christian theologians who would agree with the late Michael Foster that 'Christianity is itself opposed to idealism', and that 'the Christian should agree with almost all the criticism which the Marxist brings against idealism'.[5]

Any such agreement would entail accepting many fundamental features of the Marxist critique of 'ideology'. I have attempted elsewhere to indicate some of the senses in which the practice of Christian belief, and Christian theology, are appropriately characterized as 'ideological'.[6] In this chapter, I want to indicate some of the ways in which Christian theological enquiry, or some aspects of that enquiry, might contribute to the 'critique of ideology'. I propose to do this by making some tentative suggestions concerning the relationship between 'metaphor' and 'analogy' in religious and theological discourse. By way of introduction, however, it will be convenient to return to Donald MacKinnon's reflections on the controversy between 'idealism' and 'realism'.

The epistemological dimension of this controversy is indicated by MacKinnon's characterization of Kant's refutation of idealism as 'a necessary part of his subtle and strenuous effort . . . to hold together a view which treated learning about the world as a finding, with one that regarded such learning as a constructive act'.[7] The complexity of the relations between 'finding' and 'fashioning',[8] between discovery and construction, may be indicated by reminding ourselves that, in myth, parable, the writing of history and of the novel, *narrative* forms are not the least important of the modes of discourse that we employ in our attempts to 'discover', to lay bare, something of what is the case concerning the world in which we are, and concerning the ways in which we are and may be 'located' in a world that sets objective limits to our attempts to fashion it to our desires and fancies.

Even though Archimedes leaping from his bath could be said to have 'made' a discovery, it would still seem more immediately apparent of narrative than it is of the language of scientific discovery that we *construct* our apprehension of reality, and that in this sense construction (with its attendant risks of fantasy and illusion) is the form of all 'invention'.[9] We should, however, remember Einstein's insistence 'on the extent to which fundamental scientific progress must wait on the development, by spontaneous intellectual creativity, of more powerful branches of mathematics'.[10] Nevertheless, there does seem to be a sense in which narrative construction is more patently a 'work of art' than is the elaboration of scientific theory. And, if this is so, then that sense may be closely connected with the apparently more pervasive presence of the *metaphorical* in narrative than in theoretical discourse.

Already, several questions are suggested which should be of some interest to students of Christian theology; and they are questions which raise issues concerning the 'ideological' character of religious practice and theological reflection. In the first place, there is the question of divine revelation. A form of Christian faith which had surrendered all attempt to speak of our perception of meaning, our apprehension of hope, as fundamentally 'given' in revelation would have surrendered, without a struggle, to Feuerbach's perceptive but partial critique. And yet the way is now barred to any theology of revelation which attempts, 'positivistically', to see, in the sources and grounds of Christian hope, exceptions to the rule that it is only in risking the construction of a story that human beings have given content, shape and specificity to their hopes and fears. The narrative that declares our hope to be 'received' and not 'invented' is itself an interpretative and, in *that* sense, a 'constructive' enterprise. And we cannot avoid taking personal responsibility for the tale that we tell, even while acknowledging that the truth of the tale ultimately depends upon a fulfilment of conditions the manner of which is beyond our observation and understanding.[11]

But, with that acknowledgment, is not any possibility of the Christian legitimately laying claim to *knowledge* of the truth of the tale that he tells automatically excluded? This is no new question. Aquinas attempted to tackle it in the first question of the *Summa Theologiae*. Its contemporary exploration would demand the kind of close attention to problems concerning the relationship of 'knowledge' to 'belief' which many contemporary writers, from Christians (cheerfully disclaiming any suggestion that they 'know' that of which they speak) to Althusserian Marxists (arbitrarily restricting the range of use of the concept of 'knowledge' to the products of their 'theoretical practice'), prefer either to evade or disastrously to oversimplify.[12]

In the second place, if, as I propose to argue, there are forms of narrative discourse which have an irreducible centrality in the practice of Christianity, is not Christian religious discourse thereby rendered unavoidably 'ideological' at least in the sense that the 'truthfulness' of a tale told is partly determined by the circumstances of its production – in respect both of the 'point of view' from which it is told, and of the linguistic and imaginative resources available for its construction? In other words, does not narrative discourse lack that aspiration to universality and timelessness of expression which is characteristic of 'theoretical' or 'scientific' discourse?

In the third place, if the Christian wishes to urge that there are tales to be told whch, for all the particularity of their production and symbolic content, nevertheless 'embody' or 'signify' 'universal' truths, is he not obliged to consider questions concerning the relationship of myth, history and poetry to metaphysics? Donald MacKinnon has suggested that metaphysics sometimes emerges as 'the attempt to convert poetry into the logically admissible'.[13] In what circumstances could such 'conversion' hope to be successful? And what forms of metaphysical discourse are available, today, that are not fatally infected by idealism?

Brian Wicker, on whose stimulating study *The Story-Shaped World* I shall shortly be drawing, argues that 'Metaphor . . . raises questions that only analogy . . . can answer, while conversely analogy can only answer questions that are raised in a metaphorical form'.[14] In the light of my earlier remarks on the epistemological dimension of the controversy between idealism and realism, I suggest that Wicker's proposal might be expanded along the following lines.

The metaphysician traditionally conducts his enquiry along the 'way of analogy'. He supposes himself to be in some sense set on a voyage of discovery, at least inasmuch as only the boldest of bad metaphysicians would cheerfully admit that he was arbitrarily imposing patterns on the world of our experience. However, set on such a voyage, the theological metaphysician is prey to scepticism and discouragement in view of the fact that, appropriately mindful of the interrogative, heuristic character of his analogical extension of familiar usage, discovery is always indefinitely postponed.

The story-teller explores in a different direction. Conscious of his responsibility to help his audience to 'shape' their experience, to 'make sense' of their world, he journeys along the way, not of analogy, but of metaphor. But the attempt to 'make sense' of the world elides with dangerous ease into the attempt to make the world, in our imagination, conform to how we would have it be. The narrator is prey not so much to discouragement as to the illusion that the human quest for meaning and truth is a quest for appropriate construction.

The forms of Christian discourse are set between the poles of metaphor and analogy, of narrative and metaphysics. How, then, may the relationship between these poles be negotiated in practice and characterized in theory? And what steps can be taken to minimize the twin risks of scepticism and illusion? These are some of the issues on which, after this protracted introduction, I wish tentatively to offer some reflections.

Metaphor and autobiography

The tension between the story-teller and the philosopher, between metaphor and analogy, expression and analysis, between 'the logic of the heart' and a cooler, more dispassionate set of logical tools, is ancient and intractable. And if, in the nineteenth century, Newman attempted to sustain the tension in his exploration of the relationships between 'real' and 'notional' assent, between 'religion' and 'theology', today, in theological circles in Britain, the tension is in danger of slackening into mutual indifference. It is not that the conflict has been resolved, or even significantly clarified, but rather, as Brian Wicker suggests, that the battleground has shifted from theology to literary criticism.[15]

Wicker illuminatingly contrasts the divergent assessments of the metaphorical in two contemporary traditions of criticism, represented by Norman Mailer and Alain Robbe-Grillet. Both men see their task as 'helping to free the individual from a system of emotional and cultural constraints . . . rooted in the inherited ideology of their respective societies'.[16] Mailer would free us from the 'one-dimensionality' of technologism through 'a return to an older poetic and metaphorical way of looking at the world'.[17] According to Robbe-Grillet, the anthropomorphism that is endemic to metaphorical discourse perpetuates our enslavement to 'Nature', itself a construct of bourgeois Romanticism. He sees it as the job of the novelist to cleanse our language of anthropomorphism by banishing all metaphor.

Epistemologically, a central issue concerns the cognitive status of literary and artistic experience and expression.[18] And if, in philosophy and the social sciences, an ancient rationalism still frequently depreciates the cognitive capacity of metaphorical discourse,[19] Gadamer's study of *Truth and Method* and Ricoeur's study of *The Rule of Metaphor* signal a redressing of the balance.[20] Gadamer has sought to rehabilitate the Romantic recognition that 'art is knowledge and the experience of the work of art is a sharing of this knowledge'.[21]

Mailer would surely agree. But perhaps we should say, more cautiously, that art *may* be knowledge, because 'the recurring temptation to self-indulgence and even dishonesty that goes with a dedication to metaphorical language is far from conquered today'.[22] Robbe-Grillet's attempt to 'cleanse' our language of metaphor represents one form of the struggle against this temptation. 'We need', says Wicker, 'the corrective presence of the not-human . . . of that which is impervious to linguistic manipulation.'[23] The theological overtones are clear. But how can that which is 'impervious to linguistic manipulation', *sive Deus sive natura*, be brought to speech? Where non-human empirical reality is concerned, the answer might be sought in the quest of scientific discourse for a formal purity as little 'infected' as possible by the anthropomorphism of the metaphorical. Where the mystery of God is concerned, however, it is less clear what linguistic strategy, if any, could meet this demand. We shall return to such questions later on. I have mentioned them at this stage only to suggest that the 'corrective presence' to which Wicker refers cannot make its appearance exclusively *within* the narrative mode of discourse. Narrative without metaphor (in so far as it is possible at all) merely depicts a world devoid of meaning, and to be left alone with one's own meaninglessness is 'an ironic kind of "liberation".[24] Are these the only options available: the construction of meaning or the recognition of meaninglessness? Or is there also meaning that is not, in the last analysis, fashioned but found? Even the form of the question is, significantly, metaphysical. Thus it is that reflection on metaphor raises questions which cannot be answered metaphorically (because anthropomorphism cannot be anthropomorphically transcended) and which, in narrative discourse from which – so far as possible – metaphor has been banished, receive only the bleakest of negative responses.

I suggest that the distinction between narrative, metaphorical discourse, and those non-narrative modes of discourse to which reflection on the metaphorical gives rise appears, within Christianity, as a distinction between religious practice and critical reflection on that practice: between 'religion' and 'theology'. This is only a first approximation demanding further specification which I shall try to give to it as the argument proceeds.

The distinction between religious and theological discourse, too often obscured or elided in the work of theologians, philosophers and social scientists alike is, nevertheless, fundamental and irreducible. It is, however, formal and heuristic in character, and to insist that it must be kept in mind is not to issue a warrant for employing it with that insensitivity to the complex variety of particular instances which is the besetting sin of so many attempts at classifying or 'mapping' our linguistic usage.

Having issued that warning against mistaking the map for the countryside, I now want to suggest that the paradigm or 'focal' forms of Jewish and Christian religious discourse are not simply narrative but are, more specifically, autobiographical. They are autobiographical both in the sense that they are 'self-involving' (although this will be shown in their performance, and will not necessarily appear in their grammatical form) and in the sense that, as self-involving, they 'locate' the speaker (or the group of which he is a spokesman) in a particular cultural, historical tradition: 'My father was a wandering Aramean.' Whether the 'audience' addressed is God (in acts of supplication and worship) or other people (in acts of witness), the Christian is the teller of a tale, the narrator of a story which he tells as *his* story, as a story in which he acknowledges himself to be a participant.

From this elementary observation, a number of things follow. In the first place, Christian religious discourse, as autobiographical, will always be shaped and influenced more deeply than we know by the circumstances of its production. However 'truthfully' we try to tell our story, the narrative that we produce is always subject to ideological distortion.

In the second place, Christian religious discourse, as autobiographical, tends to attribute an unwarranted universality to the particular forms in which, in particular circumstances, it finds expression. Convinced that the tale that we tell is truly told, Christians tend to assume that the way they tell it is the way it has ever been and must ever be told.

In the third place, the construction of an autobiography, as of any narrative, entails selection, planning, the imposition of order. We do not 'merely' remember. We seek to construct, to '*make*' sense of our lives and of our history. Unless we construct the narrative, we can make no sense of our temporally ordered existence. But the very fact that the sense has to be 'made', the narrative constructed, threatens the veracity of the tale.

In the fourth place, every narrative has a beginning, a middle and an end. But 'end' ambiguously signifies both conclusion and goal, both terminus and purpose. And the Christian, like any autobiographer, stands in the middle of the history to which he seeks to give narrative expression. He is, therefore, tempted, for the sake of the coherence of the story (which is the coherence of his human and Christian experience) to claim a clearer apprehension of the 'plot' than the evidence warrants. Living in hope of resurrection, he is tempted to reduce past and present suffering to the status of necessary conditions of a 'happy ending'. 'The temptation of Hegelian and utilitarian alike', says Donald MacKinnon, 'is to find always the justification of the present in the future.'[25] And he adds: 'But the Cross utterly prevents such a trivialising of the past.'[26] The dark facticity of particular deeds and particular tragedy may not be obliterated for the sake of the coherence of the narrative. Not the least insidious of the forms of idealism by which Christian religious discourse is threatened is that which, springing from the conviction that there *is* a sense which it all makes, seeks prematurely to give to that sense unified narrative expression.

I have been trying to sketch some of the ways in which, as autobiographical (and hence as metaphorical) discourse, Christian religious speech is threatened by 'self-indulgence and even dishonesty'. Are there countervailing influences to hand which might discipline and purify faith's tendency to construct a significance which, *as* constructed, is at best distorted and, at worst, illusory? There are, I suggest, at least two such corrective influences.

I have already insisted on the importance of the distinction between 'religion' and 'theology', between the practice of faith, in worship and witness, and critical reflection on that practice. Thus the first corrective influence, or set of such influences, arises from the interaction of practice and reflection. There will be a variety of forms of reflection (or 'theological disciplines') corresponding to the variety of aspects under which the practice of faith may be critically considered. Thus, for example, because Christian religious discourse is *discourse*, it demands 'grammatical' or philosophical consideration (in the next section of this essay, I shall, therefore, consider 'theology as metaphysics'). Because Christian religious discourse is paradigmatically *narrative*, it demands literary-critical consideration. And because Christian narrative is in some sense autobiographical, it demands historical consideration.

The tendency, in contemporary English biblical studies, is to consider literary-critical and historical aspects of theological reflection as sharply distinct and to concentrate on the latter to the neglect of the former. This tendency derives from a period when positivistic conceptions of historical understanding went hand-in-hand with non-cognitive accounts of literary and poetic statement (which carried the implication that the fruit of literary-critical reflection on the biblical narratives could only be 'subjective' in character). But if it has sometimes been assumed (in theology and elsewhere) that there is 'a natural tension between the historian and the literary critic',[27] there is no timeless validity to this assumption. Thus, for example, Gadamer has powerfully argued the case for recovering a sense of the fundamental unity of the hermeneutical disciplines. From such a standpoint, it makes sense to say that 'historical understanding proves to be a kind of literary criticism writ large'.[28] Gadamer, at least as I understand him, is not seeking to obliterate the distinction between historical truth and the truth of metaphorical fiction. He is calling to our attention connections and similarities that have been too long obscured from view. At least, where Christian theology is concerned, it is surely worth remembering that the New Testament historian, for example, is dealing with narratives whose adequate elucidation demands (though it does not always receive) the most sophisticated use of literary-critical skills. And whether what those narratives express is, in the last resort, construction or discovery is, arguably, a question whose resolution is constitutive of the decision of Christian faith.

My first suggestion, then, is that Christian religious discourse is subject to purificatory and corrective criticism from the historian and the literary critic, as well as from the sociologist and psychologist of religion (to mention two other disciplines whose right to be heard is increasingly acknowledged even in the more cobwebbed theological debating-chambers). And if the tensions between practice and reflection are frequently destructive, rather than creative, this is partly because exegetes and historians have sometimes been invited to establish the grounds of belief, rather than critically to reflect upon its past and present performance and, when they have shown themselves incapable of executing this function, it has been concluded that belief has no grounds. But this is to raise questions of verification on which I shall comment briefly later on.

I have said that there are two sets of corrective influences upon the tendency of Christian belief to undergo ideological distortion. I now want to suggest, therefore, that in addition to those external correctives some of which have just been indicated, Christian religious practice also contains *internal* correctives to its own anthropomorphism. If the history of Christian faith and spirituality is a history of exuberant metaphor (verbal, ritual and iconographic), it is – just as insistently – a history of silence, simplicity and iconoclasm: of a sense that what needs to be said cannot be said. Not the least powerful of the pressures generating this apophatic dimension in Christian history has been the experience of suffering. If 'ideology . . . dulls the tragic vision's alertness to limits',[29] the experience of tragedy can sharpen that vision or (to change the metaphor) can constitute the hard rock on which the exuberance of affirmation is broken. Suffering corrupts and disfigures. And yet, it can also purify. Any description of Christian belief as 'merely ideological', as self-indulgent construction of satisfying narrative, inexcusably ignores the silent witness of that simplicity and realism which has sometimes been the fruit of a practically sustained 'alertness to limits'.

If it is true that one of the most important features of any metaphor is that we must deny its literal truth if we are to understand its metaphorical significance,[30] and hence perceive the truth which metaphor expresses, then it is perhaps not fanciful to suggest that the dialectic of affirmation and denial which is so striking a feature of the history of Christian spirituality amounts to a practical recognition of the metaphorical status of those narrative forms which I have described as paradigmatic for Christian religious discourse.

In the performance of that dialectic, Christians have been motivated by the conviction that they were responding to the 'corrective presence' of that which is 'impervious to linguistic manipulation'. This conviction, married to that unquenchable intellectual curiosity, that 'pure . . . desire simply to know',[31] which has been one of the hallmarks of Western consciousness, has sometimes provoked Christian believers to forms of reflection, of philosophical enquiry, which transcend the practical dialectic of metaphor and its negation.[32] There are questions which the recognition of paradox and, indeed, silence itself provokes rather than stifles. Metaphorical discourse, I have

suggested, raises questions which cannot be answered metaphorically. In various ways, in the past, such questions have
been explored along 'the way of analogy', to which we now,
therefore, turn.

Analogy: voie sans issue?

In the previous section, I raised the question: how can that
which is 'impervious to linguistic manipulation' be brought to
speech? When the intended referent of this question is the
transcendent mystery of God, there are several reasons for
supposing that metaphysical discourse (where metaphysics is
conceived as that branch of philosophy the logic of whose
procedures focusses on analogical usage of unrestricted generality) cannot provide the answer.

First, there are those who insist that the 'way of analogy' is
closed, and that it is only in metaphor that we can hope to speak
to God. If this were the case, then there would be no way past
the Feuerbachian critique, because we would be unable to
discriminate between the 'models' of God that we fashion
in metaphor and the discovered mystery signified by such
constructions. All that we say of God, affirmatively, is indeed
'projected' from our human experience, is anthropomorphic in
character, and we would have no way of showing the sense of
such language to be other than 'merely' projective.

Secondly, there are those who, in various ways, assimilate
the logic of analogy to that of metaphor, using the two concepts
more or less interchangeably.[33] On this account, the 'way of
analogy' is apparently open, but the appearance is illusory,
because 'analogy' turns out to be either a sub-class of metaphor
or the 'common heading' under which 'the family of metaphor'
is subsumed.[34]

Thirdly, recent studies of metaphor, standing in varied
relations of dependence on Aristotle's *Poetics*, lay the emphasis
on dissimilarity. Thus Ricoeur: 'Enigma lives on in the heart
of metaphor. In metaphor, "the same" operates *in spite of* "the
different".'[35] So far, so good. But not the least of the reasons
why I hesitated before deciding to risk using the term 'analogy'

in this essay is that it has become increasingly common to lay the emphasis, when speaking of analogy, on *similarity*: as if, along the way of analogy, 'the different' operated *in spite of* 'the same'. This is emphatically *not* the case with Aquinas' use of analogy, although it has sometimes been made to appear so in neoscholastic apologetics searching for a 'direct route', philosophically, to the knowledge of God.

In the fourth place, it could be suggested that the 'No Entry' sign across the way of analogy was most firmly planted by Kant. It is, however, at least worth asking *which* route it was that he blocked in so apparently insurmountable a manner.

According to Donald MacKinnon, Kant 'raised a problem which by dexterous use of Aristotelian analogy [the scholastics] had tried to bypass'.[36] This bypass consisted in exploiting the ontological conviction that, since 'Being . . . was an analogically participated transcendental',[37] it was possible to move from negation to affirmation, from speech concerning the conditioned to speech concerning the unconditioned ground of all conditions. 'When the schoolmen insist that agnosticism comes before anthropomorphism, we are with them all the time. But, alas, their device for allowing assertion on the basis of negation demands assumptions that we cannot make. For we have to admit in knowledge a kind of intuitive awareness of analogically participated being which we do not seem to have.'[38]

Who are these 'schoolmen', who employ this device? They undoubtedly include many of those seventeenth- and eighteenth-century scholastics against whose views Kant was reacting. But, here as elsewhere, we need to remember the sea-change undergone by late scholasticism in the seventeenth century. Thrown newly on the defensive, proof rather than enquiry became the dominant concern. Theology 'replaced the inquiry of the *quaestio* by the pedagogy of the thesis'.[39]

Nevertheless, even if the conviction that human beings had, or could have, 'a kind of intuitive awareness of analogically participated being' was of considerable assistance to a theology nervously contracting into apologetic, apologetic concerns alone can hardly have accounted for its emergence. Is the presumption of such intuitive awareness to be found further back, in thirteenth-century scholasticism? Or, since that question is impossibly large, is it to be found in Aquinas' treatment in the first thirteen Questions of the first part of his *Summa Theologiae*? For centuries, at least since Cajetan, the answer has appeared to be 'yes', and that affirmative reply is still frequently given in such neoscholasticism as survives even today.[40] In recent decades, however, historical studies of medieval thought on the one hand, and philosophical developments on the other, have made possible a reading of Aquinas that is not filtered through the systematizing transformations wrought in post-seventeenth-century scholasticism. It is beyond my competence to resolve the historical issue. I can only record the fact that I am persuaded by those whose interpretation of Aquinas' procedures, in the text to which I referred, gives us an account of his treatment of analogy which does not involve any recourse to that 'device' against which Kant protested.[41]

One of the central targets of Lonergan's *Insight* is those who persist in assuming that 'knowing consists in taking a look'. On this assumption, terms such as 'essence' and 'existence' are taken to refer to mysterious objects which 'need an extraordinary language to articulate or a superior faculty to apprehend them. Possession of such a faculty then becomes the prerequisite for being a metaphysician. Call it superior insight or the intuition of being'.[42] This model of metaphysical enquiry is in striking contrast to that with which Aquinas worked. For him, 'the mode of metaphysics is not intuitive . . . but logical'.[43] The metaphysician is distinguished from the logician 'not in possessing an arcane method but simply by the power of his intelligence'.[44] On this account there is a certain irony in H. P. Owen's criticism of G. E. M. Anscombe and P. T. Geach for being preoccupied, in their treatment of analogy, 'with logic at the expense of metaphysics'.[45] And it is significant that Owen, in common with most neoscholastics, supposes that the metaphysician's explorations along the way of analogy can furnish us with a doctrine of God.

To discover what Aquinas is up to in these Questions, it is necessary to attend to his performance, and not to be misled by the fact that the tools he uses are not those which a modern logician would employ. Thus, in spite of Aquinas' insistence that he is concerned to show 'what God is not',[46] generations of commentators have been misled by his use of 'object-language constructions to do metalinguistic jobs'[47] into supposing that he is offering a doctrine of God, at least in the sense that he is constructing a catalogue of divine attributes. In fact, 'Aquinas is not attempting to describe God at all',[48] and 'a perceptive reader would think twice before identifying a deliberate consideration of what God is not with a teaching presuming to say what God is'.[49] His treatment is resolutely grammatical and, 'while a grammatical account cannot pretend to offer a proper account of the subject in question, it can discourage improper ones'.[50] Thus, although in these Questions there are few instances of Aquinas indicating the connections between 'the more austere grammatical discipline of theology'[51] and religious discourse, a view of the relationship between religion and theology is implicit in the procedures he adopts. Theology neither reinforces nor supplants the 'image' of God built up through Christian living – in prayer, work, suffering, relation-ship – an image which, for the Christian, finds its focus in consideration of the person, words, work and death of Jesus the Christ. The role of theology, as Aquinas conceives it, is to 'exercise critical control' over this image, and over the narratives in which it finds expression, 'now unravelling confusions and inconsistencies that arise from it, now checking it with *praxis* to offset its stereotypical drift, now challenging it as a lazy simplification'.[52] On this account, then, metaphysical theology stands in a critical relationship to religious practice similar to that which I have already suggested obtains between the 'hermeneutical' theological disciplines and the practice of religion.[53]

If Burrell is justified in thus interpreting Aquinas' insistence that he is concerned, by reflecting 'grammatically' on the limits of language, to elucidate what cannot be said of God, then the gulf between Aquinas and Kant is perhaps not so wide, at this point, as has usually been supposed. But if 'we cannot pretend to offer a description of a transcendent object without betraying its transcendence',[54] does it follow that there is nothing which we can truly say of God? It would seem so, for even the discussion, in Question 13, of those predicates which *are* acceptably used of God remains under the rubric of God's 'simpleness', his 'non-compositeness', according to which 'all statements formed of subject and object – that is to say, all discourse – will falsify the reality which God is'.[55] It is at this point that the question of whether or not Aquinas sought to provide the outlines of a 'doctrine of God' is most closely linked with the question of analogy, for it has often been supposed, as we have seen, that the way of analogy provided a route by which the *via negativa* could be transcended, giving rise to a set of positive affirmations sufficiently firm and informative as to constitute the elements of a doctrine of God.[56]

In view of Burrell's insistence that Aquinas' grammatical reflections on language and its limits do not provide us with a 'doctrine of God', it comes as little surprise to find him insisting that, although Aquinas is perhaps best known for his theory of analogy, on 'closer inspection it turns out that he never had one'.[57] And Burrell's comment on Cajetan and, following him, the host of others who have tried to construct such a theory from Aquinas' scattered and unsystematic observations on analogy is somewhat caustic: 'The misunderstanding resulted in the usual way: the philosophical activity of the master became doctrine in the hands of his disciples.'[58]

In fact, the situation is more interesting than that negative comment indicates. Neoscholasticism supposed that, on the basis of a theory of analogy, it was able to construct a doctrine of God. Whereas, if Aquinas *had* had a 'theory' of analogy, he would thereby have been prevented from using analogy to speak of God at all. That remark is, I hope, sufficiently provocative to deserve unpacking a little.

Metaphor functions with the recognition of differences: 'the metaphorical statement captures its sense as metaphorical midst the ruins of the literal sense'.[59] Aquinas' distinction between metaphor and analogy stems from this recognition that, if we are to apprehend the truth which metaphor expresses, we must first deny its literal truth. There are, however, some expressions of which this denial is unnecessary, because we do not know and cannot specify the limits of their literal applicability.[60] Thus, for example, to understand what is meant by a 'living' tradition, we do not first have to deny that cultural processes are organisms. Nor, if we describe a friend as having a 'wise expression', do we have hurriedly to add: 'Of course, it's not really his *expression* that is wise.' In both cases, our usage is 'analogical'. In contrast, if we describe a talented gardener as having 'green fingers', it is necessary implicitly to deny the literal truth of the description.[61] Terms like *'wise, good* and *living* are used . . . in contexts so widely divergent that they defy comparison. . . How are such expressions related? That we cannot say'.[62] We learn how to use such terms appropriately, not by applying a theoretical maxim, but through the practical discipline of developing a sensitive appreciation of appropriate usage. Linguistic usage is an art, not a science And, if we *were* able theoretically to formulate the way in which the contexts in which we use such terms are related, then we would be unable to use them of 'a God who transcends all our contexts'.[63] It is in this sense that it is true to say that, if Aquinas had had a *theory* of analogical predication, he would thereby have been prevented from using analogy to speak of God. Those who have constructed 'theories' of analogy have usually construed 'analogy' as itself a univocal term, whereas Aquinas wisely refrained from making this move: in his hands, the notion of 'analogy' is itself highly analogical.

But what is Aquinas' justification for assuming that even terms such as 'wise', 'good' and 'living' can be applied non-metaphorically to God? The first thing to notice is that the terms selected are 'perfection terms' which occur, as a matter of fact, in the religious activity of praising God.[64] Aquinas' remarks about the applicability of such terms to radically diverse contexts, the limits of which we cannot specify, at least indicate that the believer, in thus articulating his praise of God, is not manifestly talking nonsense. We cannot specify the limits of the applicability of such terms; therefore we cannot specify the limits of their literal applicability; therefore these terms (which believers, as a matter of fact, apply to God) cannot be said to be not literally applicable to God.

At this point, however, it is necessary to notice the part played by those considerations of causality which reflect Aquinas' enduring neo-Platonism. His heuristic definition of God as the 'source' of all things affords 'the formal licence to use [perfection terms] *in divinis*.'[65] As the source of all that is, God is the source of all 'perfections'.[66] It follows, according to Aquinas, that if such terms as 'wise' and 'good' and 'living' *were* to be used literally, they would be used primarily of God and only second-arily of whatever else it is to which they are variously applicable. 'The obvious implication is that we are never in a position to employ these terms literally.'[67] By introducing this hint concerning a specification of the limits of literal applicability, Aquinas, having begun by sharply distinguishing metaphorical from analogical usage, has ended by acknowledging that there is an 'irreducibly metaphorical dimension in analogous expressions'.[68] Or, to put the point anthropomorphically (and thus metaphorically), only God would be in a position to use analogical terms without any touch of metaphor. However, to interpret this recognition as amounting to a concession that, at the end of the day, 'analogy' has been subsumed into 'metaphor' would be to ride roughshod over significant grammatical distinctions which Aquinas was at pains to elucidate.[69] After all, many philosophers of science today would be willing to recognize an irreducibly metaphorical dimension in scientific discourse. But few of them would suppose that they were thereby admitting that all scientific discourse was 'merely metaphorical'.

The philosopher, as Aquinas conceives his task, cannot show the believer *how* to use of God even those terms which are literally (and not 'merely' metaphorically) applicable to God. Just as the philosopher does not *initiate* the quest for God, 'the source and goal of all things', so also the philosopher cannot teach us the appropriate use of religious language. That use will be learnt, in religion as in cookery and politics, by disciplined practice: 'in religious matters, as in others, a philosopher can at best help to discriminate sense from nonsense'.[70]

The way of analogy serves neither as a substitute for nor, in any direct sense, as a confirmation of the way of discipleship.

At most, by shedding some light on the logically peculiar character of the linguistic dimension of our quest for God, it may 'help us through the temptation to think that reality is unintelligible'.[71]

Aquinas has often been described as 'agnostic', and my emphasis on the extent to which, in these opening Questions of the *Summa Theologiae*, he resolutely refrains from offering a 'doctrine of God', contenting himself with paying sustained logical attention to what can *not* be said of God, would seem to underline the appropriateness of that description. There are, however, at least two points of view from which the description is misleading. In the first place, Aquinas is not the only great metaphysician to have supposed that there is a sense, however obscure and indirect, in which a disciplined attention to linguistic usage can *show* us something of the character of the objects of our discourse[72] (and therefore, possibly, something of the character of our relationship to God). Of course, grammatical reflection cannot 'directly tell us whether or not there are any such objects',[73] but then it is abundantly clear from the first Question of the *Summa Theologiae* that Aquinas is not concerned to attempt to demonstrate that God exists.[74] It is no business of the philosophical theologian to seek to verify religious truth-claims. It does not follow that such verification is nobody else's business either: 'Wittgenstein did not after all say in his parenthesis "*Religion* as grammar".'[75]

In the second place, I suggest that we need to distinguish between agnosticism as a religious attitude (the practical attitude of one who refrains from worship because of his suspicion that songs of praise are sung not merely into silence but into emptiness) and as a theological policy aimed at insistently reminding the believer of the limits both of his language and of his theoretical understanding. The knowledge born of human love is frequently incapable of finding adequate expression. Lovers, and not only those with weak digestions, have been known to 'sigh and groan'. The lover does not, however, infer from his inability to 'capture the beloved in language' that the beloved is not, after all, known. The 'reticence' of the lover, his continual negation of expressions perceived as inadequate to their object, does not argue nescience, but a more penetrating knowledge than that contained in those 'neutral' descriptions of the beloved that are also available to casual acquaintances, and are found in the files of the family doctor and the social historian. On what *logical* grounds could the possibility be excluded that there is available, within human experience, a 'dark knowledge' of that transcendent mystery of which such neutral descriptions are precisely *not* available (and that they are not is part of the drift of Aquinas' grammatical reflections)? This is, of course, a dangerous line of thought because, if human love is always threatened by illusion, how much more so is man's personal knowledge of the unknown God? If love, any love, is to be responsible, it needs continual submission to a process of verification, of the corrective purification of illusion. But husband and wife do not usually set private detectives (the social equivalent of the 'natural theologian', in the sense in which Karl Barth was rightly suspicious of him?) on to each other, even though there may be circumstances in which resort to this desperate expedient is appropriate. But it is significant that these will be circumstances in which, love having grown cold, personal knowledge has been called radically into question. Burrell neatly captures the sense in which it is and is not appropriate to describe Aquinas as 'agnostic' when he says that 'Aquinas displays his religious discipline most clearly by the ease with which he is able to endure so unknown a God'.[76]

A note on 'verification'

It is fashionable to characterize the strategies available for the testing of religious truth-claims as lying between the limits of 'rationalism' on the one hand and 'fideism' on the other. By 'rationalism', I understand an approach according to which the practice of faith is judged at best irresponsible and at worst superstitious except in so far as its grounds have been established and secured by techniques of verification that are independent of specifically religious considerations. By 'fideism', I understand an approach which, insisting that appropriate criteria of assessment are only available *within* particular patterns of experience, or 'ways of life', refuses to submit the claims of faith to 'external' assessment, whether by the historian, the social scientist or the philosopher.

Christianity has, at one time or another, invested heavily in forms of rationalism in an attempt to ensure its integrity and respectability as an aspect of the human quest for truth. Thus, for example, the burgeoning of 'natural theologies' in the eighteenth century (especially in the form of 'arguments from design') represented an acceptance, by philosophers of religion, of responsibility for securing the theistic grounds of Christian belief. It was not, of course, the theistic grounds alone that needed to be secured. From the eighteenth century onwards, biblical scholars and historians of doctrine came to accept responsibility for securing, by techniques of 'secular' or 'scientific' historiography, the historical grounds of Christian belief.

In our day, both philosophers of religion and historians of Christian origins have increasingly come to admit their inability to fulfil their allotted tasks. But the apparent vulnerability to which their failure exposes Christian belief may yet be beneficial. For the rationalist strategy presupposed that, except in so far as we have succeeded in 'securing' reality *theoretically*, our patterns of action and policy are irresponsible. There is, however, an alternative and perhaps more fruitful strategy which, recognizant of the primacy of action in respect of reflection, of 'social existence' in respect of 'consciousness',[77] supposes that unless we risk seeking responsibly to live and act in the world, any theoretical 'purchase' that we imagine ourselves to have upon reality is fragile and suspect. And if this alternative strategy was put to theological use by Newman, especially in his *University Sermons*, it was put to rather different use, by a contemporary of his, as a central characteristic of Marx's 'materialism'.

The account that I have tried to give, in this chapter, of the relation between religious practice and theological reflection – whether historical, literary-critical or metaphysical – is, in this sense, 'materialist'.

To paraphrase Marx, the question whether objective truth

can be attributed to Christian believing is a practical question. The Christian must prove the truth, i.e. the reality and power, the this-sidedness of his believing in practice.[78] 'If the Christian faith is true (and unless its truth-claims can be sustained, we had better have done with it for ever), its truth is constituted by the correspondence of its credenda with harsh, human reality.'[79] That correspondence eludes theoretical demonstration. It can, however, be practically, imperfectly, partially and provisionally *shown* by the character and quality of Christian engagement in patterns of action and suffering, praise and endurance, that refuse to short-cut the quest by the erection of conceptual or institutional absolutes. The absolutization of contingent particulars is always idolatrous: the denial of divine transcendence.

Thus pragmatically to characterize the practical procedures by which Christian truth-claims are to be submitted to continual 'verification' is not, however, to endorse the strategy of the 'fideist'. For if Christian truth-claims cannot be confirmed – in any straightforward sense – by theological reflection, whether historical or philosophical, they are nevertheless such as to demand continual exposure to *dis*confirmation. Thus, for example, I should wish to argue, first, that there are constitutive features of Christian belief which are such as to be permanently exposed to historical falsification; secondly, that the narrative forms in which Christian belief finds primary expression are permanently threatened by that illusory self-indulgence the diagnosis of which is the responsibility of literary criticism; thirdly, that Christian faith in divine transcendence is permanently threatened by that incoherence in its discourse the detection of which is the responsibility of the metaphysician, or 'theological grammarian'.

In brief: the testing of Christian truth-claims occurs, or should occur, in the interplay between their practical verification and their exposure to historical, literary and philosophical criticism.

My justification for offering so outrageously oversimplified a sketch of problems of enormous complexity is that it seemed incumbent upon me to indicate, in however summary a fashion, that approach to problems of verification and falsification which is, I believe, implied by the account of the relationship between theology and religion offered in this chapter.

Conclusion

It has sometimes been suggested that Christians both can and should opt either for 'the God of Abraham, Isaac and Jacob', or for 'the God of the philosophers'; either for narrative or for metaphysics; either for 'making sense' of experience or for seeking to discover the truth-conditions of those assertions characteristic of Christian confession. In this chapter I have attempted, perhaps too obliquely, to indicate some of the reasons why none of these options is, in fact, available.

To suppose that narrative is an alternative to metaphysics, metaphor an alternative to analogy, is to overlook the fact that 'Metaphor . . . raises questions that only analogy . . . can answer, while conversely analogy can only answer questions that are raised in a metaphorical form'.[80] Similarly, to suppose that construction is an alternative to discovery is either, if one opts for construction, to settle for a Feuerbachian account of the 'essence of Christianity' (and there are surely less cumbersome ways of being an atheist than to use the paraphernalia of Christian language and imagery simply to express the form of our alienation?), or to suppose that we have access to the mystery of God other than through the hazardous enterprise of fashioning our human history.

If nothing is gained by attempting partial solutions, neither is anything to be gained by settling back into that benign pluralism ('of course, we always need *both*') which mistakes the diagnosis of a problem for its solution. I have suggested that there are two senses in which the story-teller comes first, and two senses in which, if he were left to himself, the integrity and truthfulness of Christianity would be compromised.

Thus, on the one hand, the story-teller comes first inasmuch as Christian religious discourse, as a constitutive element in the practice of Christianity, is paradigmatically narrative (and, more specifically, autobiographical) in form. From this point of view, to 'leave the story-teller to himself' would be to leave

Christian practice – unconstrained by historical, literary and philosophical criticism – exposed to the risk, endemic to all autobiography, of 'self-indulgence and even dishonesty'. (And this, even though, as I have indicated, Christian practice also embodies certain *internal* correctives.) There is thus a sense in which the indispensability of theology is the indispensability of criticism for all forms of ideology.

On the other hand, theology's hermeneutical disciplines (historical and literary-critical) also employ narrative, and hence metaphorical, modes of discourse. The historian of Christian origins, and the literary critic, are thus also 'story-tellers' after their fashion. As such, their products invite the logical attention of the metaphysician: in this sense they, too, cannot be 'left to themselves'. But yet, as story-tellers, they 'come first' inasmuch as the metaphysician, proceeding along the way of analogy, can only answer questions that are 'raised in a metaphorical form'.

The picture that emerges, I suggest, is one that would set the dialectic between construction and the disciplined quest for discovery, between narrative and metaphysics, between making sense and assessing the cost of the operation, along not one axis, but two: the 'vertical' axis of the relationship between religion and theology, and the 'horizontal' axis of the relationship between the hermeneutical and philosophical disciplines.

The schematic character of my remarks in these concluding paragraphs may have given the impression that I have sought to construct yet another 'satisfying model' of theological method with which to distract us from the harder task of tackling, both practically and theoretically, the substantive issues. That has not been my intention. Exercises in theological method that lose sight of their essentially heuristic, exploratory character are yet another form in which the temptation of idealism insinuates itself into the theologian's work.

The dialectic between narrative and nescience, anthropomorphism and agnosticism, vision and darkness, autobiographical enactment and the suffering that breaks our constructed identity, is constitutive both of Christian religious practice and of the relationships that obtain between the various patterns of theological enquiry in which that practice is critically reflected. If there are safeguards against illusion and scepticism, they are not, in the last resort, subject to our control. We can, at most, seek to take appropriate precautions.

8

Theory, Theology and Ideology

Ideology and the problem of religious truthfulness

Truthfulness is integral not only to morality but to sanity. Few of us would survive for long if we seriously supposed our deepest convictions to be false or illusory. Our marriages would founder, our political and professional projects would atrophy; the darkness would silence our whistling. And yet, honest conviction is not easily won and is only sustained in counterpoint with an awareness of its fragility.

That was, if you like, a distant paraphrase of Karl Mannheim's characterization of 'the elemental perplexity of our time'.[1] That perplexity (and now my paraphrase moves closer to his text) can be epitomized in the question: 'How is it possible for man to continue to think and live, to believe, hope and pray, when problems of ideology are being radically raised and thought through in all their implications?'[2] At the practical level, this is a question about likely or appropriate forms of survival (if any) of religious belief and practice. At the theoretical level, it is a question inviting theological reflection on the ideological status and function of religious practice and theological discourse. In attempting to respond to that invitation it is tempting to begin by offering a definition of 'ideology'. For a number of reasons, however, some of which will become clear in the course of this chapter, I prefer to take a more indirect route.

Responses to the problem

Many social scientists, influenced by any one of a number of strands in the Marxist tradition, would reply to my modified form of Mannheim's question by suggesting that religious belief and practice will either wither away in the measure that social and economic conditions are effectively transformed or, failing such transformation, will survive as ideological expressions of an ultimately doomed social order. In the first case, theology would disappear with the erosion of its practical basis; in the second case, it would only survive either as the 'symbolic organization' of a tale that continued, however falteringly, to be told, or as a form of dramatic and literary criticism.

The characterization of religious and theological discourse as 'ideological' is not, of course, confined to the Marxist tradition. It is also found in the work of those sociologists, from Mannheim to Parsons, whose method is classificatory rather than critical, and whose uses of the concept of 'ideology' correspondingly lack many of the pejorative overtones that it usually carried in Marx's writings.[3] Nevertheless, across a wide spectrum of sociological approaches, the characterization of religious and theological discourse as ideological frequently proceeds on a twofold assumption: first, that religious believers are not doing what, in the practice of their religion, they suppose themselves to be doing; secondly, that in the measure that they came to perceive this fact they would, at the very least, abandon all suggestion that religious believing implies or entails cognitive claims that cannot be redescribed, without remainder, in non-theological terms. This assumption, whatever the social conditions that generate and foster it, and whether its academic pedigree is traced, in individual cases, to Marx or to Durkheim, goes well beyond such methodological atheism or agnosticism as is stipulated by the heuristic structure of sociological explanation.

Sociologists, even sociologists of religion, rarely exhibit any close and intellectually serious familiarity with the major traditions of Christian theological enquiry and argument. The sketch I have offered of approaches to the sociology of religion perhaps indicates why this is so: quite simply, they have no need to. They 'know' that 'the criticism of religion has been essentially completed',[4] or at least that the cognitive status of such alternative accounts as theologians continue to offer has been definitively discredited. Most sociologists, including many who are themselves religious believers, would, I suspect, agree that theological discourse is not in the business of making knowledge-claims that need to be considered on their own terms.

And what of the theologians themselves? There are, as I see it, at least three widespread forms of theological response to Mannheim's question. The first consists in responding to the question in a manner sufficiently selective as to escape its full force. Thus, for example, Karl Rahner says that the concept of ideology has been used 'in so many different and contradictory ways that nothing is left to us but simply to give a brief definition . . . of what *we* mean here by ideology'.[5] The definition that he offers, while by no means arbitrary, nevertheless too easily allows him to demonstrate that 'Christianity is not an ideology',[6] even though it is always in danger of interpreting itself as such. Professor Torrance, adopting a similarly selective approach, charges those theologians, such as Schleiermacher and Troeltsch, who reflect upon 'the phenomena of faith rather than [on] that in which we have faith',[7] with thereby converting theological into ideological statements.[8] What is missing from his treatment is any serious engagement with that complex tradition which would characterize *all* theological discourse as 'ideological', whatever 'objective reference and material content'[9] was claimed for such discourse by its exponents.

The second, and by far the most widespread, form of theological response to the question of ideology consists in simply ignoring it. Most theologians pay no more attention to sociologists than sociologists do to theologians. There is, in this mutual inattention, an epistemological paradox. The sociologist, I have already suggested, confidently ignores the theologian because he 'knows' that the theologian is not in the business of making knowledge-claims that need to be considered on their own terms. The theologian, for his part, confidently ignores the sociologist because he 'knows' that the object, springs and centre of theological enquiry are, in the last instance, resistant to the reductionism which is a constitutive feature of many sociological explanations of religion. This state of affairs is paradoxical because, central to the debates that keep both traditions of enquiry on the move are fundamental and fundamentally unresolved issues concerning the character and possibility of both 'knowledge' and 'explanation'.

There is a third form of theological response to the problem of ideology. It is exemplified by the work of the Spanish Marxist theologian, Alfredo Fierro, who resolutely and uncritically embraces an Althusserian form of the distinction between 'knowledge' and 'ideology'. According to Fierro: 'Only a positivist conception of theology can entertain the idea that theology contains some sort of knowledge';[10] no more than nonbelievers do 'Christians know anything about . . . God, but they believe and hope nevertheless. . . Hoping and believing are not knowing; they are a nonknowing illustrated by parables and images'.[11]

Fierro is one of a number of theologians (the others that I have in mind being Latin Americans) who have found, in Althusser's distinction between 'knowledge', or 'science', and 'ideology', an order of service according to which the marriage between Christianity and Marxism may be celebrated in tranquillity.[12] This is intensely paradoxical in view of the use to which Althusser himself has put the distinction in order to 'save the appearances' of Communism.[13]

Considerations of space prevent me from exploring in detail my profound dissatisfaction with Fierro's characterization of 'believing' as a 'nonknowing illustrated by parable and images'. What would it be like, in the concrete, for 'believing' to take this form? What *kind* of 'illustration' of his nescience does Father Fierro expect from what 'parables and images' as he stands before the firing squad? That question seems to me not improper, since any account of Christian believing, however formal or theoretical, must surely at least plausibly indicate something of the form which that believing might take when its 'material conditions' are contracted to the point of agony. The absence, in Fierro's study, of any discussion of questions of prayer and spirituality (the concrete forms of faith) is, I believe, significant.

To put it another way. My dissatisfaction with Fierro's definition of 'believing' arises primarily neither from his insistence that believing is a 'nonknowing', nor from his claim that it is in narrative and image, in picture and story, that faith finds expression (although these are issues of far greater complexity than he indicates), but in the uninformative casualness of his recourse to the metaphor of 'illustration' in order to describe the relationship between nescience and cognition, silence and language, in the dialectic of belief.

In Fierro, as in Althusser, abstract categories and distinctions freewheel at zero gravity, unconstrained by the discipline, derived from continual attention to the concrete and particular, which we are entitled to expect of a mode of reflection which declares itself to be 'historical-materialist'.[14] My mention of Fierro's Althusserian idealism, however, may at least have served to remind us that, even if problems of ideology may not be confined within the boundaries of the epistemological, epistemological issues nevertheless remain central to its exploration inasmuch as, throughout its history, the concept of ideology has been defined in at least partial contradistinction to concepts of knowledge. To describe religious practice, or theological discourse, as 'ideological', is always to characterize them, if not as 'simply false', or 'purely illusory', at least as lacking certain essential features of whatever is held to constitute 'true knowledge'.

The bewildering variety of contemporary uses of the concept of ideology arises partly from ambiguities and imprecisions in Marx's use of the notion and partly from the complexity of its subsequent history. It also partly arises, I suggest, from the fact that 'ideology' is one of those 'basic concepts' which, in Raymond Williams's phrase, have come to be 'seen to be not concepts but problems'.[15] However, I want to risk attempting just sufficient clarification as will enable me to isolate one or two of those aspects of the problem which should especially engage the attention of students of theological method. I propose to argue that there is, first, a *practical* dimension to the problem on which it is incumbent upon theologians continually to attend but which it outstrips their competence, as theologians, to 'solve', and that there is, secondly, a *theoretical* dimension concerning the status of theological discourse and the selection of appropriate theological 'cognitive strategies'.

Marx on ideology

Omitting consideration of what we might perhaps call the 'prehistory' of the term,[16] let me plunge in at the deep end and offer some reflections on Marx's use of the concept of ideology. Marx's critics frequently belabour him for what they regard as the radically inconsistent, even contradictory, character of his treatment of the relationship between social existence and consciousness in general, and of 'ideology' in particular.[17] But these criticisms, when not stemming from mere hostility, frequently misconceive the sense in which we might expect to find in his writings the elements, consistently laid out, of a 'theory of ideology'. Not only is this expectation precluded by the explosive restlessness of an original thinker most of whose relevant writings are heavily polemical in character, but we need to bear in mind that, 'in *The German Ideology* as in the Paris Manuscripts, Marx refuses to concern himself with epistemological questions'.[18] Such questions, at least as classically conceived, are, in the sense of the second thesis on Feuerbach, 'purely scholastic'.[19] It is one thing to argue, as I should wish to do, that Marxism has paid a heavy price for this refusal, as is indicated by the solipsistic manner in which Althusserians tediously reiterate the claim that, as the expositors of Marxist 'science', they and they alone possess the key to true knowledge, but of course they cannot discuss the matter in any terms other than their own, because to do so would be to lapse into 'ideological' discourse.[20] It is quite another thing, however, to criticize Marx for inconsistency in respect of a theoretical programme which he never sought to undertake. If Marx's treatment of 'ideology' is obscure, as in many respects it undoubtedly is, that obscurity arises less from theoretical confusion than from an unfortunate choice, and a frequently slipshod use, of metaphor.[21] And few of his metaphors have caused more trouble than that of 'base' and 'superstructure', to which we shall return.

Seliger refers to Marx's 'exclusively pejorative, truth-excluding use of "ideology" '.[22] Both epithets are misleading. Neither of them is applicable, for example, to Marx's use of the term in the famous passage in the 1859 Preface to *A Contribution to the Critique of Political Economy*. In that passage, the use is, in Mannheim's sense, 'non-evaluative', and the insistence that 'It is not the consciousness of men that determines their existence, but their social existence that determines their consciousness',[23] while suffering from rhetorical overkill, says nothing about the truth or falsity of the products of consciousness, the 'ideological forms in which men become conscious of [social] conflict and fight it out'.[24]

In its most general sense, the concept of ideology refers to 'the general process of the production of meanings and ideas'.[25] if, in Marx's writings, the concept is usually employed more or less pejoratively, this is due to a series of further specifications to which he submitted it in the course of mounting his critique of the 'scientific', absolutist, ahistorical pretensions of bourgeois political economy.[26]

The first such specification arises from his insistence – the achievement of which marked the break with Feuerbach – that 'ideas are social products, which cannot be understood by the philosopher who stands outside history'.[27] The thought of those who suppose otherwise – be they philosophers, theologians, economists or politicians – is 'ideological'. And the concept has thus already acquired a sense according to which 'ideology' is a cognitively distorted and impoverished grasp of reality.

A second specification arises from Marx's preoccupation with the class-structure of society. Not only do 'the social circumstances in which the activity of individuals occurs condition their perception of the world in which they live',[28] but the particular social circumstances of nineteenth-century European societies, according to Marx, are those of societies locked in class conflict. 'Fundamental to Marx's "materialism" ' are 'the links which are drawn between *class structure* and ideology'.[29] The class struggle is not only largely invisible, but its invisibility is the result of the effective dissemination, as the accepted language and 'Weltanschauung' of a society, of the ideas and beliefs of whatever group wields economic power in that society. If Marx's polemical fire is directed most heavily at 'bourgeois' or 'capitalist' ideology, this is not because capitalist patterns of language and thought are, for some obscure reason, 'more ideological' than those of other forms of social and economic organization, but because, in nineteenth-century Europe, the structure of economic power and dominance was, in fact, capitalist. Hence, his epigrammatic slogan that 'the ideas of the ruling class are in every epoch the ruling ideas'[30] demands different application in different historical circumstances. Thus E. P. Thompson, criticizing Kolakowski, has said: 'Political organisms select from the available stock of ideas those which best suit their interests . . . they shape ideas into ideology. . . . What has happened in the Soviet Union is that Marxism as rationality or idea has been transformed into ideology.'[31]

Intellectually second-rate idealist sociologies, Marxist and other, solidify and reify Marx's analytic categories, transforming them into substantive descriptions. As such, they become historically and empirically unreferred generalizations, veering between the tautological and the patently false. Seliger is perfectly correct in saying that 'Marx did not use "ideology" according to a uniform definition, and the term itself did not occupy a central position in his work'.[32] But the moral that I would draw from this is that 'ideology', in Marx's writings, is not so much a theoretical concept as a variable pointer to a cluster of related problems his discussion of which is heavily impregnated with metaphorical usage of uneven quality. And, as E. P. Thompson has said: 'At least I know that the thinker who mistakes metaphor for fact is in for trouble.'[33] Meanwhile, he continues, 'in serious intellectual circles the argument about basis/superstructure goes *on and on and on*. . . . A whole continent of discourse is being developed . . . which rests, not upon the solid globe of historical evidence, but on the precarious point of a strained metaphor'.[34]

If we bear such warnings in mind, I suggest that those features of Marx's treatment of ideology which I have so far sketched are not lacking in historical suggestiveness and social-scientific significance. When we take the next step, however, and ask, for an epistemological point of view (if Marx will forgive me), with what ideological discourse is appropriately to be *contrasted*, we move into deeper water.

'Where speculation ends – in real life – there', says Marx, in *The German Ideology*, 'real, positive science begins: the representation . . . of the practical process of development of men. Empty talk about consciousness ceases, and real knowledge has to take its place. When reality is depicted, philosophy as an independent branch of knowledge loses its medium of existence.'[35] In the context, the general thrust of these remarks is clear enough. 'Speculation', 'empty talk about consciousness' is, to use an ancient distinction, at best 'opinion' and not 'knowledge'. Forgetful of its forgetfulness of the social, historical, 'practical' process of which it is an aspect, it 'mystifies', thereby distorting or 'falsifying' the consciousness of its practitioners. In its broad outlines, this realist criticism of freewheeling speculation, of what E. P. Thompson regrettably persists in describing as 'theology',[36] is warmly to be welcomed, not least because the contents of such speculation tend to become absolutized both in the sense that an unwarranted universality is attributed to culturally and historically particular insights, and in the sense that they tend to become hypostatized. As Terry Eagleton has remarked of contemporary antihumanist Marxist atheism, such atheism 'signifies a rejection of that process whereby, out of the pluralistic play of our signs, a single one (God, the gold standard, paternal authority) is abstracted and enthroned as a standard by which all the others must be ranked'.[37]

Unfortunately, the metaphorical and conceptual framework within which Marx mounts his criticism is doubly flawed. In the first place, from the fact that 'ideology', as described, is defective as knowledge, it does not follow that 'real knowledge' may be identified, as Marx does, with 'real science'. This confusion persists to our own day. Thus, when Althusser insists that 'a "pure" science only exists on condition that it continually frees itself from the ideology which occupies it, haunts it, or lies in wait for it',[38] he appears to be reminding us not only of the irreducible tension between 'scientific' discourse and other modes of knowledge, but also of the heightening of that tension which results from the recognition that the ordinary language of social relationships and the language of literature, for example, are permanently exposed to ideological distortion. But does not the manner in which he expresses his concern for scientific 'purity' also carry the unwarranted reductionist implication that *only* 'scientific' discourse constitutes a mode of *knowledge*? Some such depreciation of the cognitive status of non-scientific discourse is certainly suggested by his announcement that 'ideology as a system of representations, is distinguished from science in that in it the practico-social function is more important than the theoretical function (*function as knowledge*)'.[39]

The 'purity' of discourse and the rectitude of practice are, of course, two sides of the same coin. Once question the assumption that Marxist 'science' has all other modes of discourse as its 'objects', and thus cannot possibly debate with them as if they were 'epistemological equals',[40] and the springs of revolutionary action have been fatally weakened. The reductionist identification of 'real knowledge' with Marxist 'science' allows the depreciative classification of all *other* modes of knowledge as mere 'opinion' or 'belief'. However, 'the Marxist does not have a relationship of belief with his science, but rather his science allows and formulates knowledge of its object'.[41] And why cannot the Marxist add: 'this, at least, is what I believe'? Because 'If Marxism admits 'belief' as an epistemological category it will turn into its opposite, not a revolutionary praxis but an ideology of protest'.[42] Before breaking into a grin, the Christian, with his own unresolved legacy of the tension between the destructive singlemindedness apparently indispensable for effective action and the ineffective 'generosity' of the 'liberal's' perpetual seminar, should consider whether he is in any position to scoff.

The tendency to depreciate the cognitive status of informal and literary modes of discourse is not, of course, confined to the Marxist tradition. Thus, for example, Talcott Parsons, who characterizes 'religious beliefs' as 'the non-empirical homologue of ideological beliefs',[43] defines 'ideology' as 'a system of ideas which is oriented to the evaluative integration of the collect-ivity', and adds: 'In so far as the cognitive interest has clear primacy the belief system is scientific or philosophical.'[44] No justification is offered for this historically and epistemologically jejune stipulative generalization.

The second flaw in Marx's presentation stems from the manner of his characterization of ideology as thought separated from the 'practical process of development of men'. That separation, that dualism, is, for Marx, the hallmark of idealism. But his criticism of it can sometimes be read (and, subsequently, has frequently been read) not as a passionate defence of the indissoluble *unity* of the single historical process of human thought and action, life and consciousness, but as endorsing a mere reversal of that dualism. On this reversal, which is at the root of 'reductionist' readings of Marxist materialism, ' "consciousness" and "its" products can be *nothing but* "reflec-tions" of what has already occurred in the material social process'.[45] On this account, 'ideological' discourse is not only 'not scientific', but is merely 'ephiphenomenal'.

I do not for one moment believe that this was Marx's own position. I believe that Michael Foster captured the central thrust of Marx's thought on these matters when he said that 'Historical materialism does not . . . mean that ideas are devoid of all force, but that they are devoid of all original force'.[46] Nevertheless, it must be admitted that, by his choice of meta-phors – above all, the metaphor of 'base' and 'superstructure', and (for example) the notorious '*camera obscura*' image in *The German Ideology* – Marx lays himself open to dualist, and hence reductionist, interpretations.[47]

'Science' and 'ideology'

If we allow that 'ideological' discourse may usefully be contrasted with 'science', nevertheless the restrictive identification of 'science' with 'real knowledge' must certainly be disallowed and for at least two reasons. First, any such identification arbitrarily excludes from the range of modes of knowledge first-order, prereflexive modes of cognition. To follow Althusser in restricting 'knowledge' to *theoretical* apprehension is to deny that most people know the vast majority of the things that they not unreasonably suppose themselves to know. But the housewife *does* 'know' the price of butter and (to give a very different illustration of the irreducible variety of modes of knowledge) most of us may legitimately claim to 'know', albeit imperfectly, our friends.

That last illustration demands expansion, because it points the way towards my second reason for disallowing the reduction of 'knowledge' to 'science'. 'There is', says Mannheim, 'a type of knowledge . . . whose first assumption is the fact that we come to know our associates only in living and acting with them.'[48] This consideration leads him eventually to the conclusion that 'political-historical thinking produces a kind of knowledge of its own which is not pure theory, but which nevertheless embodies real insight.'[49] Thus the possibility is opened up for familiar distinctions, of some importance for considerations of theological method, between 'theoretico-scientific' and 'hermeneutic' modes of knowledge. And the practitioners of both types of enquiry should, I suggest, learn from Marx's critique of ideology to seek always to be attentive to the *limits* imposed on their discourse and imagination by their historical and social location. 'In affirming that ideologies and social consciousness were not autonomous but, instead, were grounded in "social being" ', says Gouldner, 'Marx affirms that there are *limits* on reason and rational discourse.'[50]

Two further considerations, before moving on. First, if there is *no* sense in which we may claim to 'know' our friends, or to 'know' ourselves, then, *a fortiori*, there is no sense in which we may be said to 'know' the mystery of God. And if our self-knowledge, and our knowledge of other persons, is 'conditioned' or 'determined' by the historical and social circumstances in which we exist – the stock of imaginative, conceptual and evaluative resources that are, *in practice*, available to us is indeed limited – then our knowledge of God is similarly determined. In this sense Christian belief, as the thematization or categorial expression of faith's dark knowledge of God is, like other social expressions of personal knowledge, 'ideological'. It is ideological in the further sense that, in religious matters as in secular, we tend to be forgetful of the limits to which our knowledge is subject: 'Ideology', says Gouldner, 'dulls the tragic vision's alertness to limits.'[51] But to concede that religious belief is, in both these senses, 'ideological' is by no means indiscriminately to admit its 'false' or 'illusory' character. Whether or not human experience is experience of God, and hence 'experiential knowledge' of God (whatever the conceptual and symbolic forms, theistic or other, in which such experiential knowledge is categorially 'objectified'), is not a question which can even come up for consideration in terms of the discussion so far.[52]

The second consideration that I would raise at this point concerns the possibility of 'science' in Marx's, let alone in Althusser's, sense. 'To be conditioned', says Seliger, 'is to be barred from comprehensive objective knowledge.'[53] Curiously, Seliger seems to suppose that Marx is to be criticized for endorsing this elementary truism. But in what sense, and in respect of what objects, do we usually suppose 'comprehensive objective knowledge' to be available? Gouldner highlights one important aspect of the distinction between science and ideology with his description of the 'analytic essence of ideology' as consisting in the fact that it is 'speech that does not recognize or make problematic its own grounds',[54] and by construing 'rationality' as 'the capacity to make problematic what has hitherto been treated as given'.[55] But he also comments, perceptively, that 'to make all things problematic at the *same* time is conducive not to rationality, but nihilism'.[56] And, with the shade of T. S. Kuhn peering over my shoulder, I am bound to ask: of what scientific practice that has ever occurred could it be said that it succeeded, or could hope to succeed, in making *all* of its grounds simultaneously and radically problematic?

In other words, is there not a sense in which the Marxist concept of 'science' is, in its contradistinction from 'ideology', to be construed as a *regulative ideal* rather than as the description of present practice?[57] Press this suggestion in one direction, and it would render the very notion of science practically vacuous. But, reminded by Althusser that 'the *theoretical* effects of ideology . . . are always a threat or a hindrance to scientific knowledge',[58] it can perhaps also be read as indicating that scientific theory and practice have always attentively to struggle for the establishment and retention of their own 'scientificity'. And, from this point of view, it is perhaps the case that, amongst the concerns characteristic of Christian theological enquiry, some at least are such that their pursuit is governed by a similar ideal.

Marx's critique of religion

Having so far said nothing about Marx's explicit critique of religion in general, and Christianity in particular, as ideological, I now propose briefly to remedy this. Marx is notoriously inconsistent in supposing that religion, alone amongst the forms of ideological discourse, cannot furnish genuine knowledge. On his account, whereas in a social order in which our alienation had been healed there would still be that which corresponded to law, polity, art and philosophy, there would not be that which corresponded to religion. Without being able to argue the case here, I believe that the clue to this anomaly is to be sought in the frequent analogies which Marx draws between political and religious forms of alienation. In some ideal future order, there might be that which corresponded to political practice and discourse, but the *state* would have 'withered away'. And the image of God is so unquestioningly identified, by Marx, with the image of an 'alien power', that questions concerning the forms of religion in a 'healed', non-alienated society simply do not and cannot arise.

Marx's criticism of religious practice – let us say, of religious ideology – as frequently contributive to and expressive of oppression, infantilism and social division, constitutes a far more devastating indictment of much past and present Christian practice and discourse, organization, doctrine, hymnody and preaching, than most Christians – be they laypeople, theologians or church leaders – seem willing or able to recognize. But, from a *theoretical* point of view, the form and content of that criticism are both uninformed and uninteresting. Centuries of strenuous, and by no means wholly unsuccessful, effort have been devoted to demonstrating that the God of Christian belief, a God of whom it is affirmed that the autonomy of his creation grows in direct, not in inverse, proportion to its dependence on him,[59] cannot *logically* be thought of as the alien presence (or absence) over against man which is posited by both Feuerbach and Marx.[60] Christian theology, like Jewish theology before it, has always contained its own protocols against idolatry. The dialectic between negation and affirmation, between the positing of 'images' of God, and the criticism of those images in the constructive silence of the apophatic, is a recurrent and central aspect of the history of Christianity to which Marx never at any point adverts.

A more interesting question might be: 'Why is it that Marxism needs to persist in the misrepresentation of Christianity?'[61] Brian Wicker, who raises this question, suggests that the answer may be sought not far from 'scientific' Marxism's discomfiture when confronted with the question of ethics.[62] It is at least interesting to notice that the Althusserian participant in the debate to which Wicker was contributing, while quite prepared to expatiate on the tautological character of the proposition 'God made the world',[63] and the ideological character of the proposition 'I believe in God',[64] offered nothing by way of argument or evidence in support of his contention that the proposition ' "God exists" is always false',[65] and 'shuffled', as Newman would say, when challenged on the question of ethics.

Social 'determination'

Before concluding, I must briefly return to the question of the 'conditioning' or 'determination' of language and thought by the social and economic contexts in which our language is produced. I have already noted the inadequacy of Marx's static, mechanical metaphor of 'base' and 'superstructure'. As E. P. Thompson remarks, 'the dialectic of social change cannot be fixed in any metaphor that excludes human attributes'.[66] But, when we have selected metaphors for the relationship between historical process and its ideological (and 'scientific') 'production' that do not contain an inbuilt tendency to reductionism, fundamental questions remain concerning our understanding of such concepts as 'conditioning' and 'determination'.

'No problem in Marxist cultural theory is more difficult', says Raymond Williams, 'than that of "determination".'[67] Teasing out the complexity of the relevant group of German and English words, he distinguishes between being 'determined' in the sense of being powerless in respect of iron laws or powerful external agencies (a sense frequently evoked in the Marxist tradition, especially in some of its more 'scientific' forms) and being 'determined' or 'determinate' in the sense of being set within certain objective limits. Marx, he reminds us, repeatedly used the concept in this sense: 'New social relations, and the new kinds of activity that are possible through them, may be imagined but cannot be achieved unless the determining limits of a particular mode of production are surpassed in practice, by actual social change.'[68] He adds, however, that if we are to avoid a quietism quite alien to Marx's thought, we need to remember that 'determination is never only the setting of limits; it is also the exertion of pressures'.[69]

Are these not, in this cluster of meanings, reminders for a theological tradition which, in disciplining its own tendency to speculative self-indulgence, has not only insisted that the God of Christian belief is a God who, if I may so put it, disbarred idolatry by the self-destruction of his own image, but of whom we believe that, in his practical recognition of the tightest of limits, in Gethsemane and on Calvary, and not in any ideological 'forgetfulness' of them, he *thereby* exerted definitive pressure, 'determined' the course and outcome of human history?

Conclusion

Let me now try to pull together the threads of this somewhat rambling discussion. Both the practice of faith and theological reflection are aspects of 'the general process of the production of meanings and ideas'.[70] As such, they are 'ideological' in a non-pejorative sense which should, nevertheless, remind biblical scholars and historians of doctrine that they too often neglect to study the social production of those beliefs and practices whose origins and development they seek to interpret.

The 'problem' of ideology arises, not from the fact that our ideas are social products, but from our 'forgetfulness' of this fact. We tend to be forgetful both of the objective limits set to our grasp of reality and of the extent to which the way in which we think and perceive and argue reflects underlying patterns of social division and dominance. The struggle for the accurate 'depiction' of reality, to use Marx's metaphor, thus becomes an aspect of the struggle for social change. In this sense, critical theory is an aspect of social praxis. But the quest for critical theory can, in turn, generate a 'forgetfulness' of objective limits. This, I suggest, is what happens when critical theory, or 'science' in Marx's sense, is contrasted with nonscientific modes of discourse in a manner which implies that only theoretical discourse can deliver 'real knowledge'. Thus, for example, if it is true that 'ideology dulls the tragic vision's alertness to limits',[71] it is also true that stimulating that alertness is as much the poet's duty as it is the critical theorist's. To suppose that only in theoretical discourse is truth told, reality 'depicted', is to succumb, once again, to that idealistic rationalism from which historical materialism was supposed to have delivered us.

The relevance of these remarks may become clearer when we remember that those primary modes of discourse which are constitutive elements of Christian religious practice are narrative, self-involving, autobiographical. The Christian believer is a story-teller, and the story that he tells is of a process in which he acknowledges himself to be a participant. And if it is true that the tale that he tells is, like any autobiography, threatened with illusion and distortion, it is also true that only in the telling of the tale does the process achieve conscious expression. The telling of the tale is certainly not a sufficient condition of Christian truthfulness, but it is a necessary condition. The task of theology, as critical reflection on religious practice, is to elucidate the truth-conditions of the tale and thus critically to assess the truthfulness of its telling.[72]

Implied in the distinction between 'religious practice' and 'theological reflection' is the claim that the responsibility for the critique of ideology devolves not only upon the social scientist (as 'critical theorist') but also upon the theologian. A few comments on this claim (which will seem highly implausible to many sociologists) are, therefore, in order.

In the first place, if, following Gouldner, we take 'rationality' to be 'the capacity to make problematic what had hitherto been treated as given',[73] then there will be 'objective limits', in practice, to the extent and the manner in which either the theologian or the social scientist can hope to realize this capacity. In the second place, I see no reason to suppose that, in principle, the theologian's rationality is any more circumscribed or inhibited than that of the social scientist.

In the third place, the claim that responsibility for the critique of religious ideology devolves partly upon the theologian raises the question of the possibility of 'scientific' theology. Perhaps, in view of the fact that, in current English usage, the concept of 'science' is considerably more restricted than either the French '*science*' or the German '*wissenschaft*', it would be better to ask about the possibility of theological discourse constituting a mode of 'rational knowledge'.[74] As I see it, this possibility could only legitimately be excluded if it could be shown that religious faith (the practice on which theology critically reflects) was in no sense 'experiential knowledge' of its object – even if it can never be demonstrated (and in *that* sense 'known') to be such knowledge.

These excessively condensed observations are, I hasten to add, offered as an 'agenda', as an indication of questions that arise from a consideration of the 'ideological' status of religious practice and theological reflection, not as conclusions to an argument. I began by raising the question of 'truthfulness'. The 'truthfulness' of Christianity, as of Marxism, is primarily a practical matter: it is to be 'shown' in the transformation both of individuals and of social relationships. (Most people know this, rightly recognizing that saints are more important than theologians.) And because Christian religious practice (like all other beliefs and social practices) is, in the concrete, not only 'determinate' in form and content, but subject to distortion and 'false consciousness', therefore, as with other 'ideological forms', it needs to be set in continual tension with aspects of critical reflection: historical, literary-critical and philosophical.

I have referred to the question of the 'truthfulness' of Christianity rather than to the question of its 'truth', because no discussion of the latter topic is today entitled to sidestep the issues brought into focus in Marx's *Theses on Feuerbach*. As Ernst Bloch once said, commenting on those theses: 'Correctness is not yet truth.'[75] Nevertheless, correctness does indeed matter. The characteristic assertions of Christian belief are only 'correct' if certain truth-conditions are fulfilled. The elucidation of those truth-conditions is, I have suggested, one of the responsibilities of the Christian theologian. And yet he can never afford to forget that 'the secret of the manner of their fulfilment lies with God'.[76]

PART IV

9

Human Experience and the Knowledge of God

Products and Creatures

I know of nothing whatsoever that is not a product. Every man and every mountain, every artefact and every argument, every star, every city and every symbol is a product of complex productive forces and processes. Physical and economic, chemical and psychological, biological and political: the list of descriptions by which we classify the means of production is endless, and the relationships between them endlessly complex. But everything whatsoever that we are and see, encounter and consider, is a product.

And yet somehow the suggestion that we are *only* products, only the outcome of complex processes and forces of production, chills the heart and appears to threaten our humanity. Products we may indeed be, but the suggestion that this is *all* that we are appears to discount just what we deem most precious and specific to our humanity. Whatever be the case where rocks and railway trains, stars and seagulls are concerned, the exhaustive description of *human* existence in terms of the means of its production seems to discount the personal and the spiritual, the realm of freedom. And so we are tempted to say that we are not *only* products but *also* persons; not only the outcome of complex productive processes but also free spirits; not only bound into the inexorability of temporal process but also touched by immortality.

I say that we are 'tempted' to put the matter this way because thus to register our protest against at least some versions of materialist or determinist ontology easily seduces us into supposing that, in order to safeguard the integrity of the human, it is necessary to claim that we are constituted by two kinds of component: the physical and the mental, matter and spirit.

Suppose we come at it from a slightly different angle and say that, as Christians, we are constrained to confess that there is nothing whatsoever – no man and no mountain, no artefact and no argument, no star, city or symbol – that is not a *creature*. We might defend our doctrine of creation by saying that we are not *merely* products, we are *also* creatures. But, in thus extending our description, we are not (to put it with deliberate crudeness) implying that mountains and artefacts and arguments are made up of two kinds of component: the 'produced' bits and the 'created' bits. In other words, in order to argue for the irreducibility of varities of cognitive discourse – such as scientific descriptions of modes of production and theological descriptions of our creatureliness – it is not necessary to suppose that to each type of discourse there corresponds a distinct class of substances or entities.

And yet, this is the kind of move that we tend to make when arguing for the irreducibility of our self-description as *human* creatures: as bits of the world whose unique privilege it is to have it in them, by God's grace, consciously and responsibly to relate to the mystery of God. More generally: underlying many if not most current accounts of what it is that differentiates human beings from other bits of the world we can detect one form or another of that metaphysical dualism according to which all facts, events and things fall ultimately into one of two classes: the material and the spiritual, the physical and the mental, the bound and the free.

In this chapter, I want to consider the possibility that there is much to be said, on theological, as well as on anthropoligical and political grounds, for the view that all such dualisms profoundly distort and misrepresent our human, and hence our Christian experience. There is, I would argue, no feature of human experience, nothing that we do or undergo – whether feeding a child, driving a train, creating a poem, dying of cancer or mending a fuse – which can appropriately be described as a 'purely material' or 'purely spiritual' event or experience. And I hope to show that this view of the matter has profound implications for the account that we might offer of human experience of the mystery of God.

In the first part of the chapter, I shall concentrate on the notion of 'religious experience', and especially on that account of the notion which was given powerful and influential expression by William James.

Then, in the second part, I shall try to sketch an account of human experience such that, when construed in faith as experience of God, it throws some light on why it is that the classical Christian doctrine of the unknown God is a doctrine of God as Trinity.

The argument, in a nutshell, would go like this. On the account that I shall be criticizing, it is simply taken for granted that such experience of God as we have is precisely what is *meant* by 'religious' experience, at least in its richest and purest forms. In contrast, on the account that I shall offer, our experience of God is by no means necessarily 'religious' in character nor, from the fact that a particular type of experience is appropriately characterized as 'religious', may it be inferred that it is, in any special or privileged sense, experience of God.

In a word, I want to try to *uncouple* some of the tight links that are often taken for granted between the question of 'religious experience' and questions concerning our human experience and knowledge of God.

Privacies and pathologies

In a recent paper on the theology of Austin Farrer, Brian Hebblethwaite spoke of religious experience as being, by its very nature, 'private', 'inner', 'subjective'.[1] He did not argue for this view of the matter; he did not need to, for he knew he was simply expressing the general consensus.

This notion of religious experience as essentially a matter of private, inner feelings or mental states is parasitic upon a more general account of human experience which has been very influential in modern British philosophy. Thus, for example, Professor Richard Swinburne has *defined* 'experience' as 'a conscious mental going-on'.[2]

The question I want to ask is: why on earth should this exceedingly queer account of experience in general, and of religious experience in particular, prove so persuasive that many highly intelligent people simply take it for granted? For it *is* an exceedingly queer account. If I said that I had had a painful experience in a dentist's chair, or a distressing experience after over-indulgence in food and drink, or an irritating experience in a committee meeting, I would not, in any of these cases, be referring simply to 'conscious mental goings on', but to aspects of my interaction, in the public world of flesh and fact and language, with dentist's drills and indigestion, good company and tedious discussion.

Behind the definition of experience as 'conscious mental going on' there lurks the myth, at least as old as Descartes, that the *real* 'me', the essential person, lives somewhere inside my head. From within this private citadel, in which alone are certainty and security to be sought, I attempt (not without nervousness) to make contact, through sense or argument, with such other similarly sheltered egos as may surround and greet and threaten me.

This, I think, is the general context in which the description of 'religious' experience as essentially 'private', 'inner' and 'subjective' is found at once so obvious and so appealing.

'What keeps religion going', said William James, is 'something different from faculties of theology and their professors'.[3] Very true! What keeps religion going, especially in our day, is the attraction of and the quest for, religious experience. But such experience is often construed as an oasis of delight, wonder or reassurance, a warm safe place in which the complexity and incompleteness of argument, on the one hand, and the untidy and uncontrollable turbulence and terror of fact and flesh, relationships and politics, on the other, are kept at bay. We seek a place for the spirit in which the wounds of matter may be healed or in which, at least, the conflict may find pause.

What I am suggesting is that the metaphysical dualisms

which I mentioned earlier express not simply a mistaken philosophy, but a pathological deformation, a personal and cultural disease. That is why they are so difficult both to diagnose and to heal.

The case of William James

Let us go back to William James. James was profoundly hostile to the 'scientism' that was so prevalent at the end of the nineteenth century. That is to say: he refused to acknowledge the legitimacy of the contention that only natural-scientific description and explanation could furnish us with 'objective', correct accounts of reality, and that religion, or art, or morality, were simply matters of taste – of more or less arbitrary 'subjective' preference – with no serious claim to be able to state how things truly are.

Unfortunately, however, he was, metaphysically, a dualist. Therefore, instead of trying to make a case for the irreducibility of different kinds of description, he argued for the autonomy of descriptions of different kinds of fact. Let the natural scientists confine themselves to *physical* facts; James, the psychologist, would seek to establish a scientific account of *mental* facts. And because he took it for granted that 'religious' facts – or, at least, primary religious facts – are mental facts, therefore, in *The Varieties of Religious Experience*, he offered the outlines of a scientific treatment of that class of mental facts which are appropriately described as 'religious'.

I have said that, for James, the *primary* facts about religion are mental. He knew perfectly well, of course, that religion finds institutional expression in ritual, society and story, and that it provokes intellectual enquiry and analysis. But, for him, the institutional and intellectual aspects of religion are secondary and derivative. They are but pale shadows and, at best, protections, which can never take the place of the real thing, which is the incommunicable experience of the individual touched by whatever it is that evokes his awe, compunction or obedience.

'Individuality', he says in one place, 'is founded in feeling;

and the recesses of feeling . . . are the only places in the world in which we catch real fact in the making, and directly perceive how events happen, and how work is actually done.'[4]

What is it which distinguishes 'religious' experience from other aspects of human experience? This is clearly a question of the first importance for, until it is answered, we have no means of knowing what this new discipline, the psychology or phenomenology of religion, might be *about*. As James puts it: 'The essence of religious experiences . . . must be that element or quality in them which we can meet nowhere else.'[5] He pursues this enquiry with some care, eventually arriving at the following definition: 'the feelings, acts, and experiences of individual men in their solitude, so far as they apprehend themselves to stand in relation to whatever they may consider the divine'.[6] This, and only this, is to count as 'religious experience'.

Let me pause for a moment to take stock. I have no quarrel with James's emphasis on the primacy of experience, nor with his pioneering attempt to establish a suitably disciplined, empirical or 'scientific' treatment of religious phenomena. My difficulties arise from his misidentification of the 'personal' with the 'individual', his untenable insistence that 'individual' experience is a matter of 'feeling' as *contrasted* with 'thought', and his consequent depreciation of the intellectual and institutional aspects of religion.

There can be objection to drawing distinctions between 'feeling' and 'thinking', between responding to a piece of music and constructing an argument, but to harden such distinctions into dichotomies is most misleading. Ask yourself this: when did you last find yourself *simply* 'feeling', without the slightest play or engagement of the mind, or *simply* 'thinking' without the slightest interest, excitement or boredom?

A similar hardening of distinctions into dichotomies is at work in James's attempt to identify the 'personal' with the 'individual', and the consequent underestimation of the public, institutional, structured character of all our experience. Consider, for example, the manner in which he persistently contrasts 'personal' with 'ritual' acts. Even a moment's consideration of how domestic and social rituals actually *work* should be sufficient to indicate the artificiality of any such contrast. May not birthday parties and the rituals of courtship be 'personal experiences' for the participants?

It is, of course, true that we may allow ourselves to inhabit the patterns of social relationship of which we form a part like dead wood drifting down the stream. All such relations, and the institutions and conventions which structure them – domestic, linguistic, religious, moral, political – may be reduced by us to matters of mere 'impersonal' custom and routine. When this happens, our marriages wither, our language atrophies, our religions and our politics fossilize. But it is also possible continually to seek to *appropriate* these relations, to engage – critically and responsibly – in the unending labour of sustaining and transforming the structures of our 'world', and thus to make of that world the form and content of 'personal' experience.

I said that, according to James, 'religious experience' consists in 'the feelings, acts, and experiences of individual men in their solitude, so far as they apprehend themselves to stand in relation to whatever they may consider the divine'.[7] The next question, therefore, that I want briefly to consider is this: on an account of religious experience such as that offered by James, what kind of God could be apprehended and in what manner?

Dualisms, ghosts and ideas

Where the manner of our apprehension is concerned, James's dualism leads him into a trap. 'The "objects" of our consciousness', he says, 'may be present to our senses, or they may be present only to our thought.'[8] Because he strenuously resists the suggestion that our only apprehension of God is intellectual, that we make contact with God only by argument, he is obliged to concede that the 'objects' of religious experience are, as he puts it, 'quasi-sensible realities'.[9]

The general picture operating here is something like this. The Cartesian 'ego', that private nervous 'self' inside our heads, is equipped with two 'windows' opening on to the 'external world': one marked 'sense', the other marked 'thought'. Being rightly reluctant to concede that God is encountered only in argument, James finds himself forced to suppose that religious experience is some kind of *sensation*.

Now, is seems to me self-evident that a God that could be 'sensed': seen, touched, heard or smelt, would be a particular thing which we met, or failed to meet, in the world. In classical Christian theology, the name given to particular things in the world is 'creature'. The only 'god' that could be apprehended by religious experience, as James describes it, would be a creature, and a creature encountered by only that minority of the human race who enjoy what he calls 'first-hand' religious experience; a creature encountered (in his own words) by those 'individuals for whom religion exists not as a dull habit, but as an acute fever'.[10]

It may be thought that I am being unfair to James. His interest, after all, as a psychologist, lay in mapping the varieties of religious experience, not in theological speculation concerning the ground and cause of such experience. Nevertheless, when he does tentatively formulate an hypothesis concerning that ground and cause, he does so in terms of the influence on the unconscious mind of what he calls an 'unseen', 'spiritual' or 'supernatural' 'higher part of the universe'.[11] And I still wish to insist that a God who is a 'part' of the world, even its 'highest' part, is a creature: perhaps a demiurge, but not that world's creator.

It may be worth spelling out, in very general terms, the dilemma that we have inherited from the dualisms which so massively shape and pervade our culture For the sake of clarity, I shall do so somewhat polemically!

Let us suppose that there are two and only two classes of entity: physical and mental, material and spiritual. (I am assuming, because most people seem to do so, that 'spiritual' events and experiences are to be located on the 'mental' rather than on the 'physical' side of the great divide.) Let us further suppose (because, again, most people seem to do so) that God is some kind of entity. Now, since it has been agreed, since early in the history of Western thought, that God is not a physical or material fact, he must be a kind of mental fact, a kind of idea. And, if God is an idea, he is *only* an idea.

According to some people, it is nevertheless useful to go on entertaining this idea, because it helps us to more noble deeds and loftier ambitions. According to others, the sooner we stop having this idea, and get on with the business of shouldering our responsibilities for the making of mankind and the transformation of nature, the better off and more authentically human we shall be. For the first group, 'God' is a useful, for the second a harmful fiction.

There is another direction in which we might move, but it will do little to ease the dilemma. We can resist the claim, made on behalf of modern science (though often not by scientists) that *only* 'material' entities exist. This claim is still dualistic, in the sense that, while agreeing that there could be only two classes of entity, 'material' and 'spiritual', it asserts that, as a matter of *fact*, the latter class is empty. There are no 'spiritual' entities.

This is the assertion resisted by those who insist on the importance of exploring, scientifically, that 'non-material' or 'spiritual' side of the universe which natural-scientific description leaves out of account. Before we know where we are, 'religious experience' is associated with experience of the paranormal: of phenomena for which there is some evidence but which are inexplicable by the canons of contemporary science. It is but a small step from here to the assumption that the explanation of religious experience is to be sought in the same direction as explanation of the occult. In England today, the concept of the supernatural – which once referred to that which, by God's redeeming grace, his sinful creatures are enabled to do – now refers to entities from outer space.

This is our inheritance from the dominant dualisms. 'Religious experience', on the run from painful and public fleshly fact and from the pressures of the mind's enquiring, is the prerogative of those individuals who, in the private temples of their heart, worship unwittingly either an idea or a ghost.

Requirements for a different story

The pressures exerted by the dualistic mind-set (which I have caricatured only in order to try to render 'visible' what I take to be some of its fundamental presuppositions and implications) are so powerful that it will not be easy to construct or sustain an alternative account. But at least the principal features required of such an account are not difficult to indicate.

In the first place, instead of supposing that all existence and all experience can be tidily and exhaustively distributed between two and only two classes or categories, we should risk acknowledging the irreducible, puzzling, painful and uncontrollable diversity of language, event and experience: of the things that there are and of our interactions with them.

This does not mean, in the second place, that we should refrain from drawing useful and often indispensable distinctions between (for example) thinking and feeling, arguments and institutions, custom and creativity, bondage and freedom. But it does mean that we shall be alert to the dangers inherent in hardening such distinctions into dichotomous descriptions of mutually exclusive categories of entity, event, experience and activity.

It therefore means, in the third place, that we shall refuse to identify that which makes us 'human persons' with any one particular feature or element from the complex and bewildering manifold which constitutes our identity and experience.

In the fourth place, while we may hope to find or (better) to be found by God in the world, we shall not expect to 'come across' God as some particular kind of fact or thing, and we shall therefore not expect there to be any one particular area or 'district' of human experience in which God is uniquely, or even especially, to be found.

As a preliminary illustration, consider the relationship between 'feelings' and 'institutions'. I mentioned earlier that I regarded it as a fundamental error to identify the essence of 'personal' experience with individual, private 'feeling'. This kind of dissociation of 'feeling' from public fact was brilliantly satirized by Martin Buber. 'Institutions', he said, 'are what is "out there" where for all kinds of purposes one spends time, where one works, negotiates . . . organizes, administers. . . . Feelings are what is "in here" where one lives and recovers from the institutions. . . . Here one is at home and relaxes in one's rocking chair.'[12] Monday to Friday relegated to the impersonality of the public world; the weekend kept sacred for the comforts of the personal!

Buber did not deny, of course, that personal existence is comprehensively threatened by the impersonality and brutality of the technocratic and bureaucratic structures of the age. But he believed (correctly, in my view) that the threat could not be met or countered by attempting to erect oases of the private spirit – whether within the individual heart or in the establishment of counter-cultural sects or religious conventicles.

What is required, to nullify the nightmare and sustain the spirit, is not the establishment of rocking-chairs or playgrounds for the private ego, but a redemptive transformation of structure and circumstance, language, flesh and institution; a transformation, in other words, as comprehensive as the threat. Whether such redemption is possible, whether it is worth working and suffering and waiting for is, of course, a matter not of prediction but of hope.

The pedagogy of the personal

I earlier quoted Richard Swinburne's definition of 'experience' as 'a conscious mental going on'. That definition is in striking contrast to Friedrich von Hügel's, which I find vastly more congenial. Von Hügel described what he called 'real' experience as made up of 'the endless contacts, friendly, hostile, of give, of take, between ourselves and the objects of all kinds which act upon us, and upon which we act in some degree or way'.[13]

Throughout the two rambling, untidy and fascinating volumes of *The Mystical Element of Religion*, von Hügel shows himself every bit as committed as was William James to the primacy of experience and the indispensability of the spiritual life. Unlike James, however, he persistently refuses so to isolate some one feature of our experience as to make of it alone the basis or centre either of human existence in general or of our relationship with the mystery of God.

If it is in 'religious experience' alone that we enter consciously into relationship with God, then the possibility of such conscious relationship would seem to be restricted to those people who, perhaps by accident of temperament, enjoy the kind of experience classified by the psychologist as 'religious'.

But if dependence on God, relationship with God, is simply how, as creatures, we fundamentally and ineluctably *are*, then consciousness of such relationship – what we might call the 'sense of God' – may be given, however 'dimly', confusedly, inarticulately, in each and every area and district of our existence and activity.[14] The function of religion, we might say (as a first approximation) is interpretative and transformative, rather than constitutive of our human experience and knowledge of God.

The picture painted by von Hügel is of human health and maturity as a function of the continual, practical, costly, precarious quest for the achievement of an appropriate 'balance in tension' between the factors and forces which constitute our experience in the world. In the life of the individual, as of the social group, there is an unceasing struggle between three fundamental forces or impulses: the institutional, the intellectual, the emotional; the traditional, the abstractive, the volitional; the authoritative, the scientific, the ethical. (His terminology is endlessly fluid as a reminder that the 'threefoldness' of the description is intended as an 'aid to reflection' rather than as the imposition of some abstract system of classes or categories upon the variety and complexity of our experience.)

If, in the life of the individual or of the social formation, any one or two of these aspects or impulses is allowed to dominate or crowd out the others, the result is corruption or distortion through the 'one-sided' pursuit of that which is, in principle, an indispensable constituent of human identity and excellence.

What von Hügel calls the 'three elements of religion' are simply the instances, in the context of religious activity, understanding and organization, of the factors and forces which constitute *all* human experience.

Some such threefold classification of the elements of human (and hence of religious) experience and activity has been commonplace at least since Kant.[15] You find it in Schleiermacher's permutations of 'feeling', 'knowing' and 'doing', for example, and we have already come across William James's distinction between the institutional, intellectual and personal aspects of religion. Whereas for James, however, the 'personal' was *one* of three constituent aspects of human existence and experience, for von Hügel 'persons' are what we may hope to become in the measure that we succeed in attaining that precarious balance in tension between all the elements of our existence.

I think we might say that whereas, on the account which I criticized earlier, 'persons' are what we initially, privately and 'inwardly' are (and our 'personhood' is under continual threat from the 'external' world), on the alternative account that I am sketching 'persons' are what we may hope and must struggle to become.

Human identity is ever under threat, and ever under construction. The whole complex, conflictual, unstable process of human history is a matter of the production and destruction of the 'personal'. Christianity, for von Hügel, at once discloses that this *is* the character of the process, serves as a 'school for the production of the personal' – a school whose pedagogy is structured in suffering – and promises that process's eventual achievement.

Creatures and products

I suggested at the beginning that we, and all things, and all constituent elements of us and of all things, are products. And Christian faith, I said, confesses all products to be creatures. It is not difficult to discover that we are products 'through and through'; that there is nothing in us that is not produced; that there is no safe haven or 'self' immune from the processes of production – and destruction.

But it is, I think, exceedingly difficult to make one's own the acknowledgment that we are creatures, for to be a creature – a product of *God's* 'making' – is to be absolutely dependent on our maker. And the suggestion that we are absolutely dependent is one which, in our preference for security, self-possession and autonomy, we tend strenuously to resist. There is nothing more difficult to discover than that in *absolute* dependence consists our freedom. To make such discovery, we would need a new 'grammar' of dependence: a state of affairs and its description in which, with solitude and egotism transcended, 'dependence' meant not slavery but responsible relationship: with ourselves, with each other, with all things, and with God. If this is how things are, then to characterize Christianity as 'a school for the production of the personal' is to characterize it as a school the purpose of whose pedagogy is to foster the conditions in which creatureliness, construed not as slavery but as sonship, might responsibly and effectively be acknowledged. (There, incidentally, you have in a nutshell a formal indication of the political implications of Christian belief and of why it is that those implications require a 'fundamental option' for the poor. On the other hand, of course, the Cartesian 'ego' is the paradigm of the idolatry of 'private property'.)

The Christian experience of God

At this point, we begin to see what kind of answer might be given to the final question which I earlier put on the agenda: the question concerning the character of our encounter with God, if God is not to be found or 'come across' as some particular fact or thing. It begins to look as if that encounter might consist in the responsible and effective recognition of our creatureliness, of our finitude.

If God is not to be found in any one particular 'district' of our experience (say: in 'religious' experience), but rather in all the kinds of things which we do and suffer, achieve and undergo – in politics, technology and poetry, in child care and disease, in celebration and mortality – it nevertheless does not follow that all occasions and all circumstances prompt, with equal peremptoriness, the acknowledgment of finitude: the encounter with the silence which points to God. The circumstances in which we are thus especially challenged either to confess our creatureliness or to evade its recognition might include (and the list is more or less random): the collapse of some certainty, the darkness of pure duty, the gift of a child's trust or another's love, confrontation with mortality.[16]

Now, what kind of account might we give of a God who is thus found not in the esoteric but in the limits of the ordinary? If the account is to be consonant with an account of human existence in terms of the continual, precarious, unstable quest for 'balance' between its elements, then it will be similarly marked by friction and instability. It will be an account such that each affirmation, each 'form' or 'content' that we give to our confession, will require correction by such other affirmations as are prompted by other aspects of our experience.

If we keep in mind the kind of threefold configurations of experience on which I was remarking earlier (configuration, for example, in terms of the emotional, intellectual and institutional aspects of our existence) then the account might go something like this.

We might find ourselves prompted to celebrate all life, all feeling, all freshness and inspiration, as of God; prompted to acknowledge that all vitality, all love and generosity, all fresh particular beauty, is of *absolute* significance, is a form of the divine. We could thus 'run up' a doctrine of the Spirit, a doctrine of the divinity of the '*creator spiritus*'. It might even be a true doctrine. But if, concentrating exclusively on such discovery, we *stopped* there, we would be pantheists.

There is, however (we might soon find out, if we allowed ourselves to do so) too much pain, too much chaos, too much perishing of beauty and significance, for such pantheisms to be plausible. There is too much of which we cannot make sense. Discovering that, with our fragmented language, we cannot even put together sentences which say anything appropriate about that of which we seek to speak, we might be constrained to acknowledge the utter transcendence and incomprehensibility of God. Following the 'way of negation', we might come up with a doctrine of the absolute qualitative difference between finite and infinite, creature and creator, time and eternity. It might even be a true doctrine. But if, concentrating exclusively on such discovery, we *stopped* there, we would be – at best – agnostics.

Living, however, as we are privileged to do, in the school of Christianity, we should soon be reminded that the silence of agnosticism is interrupted by a Word once spoken, by one life lived and death undergone. To that one man, that one small slice of history, we would again be invited to ascribe unsurpassable significance. That man was a prophet, but we continually rediscover that the ascription of prophetic status does not do justice to our tested conviction that what was done and seen in him is of eternal and imperishable significance and validity. And so we would be helped to come up with a doctrine of the Word incarnate, of the divinity of Christ. It might even be a true doctrine. But if, concentrating exclusively on such discovery of historical significance, we *stopped* there, we should soon risk ascribing absolute significance to the past *as* past, risk 'divinizing' the language and institutions which mediate his memory. In order not to stay trapped in this third idolatry, we would need to break up the pattern again, acknowledging that it is in freshness and creativity, not in inherited stability, in new possibilities, not ancient meanings, that God is to be glimpsed. And we would be back where we began, laying the emphasis on the elements of a doctrine of creative and transformative Spirit. It is thus, I suggest, that the dance, the '*perichoresis*', of Christian pedagogy proceeds.

As I understand it, the Christian account of God, the doctrine of the Trinity, is a doctrine of the unknown God inasmuch as it is never and nowhere appropriate to 'stop the dance', to interrupt the dialectic of experience and to say: *this* and this alone is what we mean by 'God'; *here* and here alone is his presence and activity to be discerned.

The account that I have tried to sketch, of our experience and knowledge of God, is an account which seeks simultaneously to respect the mystery of God and the mystery of human existence. What it is and what it means to be 'human' is never finally, definitively given or achieved. It is, rather, continually to be sought, in practice and theory, in action, reflection and suffering, in the precarious, costly, unending quest for reconciliation between the constitutive elements of human experience. In God, the elements are reconciled in the stillness of his unity. And in our sharing in that stillness will be our peace.

10

'Son of God': Reflections on a Metaphor

Is it really true?

Recent debates concerning the availability for contemporary use of the concept of 'incarnation' suggest that something like the following exchange could take place between an enquiring Christian and any one of a number of well-known theologians. Enquirer: ' "Jesus is the Son of God"; true or false?'. Theologian: 'Before I can answer, I need to consider a prior question which the early Christians failed to consider because they lacked our sophisticated modern awareness of the differences between various types of linguistic usage. I need to consider whether it is being asserted that Jesus is literally, or only metaphorically, the Son of God. As a purported literal description, the proposition is either unintelligible or, if intelligible, false. It is true, but only metaphorically true, that Jesus is the Son of God.'

Our enquirer now raises another question: 'Is the proposition "God exists" true or false?'. And this time the theologian (who is himself a believer) answers, unhesitatingly, 'true'. The enquirer (who has learnt a thing or two from the previous exchange) now asks: 'But is the proposition "God exists" literally or only metaphorically true?'. To this question, most of those theologians who were quite confident that the proposition 'Jesus is the Son of God' is only metaphorically true would now show themselves equally confident that the proposition 'God exists' is literally true.

At this point, a third party (another theologian, perhaps myself) joins the conversation and says that he believes the proposition 'God exists' to be true, but that it is metaphorically rather than literally true. To this suggestion, the theologian who displayed his fearless capacity for 'radical' thought in resolutely asserting that the proposition 'Jesus is the Son of God' is only metaphorically true, now reacts with some nervousness: 'But if the proposition "God exists" is only metaphorically true, then it is not *really* true that God exists.' And he suspects the third party not only of unorthodoxy (which would not trouble him) but of atheism (which would). And the latecomer would probably be accused of confusing rather than clarifying things if he said that it would only follow, from the denial that the statement 'God exists' is literally true, that God does not really exist, if the concept of 'God' functions as a proper name which, in Christian theology, it does not.

In this chapter I wish to offer some reflections on one or two issues raised by that little exchange.[1] In view of the complexity of these issues, I can only do so in a very impressionistic manner. (Thus, for example, I willingly admit that to employ a 'strategic' distinction between the 'literal' and the 'metaphorical' is crudely to oversimplify a number of fundamental issues in linguistics and the philosophy of language. Nevertheless, in view of the fact that just such a distinction has been widely appealed to in recent theological debates, I thought it might be useful to accept it but to attempt, as it were, to 'stand it on its head'.) I wish to suggest that the proposition 'Jesus is the Son of God' is true; that if it were false, Christian hope would be deprived of its grounds and Christian faith of its object: that, while 'divine sonship' is, indeed, predicated metaphorically of Jesus, it does not follow that he is not 'really' the Son of God; and that although Christian uses of the concept of 'God' are *also* metaphorical in character, it does not thereby follow that it is not 'really' true that God exists.

Metaphor, meaning and hope

There are philosophical traditions in which it is confidently assumed, first, that the distinction between literal and metaphorical uses of language is (in principle) unproblematic;

secondly, that the central and primary function of language is to make straightforward descriptive statements (and that to deny or even to question this view is to open the floodgates to 'subjectivism' and unrestrained 'relativism'); thirdly, that the further language moves from the canonical standard of literal description (by metaphorical 'extension', for example) the more suspect its objectivity, clarity and capacity unambiguously to express the truth; fourthly, that all metaphoric discourse is, in some straightforward sense, false, and that the truth which the metaphor indirectly states can always be directly stated in non-metaphorical terms.

All these assumptions, I suggest, are highly questionable. Quite apart from the arbitrary philistinism which would consign most of the world's poetic, dramatic and literary discourse to some limbo of 'merely expressive' non-cognitive ambiguity and imprecision, such a view of language paradoxically venerates 'scientific' discourse as the ideal of literal description at a time when philosophers of science increasingly draw attention to the extent to which the language of natural science is saturated with metaphor.

I am not denying the importance of distinctions between literal and metaphorical discourse. Nor am I denying that there are situations in which that distinction is drawn without difficulty (if, for example, I am told that it is 'raining cats and dogs', I do not look out of the window expecting to see the street outside littered with fallen bodies). Nevertheless, I wish, first, to insist that appropriate judgments in such matters are the fruit of practical linguistic competence rather than matter for more or less arbitrary *a priori* stipulation; and, secondly, to explore the possibility that it may nevertheless be helpful to attribute primacy to metaphorical rather than to literal usage.

Human existence is a matter of transforming, or seeking to transform, our circumstances; a matter of making ourselves at home, or of making a home for ourselves; a matter of transforming cosmos into environment. In this process, linguistic activity plays a central and indispensable role. Our struggle to 'make sense' of the world is a quest for meaning: an attempt to discern, construct and transform the meaning of things. This,

I think, is what Cornelius Ernst had in mind when, not unaware of the reasons why some philosophers have warned us that it may be misleading to speak of 'meaning' as an 'activity', he nevertheless described 'meaning' as 'primarily a praxis by which the world to which man belongs becomes the world which belongs to man'.[2]

On this account, primacy is attributed to the *transformative* potential of human action, including linguistic action. 'It is not the extension of language, by metaphor or in any other way, which is the puzzle. It is literalness which needs to be explained.'[3] We are a people on pilgrimage, a people in quest both of a home and of an identity. We have not yet succeeded in making ourselves at home, or in making a home for ourselves. And, because we have not, it is the stability, transparency and security of the 'literal' which is fragile, fitful, threatened and often questionable. It is, for example, an illusion to suppose that, merely because we can and must specify as exactly as possible our uses of the term 'human', we can give a 'literal' description of the meaning of humanity, of what it is or might be to be fully human: an illusion which supposes that we have achieved the goal, the identity, the self-understanding, which we seek.

We cannot 'literally' depict ultimate goals. As we seek, through transformative action, to open up and realize the possibilities, the most we can do is to indicate, metaphorically, what they might be 'like'. But the possibilities are not unlimited. There are boundaries and constraints beyond which we may not reasonably hope and profitably strive. Beyond these boundaries, the most formidable of which appears to be the barrier of mortality (the mortality alike of the individual and of the species), there lies not hope but fantasy.

It is at this point that the question of the rationality of human hope becomes, at one and the same time, the question of God and the question of man's resurrection.

That conclusion was reached with suspicious rapidity. We must now go back to the beginning and approach the matter by a different route.

God

In suggesting, as I did at the beginning, that the statement 'God exists' is to be understood metaphorically, I do not mean to imply that God may only metaphorically be said to 'exist', but that, having no proper name for that which, in this statement, we affirm to exist, we make do with the metaphorical expression 'God', an expression inherited from a long and complex history of religious practice and reflection.

The central question here concerns whether or not the term 'God' functions, in Christian religious and theological discourse, as a proper name. The centrality of forms of *address* in religious discourse may give the impression that 'God' is the proper name of him to whom we cry, whom we praise, adore and celebrate. This impression, however, is misleading. After all, we often address human beings without using their names: 'my brother'; 'Mr President'; 'my love'. Similarly, I suggest that the term 'God' functions as a title or description rather than as a proper name.

Most religious traditions have supposed idolatry to be both possible and reprehensible. Idolatry is the worship of a false god. The very possibility of distinguishing, or attempting to distinguish, between 'true gods' and 'false gods' suggests that the word 'god' is a description rather than a name.

But could we not say that 'God' is the proper name of the only true 'god'? Quite apart from the fact that this would be a somewhat confusing recommendation, the history of Christian extensions or transformations of Jewish and Greek concepts of divinity hardly points in this direction. Nor is it easy to see how a description, a '*nomen naturae*', becomes a proper name merely in virtue of the fact that there is only one to whom this description truly refers. We *might* say that, in the New Testament, 'God' functions 'rather like' a proper name, not in so far as the true God is distinguished from false gods, but in so far as the term is used to distinguish the Father from his Son and Spirit.[4] However, 'Father', 'Son' and 'Spirit' are not proper names either.[5]

If 'God' were taken to be a proper name, what would be the

appropriate general term to describe the relationship between 'God', 'Gott', 'Dieu', 'Yahweh' or 'Allah'? In at least some of these cases the term 'translation' would be inappropriate (and, anyway, in what sense do we usually 'translate' proper names?). Are these words, as it were, 'aliases'? And how would we know? In the case of human beings, we are able to establish whether different proper names refer to the same person inasmuch as the person is identifiable, not only by description, but also by direct or indirect acquaintance. We do not, however, know God by acquaintance, but only by description. (Or perhaps it would be better to say that, in so far as a Christian *does* suppose himself to know God as an acquaintance who can be named, his name is Jesus Christ.)

I am suggesting that 'God' is a description and not a proper name, and that to believe that God exists is not to believe something or other about God, but to believe that there is something or other which has divine attributes. It is to believe that divine attributes have reference.

The question, then, is not: what can we predicate of 'God'? but rather: what do we take to be 'divine' attributes? To ask an individual, or a group, what attributes they take to be divine is to ask them what they take to be of ultimate reality and significance. It is to ask them where they ultimately put their trust; on what their hearts and hopes are set.

The answers will vary considerably and from that variety have sprung enduring and intractable human conflicts – cultural, political and religious. Concerning this vast topic, I wish only to make four points. First, the term 'God' functions, in practice, as shorthand for some particular set of divine attributes. Secondly, the proposition 'God exists' is, logically, a confessional, 'self-involving' utterance. It declares, and the declaration is heavy with the risk of illusion and idolatry, that such-and-such are divine attributes and that these attributes have reference: that there is that on which it is appropriate thus to set all our trust, all our hope. Thirdly, those attributes we take to be divine are not mere ideas or ideals, but features of ultimate and, in that sense, transcendent reality. And, fourthly, it needs to be added (in the shadow of Feuerbach and Durkheim) that that to which such attributes refer is not reducible to any actual or possible feature or set of features of nature or history.

The suggestion that all attempts to speak of God are metaphorical, that they express (however imperfectly) the deepest convictions of those who make such language their own concerning the character and outcome of that transformative (creative and redemptive) process in which they, and others, are engaged in seeking to make sense of things, affords not the slightest licence for self-indulgence or imprecision. The crucial question is not whether we can speak of God 'literally', but whether we can speak of God truthfully. And, in our attempts to speak truthfully of God, we do not lack all criteria of appropriateness. But, for the Christian, questions of criteria are questions of christology, to which we now turn.

Son of God

Two preliminary points: In the first place, there is no reason to suppose that Christians in the early centuries were unable to distinguish between primary and secondary, 'focal' or extended, uses of words, nor that they necessarily took the concept of 'sonship' to refer only or even primarily to physical descent and relationship.[6]

In the second place, some modern philosophers of religion proceed on the assumption that christological propositions furnish 'additional information' concerning a God whose general identifying characteristics have been antecedently ascertained. Historically, it seems more correct to say that the forging of christological and trinitarian language expressed the attempt to *transform* inherited concepts of 'God' in the light of reflection on him who was confessed as 'Son' of God and on the mystery which, even in agony, he addressed as 'Father'.

In the light of these preliminary remarks, what are we to make of the notion of 'divine sonship'?

Jesus was, as we all are, a product of nature and history. As such a product, he was destructible and indeed was destroyed. We are none of us, however, *merely* 'products'. We are not merely produced: we are also, in different ways and with most varying efficacy, *cherished*. There are few human beings of whom someone, at some time, even fleetingly, has not been fond.

But, quite apart from the fact that many people are little loved, and loved with little selflessness and effective care, even the purest and most effective human loving cannot prevent the destruction, cannot transcend the mortality, of the products that we are.

To declare Jesus to be the Son of God is, I suggest, to declare that he was not only produced, but effectively, indestructibly, 'absolutely' cherished. If we take 'loving production' to be part of what we mean by 'true parenthood', and if, in declaring Jesus to be the Son of *God*, we declare 'parenthood' to be a divine attribute, then we are thereby declaring our conviction, derived from reflection on his fate, that being lovingly produced, being effectively cherished with a love that transcends destruction in mortality, is an aspect of what it ultimately is, means and will be to be human.

I suggested, in the previous section, that 'God exists' is a confessional utterance. I am now suggesting that 'Jesus is the Son of God' is, similarly, a confessional utterance, declaring our faith in his resurrection and our hope for the resurrection of all mankind. If 'parenthood' is a divine attribute, then the destruction of the product is not the last word concerning the human condition.

Two final comments. First, the anthropomorphism which seduces us into treating 'God' as a proper name has sometimes misled Christians into supposing that, if Jesus is truly God's Son, then he cannot also be (for example) Joseph's son. But this is simply a mistake. To declare Jesus to be the Son of *God* does not entail the denial that he was any other father's son.

Secondly, it is worth noting that, in confessing Jesus to be 'Son of God', it is 'parenthood', rather than either 'paternity' or 'maternity', which is declared to be a divine attribute.

Conclusion

Martin Hengel has described 'Son of God' as 'an established, unalienable metaphor of Christian theology'.[7] I have done no more, in this brief sketch, than to suggest that if this 'title' is not to be misunderstood as a piece of outmoded mythology, then it is on questions concerning the logic of the concept of 'God', and on questions concerning the character of the quest for human identity, fulfilment and self-understanding, that we should concentrate attention.

We seek so to transform our circumstances and our understanding as to make the world to which we belong a world which belongs to us.

To be able to say, in the face of human suffering and mortality, of the non-achievement of human meaning and the darkness of the future, that Jesus is *truly* the Son of God, and that therefore we also are and will be 'sons' and 'daughters', is either infantilist escapism or the mature expression of appropriate hope. That confession, I have suggested, declares our hope of resurrection, of that indefeasible transformation of nature and circumstance in which human existence attains its fulfilment and true identity in belonging to God. We can only speak truly in metaphors concerning that of which the new Jerusalem which we seek will be, we might say, the 'literal' expression.

11

Easter Meaning

The flight from the factual

In a paper on 'Infallibility and Historical Revelation', delivered in Birmingham in 1967, Austin Farrer said that the passage of time had 'served only to disgust me with the inconclusiveness and the irresponsibility of supposedly scientific New Testament scholarship or supposedly neutral historical investigation of Christian origins'.[1] He went on to add, however, that even if the Catholic historian 'has Catholic expectations, he cannot force facts'.[2] What disturbed Farrer about official Roman Catholic pronouncements concerning the Immaculate Conception and the Assumption was that they seemed to be instances of Christian authorities not only forcing the facts (affirming, for example, an unbroken tradition of belief in Mary's assumption even though no evidence for any such tradition can be found in the early church) but asserting their ability to make incorrigible historical judgments. And yet, as he said, 'history, including Catholic history, is corrigible'.[3] Farrer ended his essay by saying that what frightened him so much about the dogmatic definition of the Assumption was that it had 'the alarming appearance of an infallible fact-factory going full blast'.[4]

Harry Williams, in the last chapter of his autobiography, says that nobody present in Catholic churches on 15 August 'could fail to be aware of the power exercised over the large congregations by what was being commemorated. It obviously had the deepest and strongest meaning for them'.[5] However, he goes on, 'there isn't a single shred of historical evidence for

the corporeal assumption of our Lady. It is a pure invention of
the pious imagination. . . . The assumption, in short, never
happened'.[6] What is celebrated in Catholic churches each
August has, he says, 'nothing to do with a historical figure
called Mary. It is a spiritual reality, always contemporary,
within the hearts of the worshippers'.[7]

Already, from these two passages, we can begin to map out the
territory for our consideration of the doctrine of 'resurrection'.

In the first place, I take it that we can agree with Austin
Farrer that historical judgments (or, at least, most non-trivial
historical judgments) are not 'expectation-neutral'. What
counts as a 'fact', what counts as a relevant fact, what counts
as good evidence for a fact, will all depend, in some measure,
upon the kind of expectation – based on previous experience,
previously acquired information, belief and standards of assessment – which we bring to the matter in hand.

In the second place, I take it that we can also agree with him
that Christians are often tempted to 'force' the facts to fit their
convictions. And this, clearly, we must not do. There may be
no such thing as an expectation-neutral historical judgment,
but to admit this is by no means to allow that faith may ever
serve as a *substitute* for historical knowledge, filling in the
awkward gaps.

In the third place, both Austin Farrer and Harry Williams
agree that there is no good historical evidence for the occurrence
of that fact, that state of affairs, which they assume to be a
necessary condition for the truth of the proposition: 'Mary, the
mother of Jesus, was corporeally assumed into heaven.'

I put it in this rather cumbersome way because, although
Harry Williams roundly asserts that 'the assumption . . . never
happened', he does nevertheless believe that it is a fact. That
may sound paradoxical, but the paradox can be relieved by
pointing out that, although Williams does not believe the
assumption to be a fact about *Mary*, he insists that it is a fact,
and an important fact, about *us*, the worshippers who celebrate
the assumption. Mary, we might say (to paraphrase Bultmann)
was assumed into the liturgy.

Unlike some theologians, Harry Williams is not afraid to

make the necessary inferences, from his understanding of the assumption, for the doctrines of incarnation and resurrection. 'It seems to me', he says, 'a waste of powder and shot to try to show with immense labour that this or the other detail in the gospel narrative may after all be historical when a generation of scholars have concluded that it isn't. The real and important truth remains *whatever the status as history* of the story in which it is represented. If we have God truly present with us now, and if He can be truly incarnated in what we are today, and if we can know at first hand what it is to die and be raised again from the dead, what importance still survives in historical events alleged to have occurred two thousand years ago, apart from the power such stories have of making us aware of Emmanuel – God with us?'.[8] And again, more succinctly, 'the gospel story confronts us with inner realities and is in the end independent of what happened as a matter of history'.[9]

Harry Williams gives unusually lucid expression to a flight from the factual (or, at least, from the facts of history) which is, I think, increasingly widespread amongst Christians. However, I shall later try to argue that those of us who regard this flight from the factual, not as spiritual or intellectual maturity, but as a profoundly unsatisfactory evasion of constitutive features of the often painful complexity of Christian *credenda*, are ill-advised if we attempt, as it were, to meet the evasion 'head-on' by simply asserting that there *are* such facts, and that there is good evidence for such facts, as Harry Williams supposes not to have occurred and (anyway) to be unimportant for Christian believing. In due course, therefore, there are two questions to which we shall need to attend. First, is 'the resurrection' a fact about Jesus? Secondly, if so, what kind of a fact about Jesus is it?

The absent centre

For the time being, however, I want to approach the problem from a rather different angle. One of the oddest things about the essays in *The Myth of God Incarnate* is that the learned contributors seem to have supposed that it is appropriate to discuss the sources of Christian belief in incarnation, the meaning of that belief and its truth or falsehood while entirely neglecting to consider (as the present Bishop of Salisbury's review of the book put it) 'the affirmation from which the Christian faith began, and which apparently the contributors to this volume could not bring themselves to take seriously – the Resurrection of Jesus'.[10] ('Entirely neglect' may be a little strong: one contributor did briefly advert to the matter and disposed of it by attributing resurrection-faith to something that went 'ping' in Peter's psyche one Sunday and to mass hysteria among his friends.)[11]

What I find especially interesting about this neglect is that the two contributors to the follow-up volume who took note of Bishop Baker's criticism quite misunderstood it. They seem to have supposed that he was asking them to consider how things stood with an event quite *other* than the incarnation, an event different from that of incarnation which was related to it inasmuch as, if the occurrence of this other event could be demonstrated, or shown to be probable, then the doctrine of the incarnation would have received independent corroboration.[12]

I suggest, however, that the doctrine of the incarnation does not refer simply to something which occurred at Jesus' conception (or at his birth, or baptism, or death). It is a mistake to suppose that there was an event which we call 'incarnation' which was followed in due time by another and quite distinct event which we call 'resurrection'. That event, that fact, that state of affairs, to which we refer when we say 'The Word was made flesh and dwelt amongst us' was the event of *Jesus*, a man, a piece of history with (historically) a beginning and an end.

'Jesus is Lord' seems to have been an early, perhaps the earliest, form of Christian confession of faith in God. This confession was, at one and the same time, first, an expression of Easter faith, of faith in Christ's resurrection; secondly, an affirmation of what it was that God had worked in him; thirdly, as affirmation (at least by implication) of who this man was in whom God had worked these things, and of how this man is related to the eternal mystery of God.

In other words, I take it that the claim, in Acts 2.36, that

'God has made him both Lord and Christ, this Jesus whom you crucified' contains and entails the claim made four verses earlier in the same speech: 'This Jesus God raised up' (Acts 2.32).

On this account, the confession that Jesus is the Christ, the Lord's anointed, the bringer of the kingdom; the human, historical transcription of God's self and agency, of creative and redemptive love and power; the temporal enfleshment or incarnation of God's eternal word and deed; this confession contains and entails the conviction that Jesus is risen from the dead.

If I am right, then the mistake being made by those who say: 'the truth or falsehood of the doctrine of resurrection is a *separate issue* from that of the truth or falsehood of the doctrine of the incarnation' is more fundamentally conceptual (or 'grammatical') than historical: they have misconstrued the way in which the concepts of 'incarnation' and 'resurrection' function in Christian religious discourse.

To put it with perhaps misleading brevity: in the context of Christian belief, 'resurrection' is part of what 'incarnation' *means*. And I think that that is the right way of putting the matter even though, as Bishop Baker's remark reminds us, the doctrine of the incarnation was elaborated on the basis of, and as an implication of, faith in Christ's resurrection. That is to say: I do not think that my claim that 'resurrection' is part of what 'incarnation' means is contradicted by the fact that, in the order of discovery, belief in Christ's resurrection preceded the explicit description, as Word of God incarnate, of his identity in relation to the one who sent him.

What is the problem?

At the end of the first section of this chapter, I suggested two questions that should be included on our agenda: is 'the resurrection' a fact about Jesus and, if so, what kind of a fact about Jesus is it? We are now in a position to add two further questions: first, to what fact, event or state of affairs does the concept of 'resurrection' refer and, secondly, what does the concept mean? Another way of putting that last question might be: can we speak of that to which the concept of resurrection refers without using 'resurrection' terminology?

The logic of Harry Williams' position should lead him to assert that the resurrection of Jesus, like the assumption of Mary, 'never happened' (or, at least, that we have no good reason for supposing that it happened, and that whether it happened or not should not matter very much to us). He is, or should be, willing to say that what is celebrated in Christian churches every Easter, every Sunday and, indeed, at every celebration of the eucharist, has nothing to do with an historical figure called Jesus. It is a spiritual reality, always contemporary, within the hearts of the worshippers.

This suggests that we should begin by considering the factuality of Jesus' resurrection. I shall argue that those engaged, like Harry Williams, in the flight from the factual, and their – shall we say – 'literalist' opponents, share a common assumption concerning the *kind* of fact with which it is that we are dealing. Both agree that the resurrection of Jesus is a fact or event of the same order as the facts of his birth, life, teaching, suffering and death, which occurred (if it did) *after* this other series of facts or events was completed. The only difference between them is that the first group supposes that this further fact did not occur, or cannot be known to have occurrred, whereas the second group are confident both that it occurred and that it can be known to have occurred.

I shall suggest that there is something profoundly unsatisfactory about this view of the matter. I shall then go on to suggest that Harry Williams is more correct in what he affirms than in what he denies or ignores. The resurrection, I shall argue, is, indeed, a fact about us, but it is also a fact about Jesus and a fact about his disciples. Moreover, it is a fact not only about the present and the past, but also about our future and that of all mankind.

The fact of resurrection

The statement 'I believe in the resurrection' can be construed in at least two different ways. It might mean: it is in the light of resurrection, in the grace of resurrection, that I am able to affirm my faith and trust in God. That seems to me an appropriate and sensible thing for a Christian to say. Usually, however, when someone says 'I believe in the resurrection', they are making an assertion about what they think was, is or will be the case. This is how I shall take the statement and, thus construed, it is more like the statement 'I believe that high unemployment is likely to continue for several decades', or 'I believe that the partition of Ireland was a great mistake', than it is like the statement 'I believe in Mrs Thatcher' – where this statement means: 'I trust her and will follow her anywhere'.

I therefore feel entitled to treat the somewhat more specific or circumscribed statement, 'I believe that Jesus is risen from the dead', as a statement of the kind, 'I believe that X is the case'. It follows that, if the resurrection is not a fact, it is unbelievable, not in the sense of being 'really quite incredible', but simply in the sense that, unless it is some kind of a fact, it cannot be an object of belief.

But, what kind of fact is it? The best way to approach this question, I think, is by considering the problem of evidence. If the resurrection of Jesus is a fact, and a fact about Jesus, it can only sensibly or responsibly be believed in if there is good evidence for the fact. Geoffrey Turner, in an article in *New Blackfriars*, dismissed the suggestion that the disciples' belief that Jesus was risen could, in itself, count as 'good evidence'. 'The faith of another man', he says, 'does not count as evidence for me.'[13] Similarly, although he allows that 'in order to believe in the resurrection of Jesus we too need to experience it as something which transcends the past historical event' (we need, as he puts it, 'our own Damascus road experience'), nevertheless such experience alone 'is no basis on which to preach the Easter faith to others'.[14] We must also provide them with what Professor Michael Dummett (quoted at this point with approval by Turner) calls 'real evidence'.[15]

If I understand him, Turner is insisting that that alone could count as good evidence for the resurrection of Jesus to which access could be had, at least in principle, independently of the faith of the disciples or of twentieth-century Christians. And he considers that the evidence for the emptiness of the tomb, and for the fact that 'Jesus was seen (in the ordinary sense) by his disciples and that he spoke to them',[16] is strong enough to count, for his purposes, as good evidence.

Notice that Turner is not requiring that the fact of the resurrection should be *demonstrable* independently of faith. It is, after all, generally agreed that, even if the emptiness of the tomb could be established beyond all reasonable doubt, all that would thereby have been demonstrated was that the tomb was empty!

Nevertheless, what I find unacceptable in Turner's approach (and I have referred to his article only because it seems to me typical of the terms in which the discussion is usually conducted, at least in this country) is the empiricism which underlies it. By 'empiricism', in this context, I mean a philosophical temper which finds it necessary and unproblematic to draw a global or metaphysical distinction between 'objective' facts (what Bernard Lonergan used to call the 'already out there now real') and 'subjective' beliefs, impressions or attitudes ('in here').

Not wishing to interrupt the thread of the argument by entering into philosophical debates with which my readers will be only too wearily familiar, I content myself with asserting that there simply is no good reason why we should accept this Morton's fork of *either* 'brute' facts *or* 'merely subjective' beliefs and impressions (whether those of the disciples or of our Christian contemporaries). Instead, I suggest that we should regard the New Testament writings as a series of invitations to us to consider Jesus' history in one way rather than another. There are, we might say, two ways of 'reading' the story of Jesus, for both of which there is good evidence but yet which cannot both be exhaustively true, cannot both be the last word on the matter. We might, for the sake of convenience, label these two readings the 'story of death' and the 'story of life'.

Stories of life and death

What is the relationship, in the history of any human being, or of any social group, or (come to that) of the race as a whole, between death and life, between dying and coming alive? The apparently obvious answer, that first we live and then we die, is correct: a person can only cease to be if he or she has previously existed. Birth is the beginning, and death the end, of the historical process.

But although this answer is correct, there is a sense in which it is only trivially true and may be most misleading. At death, our bodily existence is terminated.[17] But what do we mean by our 'bodies'? My body is not simply the lump of matter by means of which I gesture and communicate with other people (or fail to do so). My body is also the world constituted by the personal, social and economic relations in which I share. My language, my family, my city, are parts of my body. When I die, the whole network of domestic and social communication of which I form a part dies a little too. The process of dying starts much earlier than the moment of terminal death. It is not only at the moment of terminal death that our world, our body, dies. Just as the physical constituents which go to make up this lump of matter are changing all the time, and many of the changes that occur amount to irretrievable loss (if you don't believe me, ask your dentist or your hairdresser) so it is with our social relationships. Friends die, relationships wither and, by our failure to communicate and care, our failure to bring each other alive, we contribute daily to each other's dying.

The story of each individual, and of every social group and, indeed, of the human race, is truly told, from start to finish, as a story of death, a narrative of mortality.

It may be objected that this is only part of the story. The story of most individuals, and of many social groups, can surely also truly be told as a story of life, of coming alive: a story of physical strength and prowess, of deepening relationships, of intellectual, practical, emotional and spiritual maturation, progress and achievement?

This is true. Were it not so, were the story of death the *only* true story, we could not bear to live. But how are these two stories, or these two parts of the story, to be related one to another? Is it possible so to weave them, however tentatively, into a single narrative as to be able to say how it *ultimately* is and will be with the individual, the group and the race?

Before trying to answer this question, there are two more points that need to be made. First, it seems clear, *prima facie*, that the last word must lie with death: every human history is bounded, terminated, by death. Even the most beautiful body corrupts, even the deepest relationship is fractured by mortality, even the most glittering civilizations decay.

The second point is that, without the willingness to die, human existence remains mere 'existence' and cannot flourish, cannot 'come alive'. In our relationships with other people, with new ideas and the challenge of fresh situations, we have continuously to be risking the unknown, the unfamiliar, the disturbing. We have to risk being changed, being transformed. We have to risk the destruction of whatever 'safe little world' we have so far succeeded in carving out of chaos. And the person who has not the courage thus to risk 'dying' throughout his or her life, is unlikely to have the courage to die at the end. The person who tries to live 'privately', to 'hang on to' possessions, friendships, certainties, will die 'privately', alone, and this (perhaps) is hell.

What this suggests is that, even if 'death' and 'life' are antagonistically related, the relationship between them is not straightforwardly antithetical. There seems to be a sense in which acceptance of mortality, engagement in mortality, is a necessary condition of coming alive. Unless a grain of wheat. . . .

Nevertheless, life and death are, even if not straightforwardly antithetical, antagonistically related: they are (to put it mythologically) locked in mortal combat.[18] And so, even though the story of death and the story of life can both be truly told, *must* both be told, it is not self-evidently inappropriate or unreasonable to try to weave them into a single narrative and to say (if we can) how it ultimately is and will be with the individual, with the group and with the race; to say where the victory lies.

When we do so, it seems clear (at least if we resolutely avoid all wishful thinking, all utopian dreaming and fantasizing that flies in the face of the evidence which surrounds us on every side) that the last word is with death. Not simply with the mere fact of termination, but with the unravelling of meaning, the destruction of relationship, the lordship of chaos. It is the light which seems ephemeral, the darkness which surrounds, determines and, again and again, 'overcomes' it. We are right to be fearful of death, afraid of the dark, to tremble in the face of chaos.

What would have to be the case for it to be otherwise? What would have to be the case for it to be possible – without illusion, evasion or fantasy – truly to tell the story of the ultimate victory of life, to tell it as a tale most truly told not of mortality but of coming alive? The answer, I suggest, is that we should have to have grounds for supposing that we live and die, although in darkness, yet not into chaos but into unconquerable light. We should have to have grounds for supposing that the ultimate truth, the last word about all that we do and suffer, enact and undergo, is with the inexhaustible vitality of 'the love that moves the sun and the other stars'.

Which brings me back, at last, to the story of Jesus. The New Testament writings are a series of invitations to us to consider Jesus' story (and, in its light, to consider our own story and that of every human being) as a story of life. It is, of course, a story of failure, suffering and death – hence the centrality of the passion narratives in the gospel accounts. And it does not cease to be so. And yet, in the last analysis, it is the darkness, not the light, which is there declared to be bounded, determined, and 'overcome'.

I suggested earlier that the 'fact' to which the doctrine of the incarnation refers is not simply the *inception* of Jesus' existence, the beginning of his history, but is, quite simply, *Jesus*: that man, that piece of history, of which we say: 'The Word was made flesh and dwelt amongst us' (John 1. 14).

Similarly, I now want to suggest that the 'fact' to which the doctrine of Jesus' resurrection refers is not simply the *termination* of his existence, the end of his history, but is, quite simply, *Jesus*: that man, that piece of history, of which we say: he was glorified, 'we have beheld his glory' (John 1. 14).

To adapt Karl Barth's imagery: the doctrine of the incarnation tells the story of Jesus as a tale of 'the way of the Son of God into the far country',[19] and the doctrine of the resurrection tells the story of Jesus as a tale of 'the homecoming of the Son of Man'.[20]

But these two stories are not stories about two consecutive sequences of events. They are the two ways in which we truly narrate one single history, one single sequence of events, the history of Jesus.

I am well aware of the fact that, by now, questions are crowding in as to what all this could possibly mean, and what the evidence for it might be. I shall attempt to attend to such questions in due course. All that I have tried to do in this section so far is to offer a framework within which to indicate what I take to be that fact, or event, or state of affairs, to which the doctrine of Jesus' resurrection refers.

My suggestion has been that, just as the doctrine of the incarnation refers to the fact of Jesus considered in the light of the question: 'who is this man and where did he come from?', so the doctrine of the resurrection refers to the fact of Jesus considered in the light of the question: 'how did it go with this man, what was the sense of his ending?'. Both doctrines are interpretations of Jesus. But thus to interpret Jesus' fact and significance is thereby to confess one's faith in the mystery of the God who thus acts in and transforms Jesus' history and ours. It makes no more sense to say 'I believe that Jesus rose from the dead but I don't believe in God' than it does to say 'I believe that Jesus is the Word incarnate but I don't believe in God'. (This last point may seem obvious, and yet much discussion of the resurrection, and especially of the evidence for the resurrection, proceeds as if the former affirmation might make sense.)

If the doctrine of the resurrection is true, it is factually true, and the fact to which it refers is a fact about Jesus. He is not here. Nor is he simply remembered. He is risen. But, once again, what *kind* of 'fact' are we speaking about? Is it an 'objective' fact? Many theologians, under the influence of the kind of empiricism that I mentioned earlier, find this an awkward question to handle.[21] But, frankly, I know of no other kind of fact. 'Facts are what statements (when true) state; they are not what statements are about.'[22] If the statement 'Christ

is risen' is true, it states a fact. And, if *Jesus* is the Christ, the
statement states a fact about Jesus.

Is that fact which the doctrine of the resurrection states an
'historical' fact? Inasmuch as the doctrine purports truly to
state how it went with Jesus, how his story is to be most truly
told, the answer must be 'Yes', at least in the sense that no
attempt to estimate the truth of stories about Jesus can ignore
the historian's testimony. If the historian could demonstrate
that what we know about Jesus is such as to render the Easter
story utterly implausible, then the truth of the doctrine would
have thereby been impugned. With all respect to Harry
Williams, the 'real and important truth' does *not* remain 'whatever the status as history of the story in which it is represented'.[23]

If we have good reason to suppose that what the doctrine of
the resurrection states about Jesus is false, then to continue to
tell it as a tale about 'spiritual reality, always contemporary,
within the hearts of the worshippers,'[24] is to issue a licence for
the kind of self-indulgent fantasy which has done damage
enough in human history. I have no doubt that the Nazis found
the myth of the master race deeply 'meaningful,' profoundly
descriptive of 'inner realities.' To suppose, however, that
'meaning' can thus be simply divorced from publicly testable
fact, significance from history, is to open the door to destructive
lunacy.

Of course, the doctrine of the resurrection says *more* about
Jesus than the historian is in a position to consider. But the
same is *also* true of the alternative version: of the story of death,
of the unravelling of meaning and the ultimacy of chaos. The
historian is not in a position to make what we might call
'metahistorical' judgments concerning what is 'ultimately' the
truth concerning the history of Jesus, or of anyone else.[25]

Evidence and Easter

If the doctrine of the resurrection states a fact about Jesus, on
the basis of what kind of evidence does it do so? Here, the first
thing that needs to be said, if only because it is too often not
said, is that the evidence for Jesus' resurrection is the evidence

of his life and teaching and the manner of his death. If Jesus, and the message which he announced and embodied, is not to be trusted on the basis of this evidence, then neither he nor his message are to be trusted at all.

If the manner of his living, and teaching, and dying, affords no basis for that trust in him which is, simultaneously, trust in the One who sends him and speaks to us through him, then nothing that happens to the disciples (or to us) after Jesus' death can be such as to warrant confessing him as the Christ of God, the Lord's anointed, him whom God raised up, him in whom the glory of God is glimpsed.

It does not follow that the evidence which the manner of his living and dying affords is *sufficient* to warrant the confession of Easter faith. Not that something was 'missing' from that life, that teaching, that costly fidelity. But that we have to be *shown* the 'sense of his ending'; we have to be shown that, not in spite of Calvary but because of it, his story can be most truly told as the story of God's unconquerably creative love, of the victory of the light which the darkness could not overcome.

How are we to be shown this? By that 'conversion process' which Edward Schillebeeckx calls 'the Easter experience'.[26] How else could we know, except by the healing gift of God's Spirit, that the fruit of his silencing was peace, of his rejection, forgiveness; that the 'end' of his death was not chaos, but daybreak; that Jesus had died, not into the darkness, but into the light of God? If that is not 'where' Jesus went, the story that we tell of him is false, and the 'Easter experience' a delusion. But, if this *is* where he went, then what else but such change, such 'conversion' could show us where he had gone, enabling us to 'find' him whom we had thought, like us, to be 'lost'? As Schillebeeckx puts it, evoking the visual metaphors that play a large part in the gospel narrative: 'Apart from this experience of Christian faith the disciples had no organ of sight that could afford them a sight of Jesus' resurrection.'[27] And I think that Karl Rahner is saying much the same thing when he says, in a much-discussed passage, that 'the resurrection of Christ is not another event *after* his passion and death . . . the resurrection is the manifestation of what happened in the death of Christ'.[28]

But in what might such 'experience' consist? How and where might such 'manifestation' occur? If we are not to fall back on unintelligible and unacceptable appeals to some kind of incommunicable 'private' experience, the answer must be sought in some public, intersubjective event or state of affairs. Here, as elsewhere, God's self-gift has created, contingent, 'form' or occurrence. Perhaps the pervasiveness of eucharistic imagery in the resurrection narratives provides us with a clue. Perhaps it was, above all, in common meals shared in his memory that the disciples were 're-called', that they came to know themselves forgiven, re-called to the presence of the crucified. And perhaps the insistence on the fact that the risen Christ first 'appears' as a 'stranger' is, in part, a comment on the perceived lack of any appropriate language, ready to hand, in which they could say what they had come to 'see'.[29]

Two footnotes, before moving on. In the first place, the account I have sketched seems to satisfy Geoffrey Turner's requirement that there should be evidence for the resurrection which is, in principle, accessible independently of the faith of the disciples. The difference between Turner's form of the requirement and mine is that I would shift the weight of the evidence to that which occurred before and at, rather than after, Jesus' death. The language in which the disciples tried, after his death, to say what they had come to 'see' is also 'evidence of resurrection', but only in the indirect sense that it constitutes an invitation to us to see what they saw; an invitation to construe Jesus' history (and hence our own and that of every human being) as a story the sense of whose ending is given by the incomparable power of God's transforming grace.

In the second place, I disagree with Harry Williams' claim that 'there isn't a single shred of historical evidence for the corporeal assumption of our Lady'.[30] There is historical evidence, however slender, of Mary's obedience and trust, from Nazareth to Calvary. And this seems to me just the kind of evidence that we would need in order to be able to see in her the 'image' of the faithfulness of Israel and thus, in the light of our faith in her son's resurrection, to trust that she, too, was brought by the grace of God to die into his glory.

The meaning of Easter

It will not have escaped your notice that, so far, I have said nothing about the question of the empty tomb. Geoffrey Turner is quite confident that even if stories about the empty tomb only came to feature in Christian proclamation of the resurrection relatively late, 'the fact of the empty tomb must have been accepted from the beginning, given Jewish beliefs at the time'.[31] He may be right, I am simply not sufficiently well-informed, historically, to pontificate on the matter. But I notice that there seem to be quite a number of learned and sober historians of the New Testament who do not share his confidence.

I take it, however, that the emphasis on 'bodily' resurrection (or 'corporeal' assumption) is, fundamentally, an emphasis on wholeness and personal identity. It is *we*, human persons, human beings, who, by God's grace, die into his glory, not some wraith-like element or partial feature of whatever constitutes our personal identity. I doubt if we can sensibly say much more. Geoffrey Turner may be correct in supposing that the emptiness of the tomb was a necessary condition of the first Christians expressing their Easter faith in terms of 'resurrection', but I am not convinced that the emptiness of the tomb is amongst the truth-conditions of the proposition 'Jesus is risen from the dead'.

This brings me, finally, to the question of what the doctrine of the resurrection means. I intend, by this question, to invite consideration of two problems: first, concerning the range of terminology and imagery that is available to us for expressing our conviction: secondly, concerning how much we can hope to *understand* of that which, in confessing the doctrine, we declare to be true.

Even if, as I suggested earlier, questions of meaning and questions of truth cannot and must not be dissociated, nevertheless they can and must be distinguished. Thus, for example, whatever we take to be the truth-conditions of the proposition 'Jesus is risen from the dead', I suggest that the unique appropriateness of the metaphor of 'resurrection' is not amongst such truth-conditions. In other words: it is, in principle, possible to make true statements abut that to which the language of resurrection refers without using the terminology, or imagery, of 'rising' from the dead.

To anyone even as cursorily familiar as I am with the New Testament evidence, this may seem obvious. And yet, theologians sometimes give the impression that a decision not to use the terminology of 'resurrection' is tantamount to a denial of the truth of the doctrine. But the early Christians used other metaphors: 'exaltation', 'glorification', and so on. And even if, in terms of linguistic history, 'resurrection-talk' is closely related to metaphors of 'waking from sleep', this notion is clearly distinguishable from that of 'resuscitation', with which 'resurrection-talk' is still too often disastrously associated. On the general issue, Léon-Dufour has argued, in some detail, the historical case for saying that 'rising' metaphors only gradually came to occupy the dominant and apparently normative place which, by and large, we continue to ascribe to them.[32]

There are, to be brief, four points that I should want to make on these matters. In the first place, to say that, in our attempts to make true statements about that to which the doctrine of resurrection refers, we are not restricted to the imagery of 'rising from the dead', is not to say, or to imply, that how we decide to tell the story (of Jesus, of ourselves, and of all mankind) is simply a matter of arbitrary choice or personal preference. It could not be so: we are constrained (as in any interpretative enterprise) by the *interpretandum*. We may, indeed, be very *tightly* constrained, if we are not to float free of the particularities of that which occurred and was transacted into some 'idealist' fantasizing of our prospects and predicament. We are constrained by what we know of Jesus' history, and by our own continuing, and continually unfinished, experience of desolation and forgiveness, tragic circumstance and obscure hope.[33] There is, nevertheless, a crucial difference (however resistant it may be to theoretical expression) between telling a story differently and telling a different story. My immediate concern is simply to suggest (and the suggestion has considerable catechetical implications) that to refrain from speaking of 'rising' is not necessarily to tell a different story.

In the second place, I am not suggesting that the expression of Easter faith could ever be a simple, unproblematic or straightforward affair. Such straightforwardness is ruled out by the fragmentariness and 'illegibility' of our circumstance, and by the fact that our 'conversion' (individually and communally, personally and politically) lacks the purity and completeness which might render our 'sight' less occluded and our speech less questionable.

In the third place, whatever imagery we employ, the story that we try to tell (and, corporately and individually, to enact) can never be, as it were, a direct transcript of its referent. Because we seek to speak of that which 'transcends' and heals all time and circumstance, we can only do so tentatively, indirectly, metaphorically, in language drawn from our present experience, which is that of a history that has *not* yet ended, not yet been given its final 'resolution', 'shape' and identity.

Therefore, fourthly, we should never lose sight of how *little* we can glimpse and understand of that of which we seek to speak. The consequent restraints upon speech and imagination work in two directions. On the one hand, we need, again and again, to allow the exuberance of unwarranted optimism to be chastened and broken by the dark facts of human experience. The 'story of death' has not ceased to be true even if it is not, perhaps, the last word. On the other hand, however, finding it too easy to say too much about the future is not the exclusive prerogative of optimism. There is also a self-indulgence of despair, a fantasy of egotism, which is or may be silenced and healed by Easter hope. The important thing is not to be able to utter that hope, to speak of resurrection, with facility, but to be able to do so at all.[34]

I have suggested that what the doctrine of the resurrection – of Jesus' resurrection and, in the light of Easter hope, of ours and of every human being – attempts to state is that the story of human history is ultimately to be told in terms, not of death, but of life, not of chaos but of God's unconquerably effective love.

It follows that, if the doctrine of the resurrection is true, then nothing whatsoever, no circumstance, no suffering, no cracking by chaos of sanity and dignity, no betrayal, no oppression, no collapse of sense, structure or relationship, can justify despair, can justify the admission that, at the end of the day, the darkness has the last word. Those who know *this* know, I think, all that it is yet possible for us to know of what 'resurrection' means.

12

The Church's Responsibility for the Future of Humanity

Discipleship and civilization

'When I was in the United States last year more than one American of the Republican party spoke gloomily to me of the decay of the English character. They were impressed by the weakness of the Government in [Northern Ireland]; by our helplessness in dealing with [radical feminists] . . . they argued for a general decay of English common sense and English courage'.[1] That was not a personal reminiscence of mine, but the opening sentences of a lecture given at the Royal Institution, in 1915, by Wilfrid Ward (shortly before his death the following year).

The lecture was entitled 'The War Spirit and Christianity'. Ward's argument for the undimmed excellence of the English character was that 'the spirit fostered by the war has brought out in the one race an outburst of Christian virtue; in the other cruelty, excess and treachery'.[2] Whereas the British troops were 'the offspring of generations in which pagan savagery has been cleansed by Christianity'[3] the ethos of the German army, under the influence of a Nietzschean rejection of Christianity, exhibited a 'reversion to pagan ideals'.[4] What the early months of the First World War demonstrated to Wilfrid Ward was that war 'makes the Christian at heart more deeply Christian. It makes the pagan at heart more evidently pagan'.[5]

The argument is distasteful and embarrassing. But, before we consign it to the history books as a relic of long-dead triumphalisms, consider how closely Ward's analysis matches descriptions which are only too familiar, of what is normally at issue in the conflict between the so-called 'free world' and Soviet Communism.

I take Ward's lecture to exemplify what we might call the 'ethical' response to questions concerning the responsibility of the church for the future of humanity. This response takes many forms, but central to most of them is the conviction that the social role, or mission, of Christianity is to be conceived in terms of 'civilization', of 'cleansing pagan savagery', and of thus contributing to the humanity or humanness of the species.

For better or worse, however, the ethical response is no longer available to us. It is not available, in the first place, because we have lost the capacity innocently to tell our story in triumphalist terms. Prompted, perhaps, by something we have learned from the sociology of knowledge, our memories of what has been said and done, in the name of Christianity, are occasions as much for repentance and transformation as for celebration.

In aspects of action and relationship, in unsung instances of gentleness and compassion, in forms of art, enquiry and organization, incalculable benefits have undoubtedly been rendered by innumerable patterns and instances of Christian discipleship. But, for every achievement a price has been paid; from each redemptive effort unforeseen dark consequences have accrued. Again and again, as the energy of conviction transposes into tyranny, the quest for the spirit into flight from the flesh, the ordering of chaos into structures of oppression, the dialectic of what we call 'Christian' history renders impossible any interpretation in straightforwardly celebratory terms.

It is not my intention to underestimate the benefits brought by Christianity. I am only insisting on the impossibility, within history, of cost-benefit analysis. The recognition of this impossibility is, arguably, an aspect of Hegel's genius: hence that obscure reference, at the end of the *Phenomenology*, to 'comprehended History' as 'the Calvary of absolute Spirit'.[6] Hegel did, nevertheless, persist in the attempt to think clearly what cannot be made transparent to thought. Most of us, not being philosophers, prefer to render tragic fact endurable not as concept but as cliché. Thus, for example, if I were to remind us that the gas-chambers of Auschwitz were not constructed without Christian influence, or that it was a culture not untouched by Christianity which dropped the bombs on Hiroshima and Nagasaki, it is quite possible that such reminders would no longer even give us nightmares, let alone lead us effectively to reconstruct our perception of Christianity's beneficent influence.

A second set of reasons for supposing that the ethical response is no longer available arise from the fact that, in order to justify the claim that the social role of Christianity is to be conceived in terms of contributing to the 'humanizing' of the species, we should have to be clearer than it is, in fact, possible to be about the relationships between Christian obedience and 'authentic' humanness.

There are two problems here. On the one hand, authentic or 'perfected' humanness cannot be *depicted* within a history that is still unfinished.[7] I am therefore more inclined than some of his critics have been to allow the coherence of Alasdair MacIntyre's characterization of 'the good life' as 'life spent in seeking for the good life'.[8] (And if someone supposes that the New Testament *does* provide us with 'pictures' of incarnate goodness they have, I think, misunderstood the ways in which memory and eschatology, narrative and proclamation, are correlated in what we might call the 'grammar' of the gospel.)

On the other hand, it is not possible to give a timelessly valid account of the relationships between Christian obedience and 'authentic' humanness because the relationships between the 'theological' and the 'moral' virtues are such that they must, again and again, be sought for and established in particular concrete circumstances of Christian 'praxis'. To put the point more simply: we cannot deduce our ethics from our faith. There are no straight lines of inference to be drawn from discipleship of the Crucified to the construction of social policy.[9]

Civil religion and prophetic criticism

Patriotism is not a vice. The particular 'places' which produce us – places with their own distinctive customs and memories, shapes and sounds, achievements and sufferings – make us the persons that we are. The plight of the refugee, of the 'dis-placed' person, is a pointer to the fact that, were there absolutely no place which we could recognize as 'home', we would have no personal existence. Human existence is structured in narrative, and, whoever we are, patriotism is the celebration of 'our' particular story. (Please notice that it is 'patriotism' and not 'nationalism' of which I speak.)

However, all attempts to give theological expression to patriotism are fraught with danger, for such expressions tend easily to absolutize the significance and excellence of particular times and places and peoples. There is a hint of this in Wilfrid Ward's contrast of British virtue with German vice. He comes close to saying that 'our' side is *God's* side. And any such claim I take to be close cousin to blasphemy.

The most powerful and destructive expressions of this absolu-tizing or idolatrous tendency are those which combine the attractiveness of 'civil religion' with the illusion of social messianism. Not being able to enter here into the extensive debates concerning the concept of 'civil religion',[10] I shall take the concept to refer, quite generally, to the assumption that the destiny of the nation and its polity are absolutely, divinely underwritten. By 'social messianism' I mean the illusion enter-tained by some particular social formation – be it a state or a revolutionary movement – that it represents, and is motivated by, not particular self-interest but simply the interests of the human race.[11] Such social messianism has been, I believe, a powerful factor in generating the *energy* with which, in our own day, both Russia and America have prosecuted their own particular interests. But whereas in Russia, of course, social messianism cannot be given explicitly theological expression, it is otherwise in the United States.

What would serve as a corrective to the idolatrous tendency of civil religion, especially in its 'messianic' forms? One answer, perhaps, would be a structure of self-criticism which drew upon theological resources that were not themselves *internal*, even as goals or ideals, to the system that it sought to correct. That is only a first approximation. To render it less abstract, let me turn to another text from another time.

'You have heard great things from New England of late . . . and indeed, great and wonderful have the things been in which God has passed before us. But now . . . the clouds have lately thickened, and our hemisphere is now much darkened with them. There is a great decay of the work of God among us.'[12] That is Jonathan Edwards, writing in May 1743. According to one of his commentators, the date is significant. Before 1742 Edwards had tended, 'albeit with caution . . . to believe that the whole cosmic drama might come to its resolution in America'.[13] After 1742, 'Such millenial tendencies had been expunged from his thinking through an eschatology which now became the principle of criticism of every historical epoch, [including] . . . his own'.[14]

My suggestion is, then, that especially in social formations infected by one form or another of the idolatrous tendencies implicit in 'civil religion' and tempted by the illusion of social messianism, the church's responsibility for the future of humanity is best exercised by having effective recourse to its eschatology as a principle of historical self-criticism.

The suggestion is hardly a novel one. It has, indeed, become something of a commonplace in contemporary theology. Nevertheless, I want to try to develop it in such a way as to indicate one or two problems which seem to me to have received insufficient attention in much of the theological literature.

In the first place, there is the problem of *power*. How is a church which conceives its social role primarily in terms not of 'civilization' or the endorsement of social policy, but rather in terms of 'prophetic criticism', to avoid falling into the trap of a new Manicheeism, a new illusion of purity, according to which all power is, in principle, suspect of sinfulness and hence to be eschewed?

In the second place, there is the problem of *knowledge*. If the church is to draw on resources of its own, which are to serve as the basis of its critique, where are such resources to be found? What is it that the church alone *knows* about the future of humanity such that, in the light of this knowledge, it is able to exercise its social responsibility?

In the third place, there is the problem of the context of criticism. If our references to 'the church' are not to remain evasively abstract, what kind of community is it that might be realistically and concretely envisaged as the symbolic or sacramental expression of eschatological hope, of a hope that is effectively critical of all idolatrous absolutization of particular places and times, nations and destinies, projects and policies?

This, then, is my ridiculously ambitious agenda for the remainder of this chapter. (It will be noticed that the three points I have placed on it have something in common with the three articles of the Creed: with our confession of God's almightiness, of his utterance to us of his Word, and of his Spirit in which we are to dwell.)

The problem of power

'Jesus' whole ministry', it has been said, 'is a challenge to . . . those constraints and conditions of this world which the kings of this world regard as defining the absolute limits of their power.'[15] The Gospels, and especially the passion narratives, challenge us to acknowledge that what counts as worldly power may be (as in Pilate's case) only a kind of impotence, and that what counts as impotence may be (as in Jesus' case) the direct transcription of God's almighty power.

The New Testament, in other words, takes out of our control the 'grammar' of power and authority, depriving us of all assurance that the powers which we acknowledge and exercise, or in whose grip we are held, may not, in fact, be counterfeit. Effectiveness is not a criterion of conformity with God's fruitful purposes.

What the New Testament does not do, however, is to equate effectiveness with sin. And yet, especially on the rebound from centuries of complicity between church authority and secular power – centuries which have seen all manner of domination and exploitation perpetrated in the name of the gospel – Christians may nowadays be tempted towards this equation. And, since domination is antithetical to freedom, the Christian responsibility to contribute to society's liberation from the idolatry endemic in civil religion[16] will be construed as a responsibility to remain untarnished by power.

This flight from the ambiguities of flesh and force and fact is reinforced by the illusion (an illusion which saturates the imagination of modern Western culture) that 'matter' and 'mind', or 'flesh' and 'spirit', are the names of irreducibly distinct classes of entity. The inference is then easily drawn that the 'spiritual' life is concerned with changing one's mind and not with the transformation of the material conditions of human existence. But the paradoxes of power in the New Testament have nothing to do with metaphysical dualism. The authors of the Gospels were not disciples of Descartes.

When power is equated (theologically) with sin and (sociologically) with domination, it is but a small step to the supposition that servitude and impotence are, simply *as such*, potentially virtuous or redemptive. And here, I think, we touch on another and perhaps surprising source of the failure of so much current theology to engage in detailed analysis of the problem of power. This view that slavery and powerlessness are in themselves sources of liberation comes close to Marx's analysis of the revolutionary potential of the proletariat. Central to that analysis was a concept of the proletariat defined in terms of 'pure negativity', a concept infected by mythological elements derived in part (I believe) from Hegel's philosophical dialectic of lordship and bondage.[17] It is not without interest for my argument, therefore, that there are social theorists who would now insist that a major limitation of Marx's social and historical analysis was his failure adequately to come to grips with the problem of power.[18]

My suggestion is, then, that whereas the failure of theologians on the 'right' adequately to engage with the problem of power is partly attributable to the dualisms which disease the Western mind, the failure of theologians on the 'left' so to engage is partly attributable to acknowledged inadequacies in the Marxist tradition.

Power, in the sense of effectiveness, is not, I said, to be equated with sin. But neither is it to be contrasted with freedom. 'Power and freedom in human society', says Anthony Giddens, 'are not opposites . . . power is rooted in the very nature of human agency, and thus in the "freedom to act otherwise".'[19] Power is capacity, skill, competence, entitlement and access to resources. Just as power cannot be contrasted coherently with freedom, so also it cannot be identified plausibly with domination or exploitation. As a human phenomenon, power is inherently ambivalent. And there is no virtue or liberating potential in powerlessness simply as such.

Articulateness is power. Memory is power. Were the Christian community to 'lose its memory' (through the destruction, for example, of libraries and monuments, for memory has material conditions) it would, indeed, be rendered powerless to exert its critical or liberating influence through the effective remembrance of the crucified Christ.

I remarked earlier that there are no straight lines to be drawn from discipleship of the Crucified to the construction of social policy. This is a theme which the critics of 'liberation theology' are fond of emphasizing. But they then proceed to draw the quite unwarranted inference that *therefore* discipleship has little or nothing to do with social policy, and so priests must keep out of politics (except in Poland). What is required, however, and what is still too often lacking, is the establishment of connections between discipleship and policy through the permanently unfinished labour of critical engagement with specific situations and states of affairs, specific instances and aspects of power and impotence.[20]

By taking out of our control the grammar of power and authority, the New Testament prevents us from equating effectiveness with either sin or virtue. Power, as a human phenomenon, is inherently ambivalent. It does not follow that there are not clear choices placed before us. It does, however, follow that a 'preferential option for the poor' (for example) is *not* to be construed as an option in favour of powerlessness, an option against the possession and use of power. It is an option which, in the light of hope sprung from the memory of the Crucified, equips us with a criterion of discrimination concerning the forms and uses of power.

Hope and nescience

If, as I have suggested, Christian eschatological hope is to function as a principle of historical self-criticism, a criterion of discrimination concerning the uses and abuses of power, what is to be said about the character and content of this hope? Or, as I put it earlier, what is it that the church alone knows about the future of humanity such that, in the light of this knowledge, it is able to exercise its social responsibility? The short answer is that the church alone knows that we know absolutely nothing about our absolute or ultimate future except that we *have* a future in the mystery that we call God. We are not, therefore, in a position either to predict or to control the form or outcome of history, to determine the end of history. It is not in our hands.

But surely, however unwarranted our long-term predictions, however totalitarian our attempts at large-scale control, the one thing that we do know about history's outcome is that history *ends*; that the story of each individual, each social formation, and of the human race, is bounded by mortality? Yes, but what is to be made of mortality? Is it matter for joy, or despair, or stoic resignation making what we can of the interim?

Most modern large-scale descriptions of historical process are *evolutionary* in character (whether the pattern of that description be 'dialectical' or 'gradualist'), and most proponents of evolutionary accounts have supposed themselves to 'know' the outcome of the process, and to know that it will be excellent, however laborious the route. Evolutionary views of history, therefore, tend to be optimistic in their expectations, and characteristically neglectful of the implications of individual and social mortality. It is the *outcome* of the process on which the evolutionist concentrates attention. And, because that outcome is known to be excellent, all the darkness and the horror that precede and surround us are deemed, in that excellent outcome, to find their justification or (at least) their explanation. Thus it is that optimism, with its sights set on the far horizon, is often destructive – in the 'interim' – of that very freedom whose eventual fulfilment it confidently predicts.

It is not, however, the optimist alone who knows too much about the future, idolatrously absolutizing the supposed object of his knowledge. Especially in the shadow of the bomb, ideologies of 'progress' and evolution get displaced by a darker certainty: the certainty that we have no future or, at the very least (and this is the characteristic voice of conservatism) that we have no alternative but to accept the insurmountability of the existing 'limits' set to human flourishing. 'Be realistic' is a polite way of saying: 'Cease to hope'.

Both optimism and despair know too much about the future. They take it upon themselves to provide the unfinished narrative of history with the conclusion which it has not, in fact, achieved. They foreclose the question of the future, lifting what Newman called 'the curtain hung over [our] futurity'.[21] What style of life, what kind of praxis, would it be, then, which could enable us to resist these foreclosures, and to keep the question open? It would be, I suggest, a praxis, a 'culture' (if you will), characterized, on the one hand, by the *reticence* enjoined upon it by the recognition that the curtain hung over our futurity *cannot* be lifted – not by science, not by astrology, and not by revelation – and, on the other hand, by the acknowledgment that past and present particular sufferings and particular joys may not be forgotten or discounted for the sake of completing the narrative, of 'solving the plot'.

Christian eschatology has often fallen into the trap of supposing that faith can furnish us with 'previews of future events'.[22] But thus to suppose is to cut eschatology loose from its content in christology. Christian hope springs from the memory of the Crucified. Gethsemane and Calvary remain the unsurpassable context of eschatology. Theologically, we have no source of information which Jesus lacked. *We* do not know something about the future which he did *not* know. Cognitively, we stand where he stood, bounded by nescience. But, in that darkness, he did not despair. He addressed the darkness as 'Father'. To live by Easter faith, interpreting his death as resurrection, is to be enabled to live, and to struggle, and to die, in that same unswervingly trustful nescience.

The Christian, Karl Rahner once said, must 'impress the form of his hope upon the framework of the world he lives in'.[23] But, if the form of that hope is as I have tried to characterize it, it will make its 'impression' through the continual reappraisal and critique of the 'bounds' or 'limits' set to our existence, practically and conceptually, by that existing framework, for the question of the future remains *open*.[24]

One further thought. I have hinted that conceptions of history (and the modes of production that generate them) which foreclose the question of the future discount the significance of the interim: of small times and small places, of particular joys and sufferings, relationships and achievements. In place of the richness and diversity of the particular, existence is mechanized and routinized: 'time is money', and ceases to have any other value than as commodity.[25] The mechanical emptiness of the routine, of a world in which times and places are deprived of significance, is decorated by triviality and punctuated by nightmare. In what Anthony Giddens has desribed as this 'unique conjunction of the banal and the apocalyptic',[26] Dallas alternates with Doomwatch, Disneyland with Apocalypse Now.

If there is something in this, it suggests that a form of Christianity whose stance in respect of the future was character-ized by the kind of respect for the interim, the kind of trustful nescience, which I have tried to indicate, might (after all) have a civilizing or 'culturing' influence. Not, indeed, as its primary objective (this I have ruled out from the start) but rather as an unsought by-product of its central concern, which is to 'impress the form of its hope upon the framework of the world' by keeping the question of the future open in prophetically critical obedience to the memory of the Crucified. What form of Christianity might this be? I am thus brought, finally, to consider the question: in what sort of context or community could such hope be sustained, embodied and exhibited?

Contexts of hope

Alasdair MacIntyre has argued, in *After Virtue*, that what he calls a 'shared vision of the good' can only be sustained by 'a network of small groups of friends'. This proposal, he acknowledges, will be almost unintelligible in a society in which, with friendship relegated to the privacy of individuals, the political order is restricted to the calculus of administration and control.[27] Despairing, therefore, of 'modern systematic politics, whether liberal, conservative, radical or socialist',[28] MacIntyre sees the only hope for our humanness in 'the construction of local forms of community within which civility and the intellectual and moral life can be sustained through the new dark ages which are already upon us'.[29]

The model he is invoking here, of course, is that of the social function of monasticism in an earlier 'dark ages'. But, quite apart from the fact that he sees the civilizing function of early medieval monasticism as more of a motive, and less of a 'by-product', than I would be inclined to do,[30] I believe that his proposal, while admirably lacking in optimism, stands too near the side of despair and, in so doing, surrenders too much to tyrannical and destructive uses of social and political power. In other words, while there would certainly by nothing 'constantinian' about a church modelled on MacIntyre's lines, such a church would (I think) be sustained by stoicism rather than by prophetically critical engagement. I see no scope for *joy* in MacIntyre's communities. And yet there is, I take it, a *joyfulness* which characterizes even the 'darkest' and most ascetically nescient expressions of authentically Christian hope.

After Virtue is only one of a number of recent studies, operating in the borderlands between moral philosophy and social theory, which conclude with consideration of the kinds of *community* which are necessary or desirable in our present predicament. In several of these studies, however, the question of community is tackled with an abstractness which is tantamount to evasion.

Richard Rorty, for example, although he talks about a 'renewed sense of community',[31] confines his attention to the marginal world of the academic seminar, and when he speaks about what 'we' might be able to do or say, he is honest enough to acknowledge that by 'us' he means 'relatively leisured intellectuals, inhabiting a stable and prosperous part of the world'.[32]

Richard Bernstein, in his fascinating study *Beyond Objectivism and Relativism*, compliments MacIntyre for 'constantly pointing us in the direction of a politics of everyday life in which individuals act together to form new specific and local forms of community'.[33] According to Bernstein, the thinkers whom he has been considering – Gadamer, Habermas, Rorty and Arendt – all 'help us to think about our situation, our history, and our prospects'.[34] Now, on the page from which I have taken that quotation, there are no fewer than nineteen first-person plurals: 'we', 'us', 'our'. But who are 'we'? Who are the subjects of these sentences, the objects of these proposals?

One tempting reply to such questions is: it is up to each reader to answer for him or herself. The reply is tempting because, though correct, it is inadequate. It is inadequate because, if studies such as MacIntyre's and Bernstein's are to count as contributions to social analysis, and not as mere speculation, it must be possible to indicate where the kinds of community which they deem indispensable for the survival of humanity are, at least incipiently, to be found.

I have now brought the discussion round to the point at which the *theological* questions that need to be considered (and which I shall shortly attempt to consider) are: where is the *church* to be found, and what forms might it appropriately take in the circumstances of our culture?

What all the writers I have mentioned have in common is a conviction that the political 'macro-structures' of both West and East, and the ideologies which inform them, are deeply infected by a kind of disseminated sclerosis requiring, for the survival of our humanity, the corrective influence or at least (in MacIntyre's form) the alternative presence of 'local forms of community'. This conviction seems to be at least consonant with my suggestion that Christian hope, resisting the illusory long-term visions of both optimism and despair, and prophetically critical of the structures of prediction and control in which these dreams and nightmares are embodied, should find form and focus in the 'interim': in the concrete occurrence of particular joys and sufferings, relationships and achievements, none of which may be discounted or simply overriden in the name of some master strategy or finished narrative of our still unfinished history.

So successful, so thorough, has been the exile (often self-inflicted) of theological considerations from the sophisticated discourse and imagination of our culture, that none of the authors to whom I have referred makes mention of the celebration of the Christian eucharist. And yet it is surely here, in the celebration of the eucharist, that the kind of 'local community' that is sought for finds (or should find) a form of indirect, symbolic, expression or 'dramatic' instantiation.

I believe that none of the changes in Catholic Christianity which have occurred in recent decades are of more far-reaching potential significance than what we might call the recovery of the 'congregationalist' element in Catholicism. And the focus of this recovery, this transformation in our self-perception, has undoubtedly been our eucharistic self-understanding.

'This Church of Christ', said Vatican II, 'is truly present in all legitimate local congregations of the faithful.'[35] It has begun to dawn on us that when a group of people express, in the breaking of bread, hope sprung from the memory of the Crucified, then – however small and undistinguished the company, however ritually unimpressive the circumstances – *what* they are is not a 'bit' of something bigger, not an obscure branch office of a multinational corporation, but, quite simply, the church of Christ, in its entirety. It is an excellent rule in ecclesiology, a rule only broken by schism, that one plus one equals one.

Had the transformation *stopped* there, it would not, of course, have gone far enough. For the rule I have just mentioned has long been a principle in the ecclesiology of Eastern Orthodoxy, and yet the sacramentality of the Orthodox Churches seems rarely to have stimulated political criticism. But, in Catholicism, the changes in eucharistic self-understanding are now part and parcel of a more profound transformation.

It is now twenty years since Karl Rahner, reflecting on the 'diaspora' situation of contemporary Christianity, spoke of the 'transition from the regional or national Church to the Church of believers'.[36] Ten years later, he could say, more simply, that 'the Church of the future will be one built from below by basic communities as a result of free initiatives and association'.[37] I find it difficult not to believe that, in the burgeoning of such communities – from Latin America to Africa, from Asia to the United States; communities that have grown up primarily among the poor, the oppressed, the 'invisible' – we have the most striking single sign of the vitality of Christianity.

Each community, suffering and striving and praying in its place, *is* the church of God. But, just because it is the church in its particular place, its very engagment in the requirements of that place can engender narrowness and parochialism, 'tribal' and sectarian attitudes. It is, in that place, the church, but what it is required to be, in that particular place, is the 'sacrament of intimate union with God and of unity for the whole human race'.[38] Therefore, the congregationalist impulse in Catholicism stands in need of permanent corrective pressure from the 'catholic' impulse. We need not worry: such corrective pressure will most certainly be supplied by those who at present regard the 'basic communities' as a disruptive element in the smooth running of a world-wide corporation!

It has been argued, and – in view of the shift from countryside to megalopolis – the argument is not without its element of conscious paradox, that, with the development of modern capitalism, the nation-state replaced the city as the 'crucible of power'.[39] Now, although it would be 'a mistake to suppose that the end of the era of the nation-state has at last arrived . . . for, after all, the super-powers are still nation-states, and there are no more embracing world organisations that even remotely threaten their power',[40] nevertheless, there does seem to be a case for suggesting that, unless the human race is to perish prematurely, it must seek some means of transcending the nation-state, some means of superceding its autonomy into a system of global government.

This may never happen. We may not find the necessary

moral, imaginative and technical resources. And so, perhaps, we perish. But it is not, I think, fanciful to suggest that, in the 'interim', a not unimportant responsibility for the future of humanity could be exercised by a transcultural, global 'network' of local communities, each of which conceived its primary duty to be that of sustaining, in its particular place, the memory of him in whose dying we discern the transformative presence of God; communities which, in that act and process of remembrance, sustain an absolute hope for all humanity in the light of which to stimulate resistance to those dreams and nightmares in which individual nations and destinies, individual projects and policies, are destructively idolized.

Conclusion

Earlier I described my agenda for this chapter as ridiculously ambitious. By now, it will have been realized that the agenda was much more modest than I then suggested. All that I have tried to do, within a familiar framework, has been to indicate three interrelated areas – the problem of power, the problem of the cognitive character of eschatological hope, and the problem of community – in which (it seems to me) a very great deal of theological work needs urgently to be done, and to be done in collaboration with the philosophers and social scientists.

But, since it is Christian theology that is in question, the context in which such work will appropriately be done is certainly not merely that of the academic seminar (indispensable as I believe academics, in their own small way, to be!). That context is today, as it has always been, a community of disciples on a journey, their memory shaped by a particular darkness, who talk with each other about these things that happen; a community who, then as now, are accompanied, and who, although they often cannot understand their company, are still enabled to recognize him in the breaking of bread.[41]

13

All Shall Be Well: Christian and Marxist Hope

Most people would agree that there are differences between Christian hope and Marxist hope. But where do these differences lie, and how are they to be specified? According to one widely accepted account, Marxists entertain high hopes for the future of the world, convinced that nothing can stand in the way of their realization. Christians, on the other hand, entertain no such hopes. They are prepared to tolerate, or endure, the state of the world as it is, hoping only for a future 'beyond' all futures, an eternity that will redress the tragedy of time.

Even if we leave on one side the problem of how to establish criteria on the basis of which an attitude or opinion is to be judged 'Marxist' or 'Christian', this account cannot usefully serve as a starting-point for our discussion because it distorts by obscuring just those features of both Marxist and Christian hope which might make a comparison between them illuminating.

Consider, for example, the question: what is the mechanism or agency by which, on a Marxist or on a Christian account, that which is hoped for is to be brought about? Or again, consider the fact that both Marxist and Christian hope are often criticized for illegitimately 'over-riding' the tragic dimension of human existence.

In this chapter, I want to offer some comments on these two issues, and to suggest some of the ways in which they hang together.

Christ and Prometheus: agents of redemption

In framing my first question, I spoke of mechanism *or* agency, because there are some characterizations of Marxist hope which seem to discount the 'relative autonomy' of human freedom, reducing human agency to an aspect of ineluctable natural process: a form of 'mechanism'. If this were a correct account, then the hoped-for future would be realized *whatever* anybody did about it. There would be no possibility of failure.

However, such views of the matter are distortions or caricatures of Marxist hope. I shall, therefore, assume that human agency, as an aspect of 'natural' agency which is, nevertheless, not reducible to *other* aspects of natural agency, plays an indispensable part in the fulfilment or failure of human hope.

This raises a question of considerable importance: by *whose* agency will the hoped for future be realized? Marx answered this question, in his time, with reference to the industrial proletariat (as at least the 'inaugurating agent' of the definitive stage of the redemptive process), whereas the answers given in contemporary Marxism are very varied. However, no Marxist could conceivably answer the question 'by whose agency?' except by reference to human beings. Man himself is and must be his own redeemer: hence the 'Promethean' strand in Marxism.

Christian characterizations of hope are 'personalist' from the start, in the sense that they assume answers to the question 'By *whom* are we redeemed, are our hopes realized?' to be more fundamental than answers to the question 'By *what*, by what means, are we redeemed?'. And, of course, put like that, there is only one answer: we are redeemed by the grace of God. More specifically, we are redeemed by the grace of God in Christ Jesus our Lord.

All I have done so far is to indicate why the Czech theologian, Jan Lochman, should have said of the question 'Is Christ the opposite of Prometheus?' that it is 'the question at the heart of every Christian-Marxist dialogue'.[1]

'The criticism of religion', said Marx in 1843, 'ends with the doctrine that for man the supreme being is man, and thus with the categorical imperative to overthrow all conditions in which man is a debased, enslaved, neglected and contemptible being.'[2] According to Lochman, the fulfilment of that categorical imperative is 'the true Promethean mission – for Christians and for Marxists'.[3]

Marx, like many Christians, supposed the images of Christ and Prometheus to be necessarily antithetical. And an antithetical account of the relationship between divine grace and human freedom always *expects too little* of human beings. This is still, in practice and in theory, the dominant Christian temptation.

In a later section of this chapter, I shall suggest that Marxian Prometheanism *expects too much* of human beings. And Christians, on the rebound from those dualisms – of matter and spirit, time and eternity, the political kingdom and the kingdom of God – which have too often enabled them simply to tolerate the conditions of human enslavement, may nowadays be tempted to repeat the Marxian mistake.

However, even though the images of Christ and Prometheus are not to be seen as antithetical – for Christ's passion, that which he *underwent*, and which we undergo in him, is nevertheless correctly described as agency, as the *work* of our redemption – neither may these images be simply superimposed, elided, reduced one to another.

By those agency is that which we hope for to be brought about? If we have successfully transcended, in action and thought, the dualisms to which I have referred, we should be able to say, quite simply: by our own effort. But if this is to be a *Christian* answer, a comment on our christology, and not an expression either of *hubris* or of stoic resignation in the face of our servitude, it will be a celebration of God's continual self-gift and an entreaty for that gift's endurance. The effort that we acknowledge to be our own is not some fragile *possession*, some mere artefact or commodity that might crack under the strain, but the historical human form of God's unconquerable grace.

'*An energetic revision of our anthropology*'

Marxist materialism, and the hope which it embodies, represents one way of seeking to transcend the dualisms that I have mentioned. The challenge to Christian thought and action contained in this attempt is spelt out, in a most suggestive manner, in one of those small-print excursuses in the *Church Dogmatics* which are regularly ignored by English theologians patronizing Barth from a safe distance. A summary of this excursus can serve as a bridge passage between my remarks about agency and the question of tragedy.

The discussion occurs in §46, on 'Man as Soul and Body', in *Church Dogmatics*, III/2, in a sub-section on 'the inner unity of human creatureliness', the 'interconnection' of soul and body.[4] Barth locates the 'foundation' of modern monistic, reductionist materialism, not in the wealth of 'scientific' description with which it decked itself out, justified itself, but in the emergence of a particular anthropology, a particular lived account of human essence and excellence: ' "only he who lives in prosperity lives agreeably" – so thinks the big man contentedly and the little man discontentedly, except that the big man is perhaps seldom honest enough to admit to himself that this is how he thinks'.[5]

For Marx, this 'materialism' served only as 'a necessary weapon . . . and polemical ally'. Barth insists, quite rightly, that Marx's 'historical materialism' will be misunderstood if 'we take it to be *grounded*' on this 'ostensibly scientific materialism'. Nevertheless, he also regrets (again, I believe, correctly) that Marxism, as it developed, 'bound itself' as tightly as it did to this philosophical and pseudo-scientific doctrine.[6]

Barth presents 'historical materialism' as 'a critique of the previous course of human history', 'a summons . . . not issued to all, and therefore not to the dominant middle class', and as 'a prediction concerning the future course of the history of mankind'. 'It will not', he says, 'be ideologies that will lead mankind' to that end which is the object of Marxist hope, to a state of affairs in which, with exploitation abolished, 'all other social sicknesses vanish with their common cause', but only 'economic material development as this is rightly understood and therefore directed at the right moment by the right intervention.' 'This', he says, 'was the hope, the eschatology, which Karl Marx gave to his followers.'[7]

One may regret that it 'came about that the scientifically inadmissible deduction that the soul is material because materially conditioned became', as Marxism developed, 'the received dogma of historical materialism'.[8] Barth *does* regret it but, unlike some Christian theologians, he acknowledges the responsibility which Christians bear for this development. 'In all the centuries', he asks (with, we may feel, an element of rhetorical overkill), 'what has [the church] done positively to prevent the rise of that figure of the soulless man? Has it not always stood on the side of the "ruling classes"? . . . And has it not with its doctrine of soul and body at least shown a culpable indifference towards the problem of matter, of bodily life, and therefore of contemporary economics? Has it not made a point of teaching the immortality of the soul instead of attesting to society, with its proclamation of the resurrection of the dead, that the judgment and promise of God compass the whole man?'[9]

Entrapped in its dualisms of soul and body, spirit and matter, time and eternity, Christianity has done little, since the rise of the 'soulless man', and of the structures that enslave him, except 'complain and scold'. Nor, he concludes, 'will it have anything [more constructive] to say in the future . . . so long as it does not undertake an energetic revision of its anthropology . . . in the light of its eschatology'.[10]

I have summarized this passage from the *Church Dogmatics* at what may seem disproportionate length in order to indicate my conviction that British theologians are ill-advised to suppose that they can prudently bypass Barth in their attempts to reappropriate and reconstruct, in our contemporary context, the elements of Christian doctrine. If we are, as Christians, to expect neither too much nor too little of human beings, of ourselves and of others, nothing less is required of us than an 'energetic revision' of our anthropology in the light of our eschatology. (And the 'energy' expended will, of course, be an expenditure as much of heart and muscle as of mind; the laborious production of patterns of relationship, hope and organization, and not merely the elaboration of appropriate theoretical constructs.)

Over-riding the tragic

In *A Matter of Hope*,[11] I agreed that there is, indeed, a tragic dimension to the Marxian view of history, and I therefore rejected George Steiner's claim that 'Marx repudiated the entire concept of tragedy'.[12] But I nevertheless agreed with Steiner that, in the last resort, 'the Marxist creed is immensely, perhaps naively optimistic'.[13] The source of the incoherence at the heart of Marx's vision is to be sought, I suggested, in the abstract character of his account of the 'essence' of the human as 'true community', and of the circumstances in which that 'essence' might be 'born' from its tragic 'pre-history'. This criticism has three principal components.

In the first place, Marx was unduly neglectful of the implications of human mortality: a mortality not only of the individual but also (as the shadow of the bomb helps us to remember) of the species. In the second place, he was unwarrantedly optimistic in his conviction that transformation of structures and circumstances would lead, not simply to a corresponding transformation of consciousness (i.e. of language and mental attitude), but to a *moral* transformation: a transformation of patterns of behaviour and relationship, such that human egotism would have been irreversibly uprooted and 'abolished'. In the third place, Marx's account of the process whereby capitalism was to be overthrown as a process constituting the last, irreversible (and, hence, eschatological) revolution, a revolution to be achieved by an agent whose radical poverty would guarantee his purity, his absence of 'particular interest', is unrealizable and dangerously infected with mythology.

Marx, in provoking people to work and suffer for an unrealizable future, asked too much of them. That is the hallmark of one form of optimism. But the pessimist, the spokesman of apathy and despair, asks too little. He implores us to be 'realistic'. But how are we to avoid always asking too much of each other if we are to break the bounds of present possibility, to sustain the vision and the energy that will enable us to continue to love, and suffer, and struggle, for the transformation of 'all conditions in which man is a debased, enslaved, neglected and contemptible being'? The 'energetic revision of our anthropology in the light of our eschatology' appears to be not merely a daunting but a baffling task.

If 'asking too much' and 'asking too little' do not exhaust the range of options available to us, the alternative cannot consist in cloudy compromise between the two. To suppose that there is something which would count as sensibly and realistically asking for just the right amount is to forget that excessive and inadequate expectation express the antithetical stances of optimism and resignation or despair.

Simply to *accept* the insurmountability of existing 'limits' is to surrender the future (the more 'moderate' case for policies of nuclear deterrence would be an instance of this), whereas optimism, with its sights set on the far horizon, is only too often destructive of that very freedom whose eventual fulfilment it so confidently announces.

Therefore, in *A Matter of Hope*, I tried to sketch an account of Christian hope as that form of the tragic vision which refuses to succumb to the twin temptations of an optimism which sacrifices the present (and forgets the past) and a despair which surrenders the future. On this account, the precariousness of hope arises from its refusal to tolerate either of these destructive renunciations.

Both optimism and despair, I suggested, 'know the answer'. They take it upon themselves to provide the unfinished narrative of human history with the ending which it has not yet, in fact, achieved. They confidently predict the outcome. Hope, as one form of expression of the tragic vision, is more *reticent*. The mood of its discourse is less that of assertion and prediction than of interrogation and request.

Because several of the more constructive critics of *A Matter of Hope* have found all this talk of the 'interrogative mood' either unclear or objectionable, I want to try, in the final section of this chapter, to see if I can clarify the suggestion, spell it out in a little more detail, and do so in a way which will connect the question of how Christianity can avoid illegitimately over-riding the tragic with the remarks that I briefly made at the end of the section on agency.

All manner of thing shall be well

'All shall be well and all shall be well and all manner of thing shall be well.' That (I take it) is, or may be, an expression of Christian hope. It need not be. It could simply be an expression of unwarranted optimism, or facile evasion of particular pain and responsibility. In order for it to be, in practice, an expression of authentically Christian hope, what would the character and context of its utterance have to be? This is the question which, as I take up again some of the topics that I have already touched upon, I now want to consider.

I admit that the Lady Julian's statement seems an improbable candidate to stand as expression of the tragic vision. Its exuber-ance seems at odds with that reticence which I contrasted with the confident eloquence of optimism and despair, both of which claim to 'know the answer', to be able to complete the unfinished narrative of human history. And yet (and this point can serve as a general clue to what follows) a lot perhaps depends on who utters such a statement in what circumstances.

In Julian's case, we remember, the statement occurs in the context of her consideration of 'all the suffering and pain of . . . creation, both spiritual and physical'.[14] If what she says can be said, with integrity, there, in that darkness; if, from within that darkness (and not, as it were, from some imaginary external vantage point for the contemplation of chaos) it is nevertheless the one thing that we find ourselves able to say; then perhaps its utterance, for all the apparent exuberance of form, could be characterized by the kind of reticence that I had in mind.

In the second place, the form of her statement undoubtedly seems to be that of confident, predictive assertion, rather than of interrogation, or request. However, the issue is not to be decided in the abstract, by consideration of grammatical form, but only by attending to particular instances and contexts of use and performance.

The central issue at this point (indeed, I suspect that it is the central issue of the entire discussion) is the doctrine of creative and redemptive grace, the conviction of our creatureliness.

It is this which our hope confesses: that we are creatures of grace. To be a creature is to be a product. And we are, all of us, products of nature and history (or, if you prefer, of natural history). To be creatures of *God*, as all nature and history are, is to be, not merely produced, but to be *absolutely* produced, beyond all structures of causality. And to be creatures of *grace*, as all nature and history are, is to be, not merely produced, but cherished; and not merely cherished, but absolutely and indefeasibly cherished. To confess that we are creatures of grace is to acknowledge effective cherishing to be, we might say, God's mode of production. (It perhaps follows that the fundamental principle of Christian ethics is that production, if it is to be authentically *human* production, whether of things or relationships, ideas or institutions, has in turn to consist of effective cherishing.)

But how does the recognition of our dependence, our creatureliness, *show* itself in the language in which we bring it to speech? Here, the first thing to be said is that it does not necessarily do so in its grammatical form. There is no form of words, no tense or construction, which can be such as to guarantee that whoever uses it, in whatever circumstances, is giving expression to authentically Christian hope. 'God is love', 'Christ is risen', 'I believe in the Holy Spirit': all these statements can be and have been used, without deliberate dishonesty or conscious impropriety, as instruments of evasion, optimism and even oppression.

Correlatively, even statements whose grammatical form, or 'surface structure', is that of assertion or confident prediction concerning the future, concerning the outcome of the processes in which we participate, *may* be, in the actual conditions and circumstances of their use, instances of the acknowledgment of our dependence, our creatureliness – and hence expressions of trust in God, pleas or requests for the realization, the accomplishment, the 'appearance' (to use the language of the Pastoral Epistles) of that which we trust to be the heart of the matter.

Furthermore, if the statements which we utter, and the actions and policies which the statements interpret, have *not* this character of acknowledged creatureliness, of request, then they are not authentic expressions of Christian hope. To put it as briefly and simply as possible, if the assertion that 'all shall be well and all shall be well and all manner of thing shall be well' is not an instance of petitionary prayer, then it is not an expression of Christian hope.

This is what I meant when I said that, if hope is not to topple over into optimism, then the character of its discourse must be more fundamentally a matter of interrogation and request than of assertion and prediction. It is only in our acknowledged dependence on the mystery of *God* that our autonomy, responsibility, freedom and hope are celebrated. The precariousness of Christian hope arises from the fact that nothing is less obvious than that we are creatures of grace. Prometheanism forgets this, as does the setting up of divine grace as the antithesis of promethean effort. Both optimism and pessimism make much more obvious, though ultimately illusory, sense.

In the third place, I criticized 'mechanistic' readings of Marxist materialism for their inability seriously to entertain the possibility of failure. The Lady Julian's statement seems to invite the same criticism inasmuch as, even though its context is the consideration of 'all the suffering and pain of . . . creation', it appears to disallow the possibility of *ultimate* failure: it announces that, in spite of all suffering and slavery, chaos and incapacity, all shall most certainly *eventually* be well.

The theological correlate of necessitarian forms of Marxist hope would be those versions of the doctrine of predestination which invite either passivity and fatalism or the ruthlessness and arrogance of those self-described as God's elect. But, just as there are non-necessitarian forms of Marxism, so also there are forms of the doctrine of election and predestination which hold in tension the conviction that 'ultimate' failure has been ruled out with the recognition that all our projects are threat-

ened with failure and eventually fail; that all our choices are
heavy with ineluctable, unforeseeable and frequently disastrous
consequences. As we continue to contribute to the destruction
which threatens to engulf us, there is no darker or more obscure
knowledge than that despair is unjustified.

In the fourth place, I charged the optimist with asking too
much of human beings, with setting them unrealizable goals.
But Marxist optimism looks modest beside Julian's statement
that *all* shall be well and *all* manner of thing shall be well. We
could, of course, point out that she is not indulging in some
armchair utopian description of future states of affairs; that it
would be possible to make her statement our own while
acknowledging that what *counts* as 'well being' can only be
indicated indirectly, in the analysis of and the struggle against
particular instances of 'ill being': of the debasement, enslavement and neglect of human beings and their needs; in other
words, that 'well being' can only be specified in the 'negating
of negations'.

We could also point out that Christianity, unlike Marxism,
does at least attempt to confront the 'barriers' of egotism and
mortality in its doctrines of justification and resurrection. It
declares (even though its practice usually fails to exhibit the
truth of the declaration) that egotism and mortality are being
and will be dealt with by the historical forms of God's eternal
grace, the human forms of God's fidelity.

Where mortality is concerned, we do not, of course, know
what this means, except indirectly. 'All shall be well.' Therefore
nothing, no circumstance, not even those in which all sanity and
dignity, sense, structure and relationship, are cracked by chaos,
disfigured by darkness, could justify resignation and despair.
Those who know *this* know all that we can yet know of what
'resurrection' means.[15]

Nevertheless, even when all this has been said (and it certainly
needs to be said) the fact remains that we are permanently
tempted, as Christians, to say: No, we do not expect too much
of people, ask too much *from* them, but we ask and expect
everything *for* them: we ask and expect that 'all shall be well'.
I call this a temptation because it is an exceedingly dangerous

way of expressing the truth that Christian hope is a celebration of our creatureliness, not an exercise in self-aggrandizement.

It is dangerous because it too easily allows us to reintroduce antithetical expressions of the relationship between divine grace and human effort, between Christ and Prometheus. Is there not a sense in which, in asking (as we do) everything *for* us, it is only *of* ourselves and of each other that we can ask it? Grace is gift, but it is gift constitutive and transformative of, not intrusive into, ourselves and our circumstances. There is no *deus ex machina* for us, any more than there was for Christ on Calvary. (This may be the point at which to remind ourselves that Julian's statement, though uttered as 'not her own', as the statement of redeeming grace, the voice of Christ, yet was and had to be uttered *by* her, as her conviction.)

This brings me, finally, to some brief remarks on the relation-ship between hope and memory. I said earlier that Marxist hope is able the more easily to over-ride the tragic and to topple over into optimism in the measure that it gives an unduly *abstract* account of the 'essence' of the human as consisting in 'true community'.

The charge of 'abstractness' refers not only to a lack of specificity, to aspects of human need and existence, consider-ation of which is omitted or unduly neglected, but also to the tendency to suppose that, with the 'birth' of humanity from its tragic 'pre-history', the tragic dimension can, with the passage of time and the fading of the 'birth-marks',[16] be obliterated from memory. The dead can be left to bury the dead.

Christians, like Marxists, describe the 'essence' of the human, that which is being brought to birth in history, as 'true community': the communion of saints in the new Jerusalem. But, if this account is not to suffer from the same twofold 'abstractness' then, in the first place, it must always derive its sense primarily from the memory of one actual, historical individual; from the unending attempt to understand him, to 'follow' him, and to discover, in the practice of that discipleship, what 'true community' might mean.

In the second place, no Christian account of the future of humanity will be adequate to the memory of Jesus unless it includes the effective remembrance of *all* past suffering and slavery, debasement and death. To understand Calvary as the place where *God* died is to understand all other places of death as Calvary.

The Marxist has no need to 'justify' the horrors of the past. It is sufficient for his purposes if he can provide them with some plausible explanation. But the question of theodicy, of the justification of past and present suffering, cannot be evaded by a Christian who wishes to claim that all that occurs, in nature and history, is the contingent expression of a God to whom the moral quality of 'goodness' is ascribed.

And yet, all theodicies – in the sense of theoretical attempts to demonstrate the compatibility of 'tragic disorder' with the goodness of God – are suspect as rationalizations of other people's meaningless suffering. Armed with a satisfactory theodicy, the need to contribute, in practice, to the redemptive liberation of human beings is sometimes less sharply felt. Christian hope remains a form of the tragic vision in the measure that it refuses to foreclose the question of the future by postulating, in the imagination, some resolution to past and present tragedy, that in fact, has not been resolved.

Whatever we are able to say and do has to be said and done as a response to, an interpretation of, an expression of solidarity with, what has been and still is *going on* in all weakness, darkness and destruction.

In an interview which he gave in 1947, Karl Barth asked: 'Has the Church realised that Marxist materialism contains something of the message of the resurrection of the flesh?'[17] That 'something' is obscured by the incoherent juxtaposition of a tragic reading of the past with an unwarranted optimism in face of the eventual future; a juxtaposition which has enabled 'orthodox' Marxism to wreak untold practical havoc. Overriding the tragic regularly entails trampling on the tragedians.

If Christianity, for its part, could unlearn its own incoherent juxtaposition (hinted at in my opening remarks) of historical pessimism and eschatological optimism, and could instead recover and sustain the precariousness of its hope, it might proclaim the message of the resurrection of the flesh more effectively, in socially and individually transformative response to, interpretation of and solidarity with, the suffering of human beings.

The focal point of both memory and hope is Gethsemane and Calvary. It was *there* that God died, and resurrection began. To understand all places of darkness and death to be that garden and that hilltop is, therefore, to refuse to give the last word to all that entombs the body and the mind of man. Jesus taught us to address the darkness as 'Father'. But we only learn appropriately to do so at the place where he did it. It is only there, at the heart of darkness, that we are enabled and entitled to pray: 'All shall be well and all shall be well and all manner of thing shall be well.'

Notes

Introduction

1. For an indication of where and how I believe some of the lines between 'philosophy' and 'theology' are to be drawn, cf. 'Doing Theology on Dover Beach', *Theology on Dover Beach*, Darton, Longman & Todd 1979, pp. 5–13.

2. Wolfhart Pannenberg, *Theology and the Philosophy of Science*, Darton, Longman & Todd, 1976, p. 404.

3. S. W. Sykes, 'Systematic Theology', *A New Dictionary of Christian Theology*, ed. Alan Richardson and John Bowden, SCM Press, 1983, p. 560.

4. Eamon Duffy, 'Urbi, but not Orbi . . . the Cardinal, the Church, and the World', *New Blackfriars*, LXVI, 1985, p. 276.

5. Cf. below, pp. 29, 82, 99–106.

6. Cf. below, pp. 6, 23–4, 68–9, 200.

7. Cf. below, pp. 201.

PART I

1. Criticism or Construction? The Task of the Theologian

The annual Aquinas Lecture, delivered at Blackfriars, Oxford, in January 1982, and originally published in *New Blackfriars*, LXIII, 1982, pp. 148–59.

1. J.-B. Metz, *Faith in History and Society*, Burns & Oates 1980, pp. 58–9.

2. Dogmatic Constitution on the Church (*Lumen Gentium*), art. 1.

3. Cf. *Summa Theologiae*, Ia, q.1, art. 7.

4. Cf. R. Bultmann, *Faith and Understanding I*, ed. Robert W. Funk, SCM Press 1969, p. 30. Bultmann here acknowledges his 'debt of gratitude' to G. Kruger for this view of the matter.

2. Theologies at the Service of a Common Tradition

Originally published in Claude Geffré, Gustavo Gutierrez and Virgil Elizondo (eds), *Different Theologies, Common Responsibility: Babel or Pentecost? (Concilium 171)*, T. & T. Clark 1984, pp. 74–83.

1. B. J. F. Lonergan, *Method in Theology*, Darton, Longman & Todd 1972, pp. 326–7.

2. Ibid., p. 301.

3. Nor only in Catholicism. Protestant Christians are apt to overlook the fact that there are Protestant 'classicisms', the theological indicators of which include, for example, certain forms of 'biblicism', and of the appeal to the principle of 'justification by faith' or to the doctrine of the Atonement.

4.Cf. Nicholas Lash, *Voices of Authority*, Sheed & Ward 1976, pp. 84–100.

5. Dogmatic Constitution on the Church (*Lumen Gentium*), art. 1.

6. Cf. Nicholas Lash, *A Matter of Hope: A Theologian's Reflections on the Thought of Karl Marx*, Darton, Longman & Todd 1981, pp. 237, 252.

7. Cf. Acts 11.15.

8. Anyone who supposes that the incarnation of the Word constitutes an exemption to this rule has overlooked distinctions drawn with great care by the Councils of the early church.

9. Cf. R. Panikkar, 'Faith, a Constitutive Dimension of Man', *Journal of Ecumenical Studies*, VIII, 1971, pp. 223–54.

10. Even in 'the shadow of the bomb' these things are more easily said in a climate of relative economic prosperity and political stability than they might be elsewhere. Nevertheless, whatever one's situation, to refrain from saying them would be to refrain from acknowledging one's *own* need for forgiveness.

11. K. Rahner, 'Reflections on the Problems Involved in Devising a Short Formula of the Faith', *Theological Investigations* XI, Darton, Longman & Todd 1974, p. 233. On the general issue, cf. Rahner, 'Pluralism in Theology and the Unity of the Creed in the Church', *Investigations* XI, pp. 11–23; 'The Foundation of Belief Today', *Investigations* XVI, 1979, pp. 3–23.

12. Cf. Nicholas Lash, 'Credal Affirmation as a Criterion of Church Membership', *Church Membership and Intercommunion*, ed. J. Kent and R. Murray, Darton, Longman & Todd 1973, pp. 51–73.

13. Cf. B.J. F. Lonergan, 'Theology in its New Context', *A Second Collection*, Darton, Longman & Todd 1974, pp. 55–67.

14. Cf. K. Rahner, 'Philosophy and Philosophising in Theology', *Theological Investigations* IX, Darton, Longman & Todd 1972, pp. 46–63.

PART II

3. Performing the Scriptures

Originally published in *The Furrow*, in 1982, as one of a series of articles which were collected as Ronan Drury (ed.), *The New Testament as Personal Reading*, Springfield, Illinois, Templegate Publishers 1983.

4. What Authority has our Past?

A revised version of a lecture originally given in Cambridge, in 1979, as one of a series of Open Lectures on the theme of 'Revelation and Authority'.

1. H. Küng, *On Being a Christian*, Collins 1977, p. 20, his stress.

2. M. Kähler, *The So-Called Historical Jesus and the Historic Biblical Christ*, Fortress Press 1964, p. 118.

3. Loc. cit.

4. M. F. Wiles, *Explorations in Theology 4*, SCM Press 1979, p. 64.

5. Loc. cit.

6. For some further comments on 'idealism' and 'realism', see the 'Introduction' to 'Ideology, Metaphor and Analogy', Ch. 7, pp. 95–9 below.

7. I. Kant, 'An Answer to the Question: "What is Enlightenment?" ', *Kant's Political Writings*, ed. Hans Reiss, tr. H. B. Nisbet, Cambridge University Press 1970, p. 54.

8. Paul Ricoeur, 'Ethics and Culture: Habermas and Gadamer in Dialogue', *Philosophy Today*, XVII, 1973, p. 157.

9. Jürgen Habermas, *Zur Logik der Sozialwissenschaften*, Suhrkamp Verlag, Frankfurt ²1970, p. 142; quoted from Thomas McCarthy, *The Critical Theory of Jürgen Habermas*, Hutchinson 1978, p. 147.

10. Karl Marx and Frederick Engels, 'The German Ideology', *Collected Works*, V, Lawrence & Wishart 1976, p. 24.

5. How Do We Know Where We Are?

A revised version of a paper read to the Society for the Study of Theology in March 1982.

1. J. Butler, *The Works of Joseph Butler* I, ed. W. E. Gladstone, Clarendon Press 1896, pp. 303–4.

2. On 'taking a view' in Newman's thought, cf. Nicholas Lash, *Newman on Development*, Sheed & Ward 1975, pp. 34–8, 164–6.

3. J. H. Newman, *The Letters and Diaries of John Henry Newman* XI, ed. C. S. Dessain, Thomas Nelson and Sons 1961, p. 69.

4. Newman, *Letters and Diaries* XXIII, Clarendon Press 1973, p. 227.

5. W. B. Gallie, *Philosophy and the Historical Understanding*, Chatto and Windus 1964.

6. This English translation is given by Gallie on p. 226. The last two lines are uncomfortably evocative of what I have elsewhere described as the 'tourism' model of historical understanding; cf. ch. 6 below, 'What Might Martyrdom Mean?', pp. 82–7.

7. As expounded in R. G. Collingwood, *An Essay on Metaphysics*, Clarendon Press 1940.

8. T. M. Knox, 'Editor's Preface' to R. G. Collingwood, *The Idea of History*, Clarendon Press 1946, p. xviii.

9. Fergus Kerr, 'Rahner Retrospective. III: Transcendence or Finitude', *New Blackfriars*, LXII, 1981, p. 378.

10. Loc. cit.

11. It is of interest that Ernest Gellner's uncompromising rationalism, in *The Legitimation of Belief*, Cambridge University Press 1974, is declared to be a strategy for coping with a situation in which we know ourselves to be 'badly lost, really lost' (p. 10).

12. Cf. Matt 4.8; Luke 4.5

13. Cf. J. H. Newman, 'The Pillar of the Cloud', better known by its opening words: 'Lead, kindly light'.

14. My use of this metaphor is rather different from J. P. Stern's, which has been described as 'perhaps the most valuable single concept for clarifying Barth's handling of narrative' (David Ford, *Barth and God's Story*, Frankfurt, Verlag Peter Lang 1981, p. 55). Stern describes 'the middle distance of realism' as 'the most familiar thing in all literature: it is the fictional creation of *people*, of individual characters and lives informed by what in any one age is agreed to constitute a certain integrity and coherence' (J. P. Stern, *On Realism*, Routledge & Kegan Paul 1973, p. 120; quoted from Ford, loc. cit.). It is a matter of accuracy of narrative depiction, between the 'proximity' of (for example) 'existential' narration and the 'distance' of more timeless or abstract tales that do not intend any such particularity of perspective or description.

My use of the metaphor is ethical, prescriptive, in a way that I take Stern's not to be. Nevertheless, the two uses are not, perhaps, quite alien to each other. It could be that 'realism' (in Stern's sense) in our telling of the story of Jesus the Christ is an important factor in enabling Christians to sustain that 'middle distance' (in my sense) hold on memory and expectation that I am advocating.

15. Cf. Nicholas Lash, *A Matter of Hope*, Darton, Longman & Todd 1981, p. 270.

16. And, of course, of sin. But sin is the refusal of grace, and can only be spoken of, *as* sin, in the light of the history of that which it refuses.

17. This is the burden of Richard Roberts' trenchant criticism of Karl Barth's doctrine of time. In the *Church Dogmatics*, according to Roberts, eternity 'annihilates time', and a 'vast and "unnatural" theological growth chokes and smothers the natural order and its reality' (Richard H. Roberts, 'Karl Barth's Doctrine of Time: its Nature and Implications', *Karl Barth: Studies of his Theological Method*, ed. S. W. Sykes, Clarendon Press 1979, p. 124).

18. Karl Rahner, 'Consecration in the Life and Reflection of the Church', *Theological Investigations*, XIX, Darton, Longman & Todd 1984, p. 60.

19. Rahner, 'History of the World and Salvation-History', *Theological Investigations* V, Darton, Longman & Todd 1961, p. 102.

20. Cf. A. Giddens, *A Contemporary Critique of Historical Materialism, I: Power, Property and the State*, Macmillan 1981, p. 133. Giddens is drawing upon G. J. Whitrow, 'Reflections on the History of the Concept of Time', in J. T. Fraser et al., *The Study of Time*, Berlin, Springer 1972. In my opinion, Whitrow overstates the differences between Christian and Jewish conceptions of time: cf. G. J. Whitrow, *The Nature of Time*, Thames & Hudson 1972, p. 18. Cf. D. M. MacKinnon, 'Some Notes on the Irreversibility of Time', *Explorations in Theology 5*, SCM Press 1976, pp. 90–98.

21. Cf. Giddens, op. cit., p. 38, on 'time-space convergence'.

22. Cf. F. Kermode, *The Genesis of Secrecy*, Harvard University Press 1979,

p. 117. Kermode borrowed the concept from Gallie's *Philosophy and the Historical Understanding*.

23. Kermode, op. cit., p. 145.

24. W. Kasper, 'Theology of History', *Sacramentum Mundi*, III, ed. K. Rahner et al., Burns & Oates 1969, pp. 46–7.

6. What Might Martyrdom Mean?

Originally published in W. Horbury and B. McNeil (eds), *Suffering and Martyrdom in the New Testament*, Cambridge University Press 1981, pp. 183–98.

1. L. E. Keck and G. M. Tucker, 'Exegesis', *The Interpreter's Dictionary of the Bible, Supplementary Volume*, Nashville, Abingdon Press 1976, p. 297.

2. Loc. cit.

3. Cf. K. Stendahl, 'Biblical Theology, Contemporary', *The Interpreter's Dictionary of the Bible*, I, New York and Nashville, Abingdon Press 1962, pp. 418–32.

4. Stendahl, ibid., p. 419.

5. Ibid., p. 422.

6. Ibid., p. 425.

7. Ibid., p. 427.

8. Cf. D. E. Nineham, 'New Testament Interpretation in an Historical Age', *Explorations in Theology 1*, SCM Press 1977, p. 163.

9. I should in fact wish to argue that even textual criticism is inevitably an interpretative activity.

10. B. J. F. Lonergan, *Method in Theology*, Darton, Longman & Todd 1971, p. 157.

11. Loc. cit.

12. Stendahl, 'Biblical Theology', p. 427 (my italics).

13. R. Bultmann, *Existence and Faith*, Collins, Fontana 1964, p. 346.

14. Cf. Stendahl, art. cit., pp. 427, 430.

15. D. H. Kelsey, *The Uses of Scripture in Recent Theology*, SCM Press 1975, p. 186.

16. Ibid., pp. 189–90 (his italics).

17. Cf. ibid., pp. 185–6. As I see it, the main thrust of Kelsey's criticism retains its validity notwithstanding the fact that his manner of making it rests, in part, upon the mistaken belief that there could be non-interpretative 'translation': cf. A. C. Thiselton, *The Two Horizons*, Paternoster Press 1980, pp. 130–33.

18. Nicholas Lash, 'Interpretation and Imagination', *Incarnation and Myth: the Debate Continued*, ed. M. Goulder, SCM Press 1979, pp. 24–5.

19. Barnabas Lindars, 'The Persecution of Christians in John 15.18 – 16.4a', *Suffering and Martyrdom in the New Testament*, p. 61.

20. Brian E. Beck, '*Imitatio Christi* and the Lucan Passion narrative', *Suffering and Martyrdom*, p. 40.

21. Nineham, 'New Testament Interpretation', p. 145.

22. From the Cambridge Board of Graduate Studies description of requirements for the PhD Degree.

23. Nineham, 'The Genealogy in St Matthew's Gospel and its Significance for the Study of the Gospels', *Explorations*, p. 186.

24. J. S. Dunne, *The Way of All the Earth*, Sheldon Press 1973, p. vii.

25. R. Williams, 'Base and Superstructure in Marxist Cultural Theory', *New Left Review*, LXXXII, 1973, p. 14.

26. ibid., p. 15.

27. Keck and Tucker, 'Exegesis', p. 297 (my italics).

28. Stendahl, 'Biblical Theology', p. 425.

29. Nineham, 'The Genealogy in St Matthew's Gospel', p. 186.

30. J. C. O'Neill, 'Did Jesus teach that his death would be vicarious as well as typical?', *Suffering and Martyrdom in the New Testament*, p. 10.

31. Cf. O'Neill, art. cit., p. 27.

32. Cf. J. P. M. Sweet, 'Maintaining the testimony of Jesus: the suffering of Christians in the Revelation of John', *Suffering and Martyrdom*, pp. 101, 103f.

33. W. F. Flemington, 'On the interpretation of Colossians 1.24', *Suffering and Martyrdom*, p. 90.

34. For a sketch of how the argument might go, cf. above Ch. 3, 'Performing the Scriptures'.

PART III

7. Ideology, Metaphor and Analogy

Originally published in Brian Hebblethwaite and Stewart Sutherland (eds), *The Philosophical Frontiers of Christian Theology*, Cambridge University Press 1982, pp. 68–94.

1. D. M. MacKinnon, 'The Conflict Between Realism and Idealism', *Explorations in Theology 5*, SCM Press 1979, p. 164.

2. MacKinnon, 'Absolute and Relative in History', *Explorations*, p. 57. In the same volume, cf. 'Lenin and Theology', p. 22.

3. D. M. MacKinnon, 'Christian and Marxist Dialectic', *Christian Faith and Communist Faith*, ed. D. M. Mackinnon, Macmillan 1953, p. 236.

4. MacKinnon, *Explorations*, p. 57.

5. M. B. Foster, 'Historical Materialism', in MacKinnon, *Christian Faith and Communist Faith*, p. 90. The meaning of terms descriptive of philosophical positions or strategies undergoes, in the course of their history, bewildering shifts and diversifications. I hope that, in this paper, the contexts will sufficiently indicate the sense in which the term 'idealism' is being used.

6. Cf. below, Ch. 8, 'Theory, Theology and Ideology' and, in the context of a more extended discussion of Marx's views on these matters: Nicholas Lash, *A Matter of Hope*, Darton, Longman & Todd 1981, pp. 125–34.

7. MacKinnon, 'Idealism and Realism: An Old Controversy Renewed', *Explorations*, p. 138.

8. Cf. D. M. MacKinnon, *The Problem of Metaphysics*, Cambridge University Press 1974, p. 7.

9. The restless ambivalence of that term is not, I think, without significance.

10. MacKinnon, *Explorations*, p. 153.

11. Cf. ibid., p. 165.

12. It is disappointing to find as sophisticated a philosopher as Anthony Kenny apparently taking for granted a sharp disjunction between 'knowledge' and 'belief': 'I suppose that few people claim to know that there is a God; most believe it as a matter of faith' (Anthony Kenny, *The God of the Philosophers*, Clarendon Press 1979, p. 127).

13. D. M. MacKinnon, 'Metaphysical and Religious Language', *Borderlands of Theology and Other Essays*, Lutterworth Press 1968, p. 214.

14. Brian Wicker, *The Story-Shaped World*, Athlone Press 1975, p. 27. In context, this thesis is far from being as uninformatively abstract as it appears here. It arises from an interpretation of the relationship between the octet and sestet in Gerard Manley Hopkins' sonnet, 'God's Grandeur'.

15. Cf. Wicker, *Story-Shaped World*, p. 7.

16. Wicker, loc. cit.

17. Ibid., p. 2.

18. 'Mr Moore', said a writer in the first number of the *Westminster Review*, in 1824, '*is* a poet, and therefore is *not* a reasoner' (cited with disapproval in J. S. Mill, *Autobiography*, New York, Signet Classics 1964, p. 93). As Gadamer puts it: 'It is not now said that poets tell lies, but that they are incapable of saying anything true' (H.-G. Gadamer, *Truth and Method*, Sheed & Ward 1975, p. 243).

19. As, for example, in the Althusserian manner of distinguishing between 'science' and 'ideology', according to which only the former can furnish knowledge, or in the epistemological strategy for which Ernest Gellner pleads so eloquently in *Legitimation of Belief*, Cambridge University Press 1974.

20. Cf. Paul Ricoeur, *The Rule of Metaphor*, Routledge & Kegan Paul 1978. For an historical sketch of the erosion of metaphor from the cognitive to the merely expressive or decorative, cf. Ricoeur's discussion of 'the decline of rhetoric' (pp. 44–64).

21. *Truth and Method*, p. 87.

22. Wicker, *Story-Shaped World*, p. 12.

23. Loc. cit.

24. Ibid., p. 190.

25. MacKinnon, 'Prayer, Worship, and Life', *Christian Faith and Communist Faith*, p. 248.

26. Loc. cit.

27. Gadamer, *Truth and Method*, p. 301.

28. Ibid., p. 304.

29. Alvin W. Gouldner, *The Dialectic of Ideology and Technology*, Macmillan 1976, p. 75.

30. Cf. Wicker, *Story-Shaped World*, p. 26.

31. B. J. F. Lonergan, *Insight*, Longmans Green 1957, p. 74. 'Deep within us all, emergent when the noise of other appetites is stilled, there is a desire to know, to understand, to see why, to discover the reason, to find the cause, to explain' (ibid., p. 4). This pursuit of truth 'for its own sake', and the practical and moral dilemmas to which it gives rise today, formed the theme of Professor George Steiner's Bronowski Lecture, *Has Truth a Future?*, BBC Publications 1978, which I have elsewhere attempted to 'read' theologically: cf. Nicholas Lash, 'Christology and the Future of Truth', *Incarnation and Myth: the Debate Continued*, ed. Michael Goulder, SCM Press 1979, pp. 224–32.

32. This is one way of reading the phenomenon of so-called 'hellenization': cf. Wolfhart Pannenberg, 'The Appropriation of the Philosophical Concept of God as a Dogmatic Problem of Early Christian Theology', *Basic Questions in Theology 2*, SCM Press 1971, pp. 119–83.

33. This happens even in Pannenberg's interesting essay, 'Analogy and Doxology', *Basic Questions in Theology 1*, SCM Press 1970, pp. 211–38; cf. e. g. pp. 212, 228.

34. Cf. Ricoeur, *Metaphor*, p. 260. It is, of course, possible to take the *term* 'analogy' (rather than, as Ricoeur does, the term 'metaphor') to cover the entire 'family' of problems, while yet remaining sensitive to the distinctions which I am urging: cf. e.g. James Ross, *Portraying Analogy*, Cambridge University Press 1981.

35. Ricoeur, *Metaphor*, p. 196.

36. MacKinnon, *Borderlands*, p. 209.

37. Loc. cit.

38. *Borderlands*, p. 210. Where the Kantian sources of Barth's rejection of that 'invention of Antichrist' (*Church Dogmatics*, I/1, T. & T. Clark 1936, p. x), the *analogia entis*, are concerned, it is worth comparing MacKinnon's comments with Barth's sketch of Kant's rejection of the possibility of metaphysics, 'if one understands by it a theoretical knowledge of objects, the concepts of which must be devoid of corresponding *intuitions*' (*Protestant Theology in the Nineteenth Century*, SCM Press 1972, p. 275, my stress).

39. B. J. F. Lonergan, 'Theology in its New Context', *A Second Collection*. Darton, Longman & Todd 1974, p. 57.

40. Thus, for example, according to Professor Eric Mascall, 'St Thomas's doctrine, because it is rooted in the act of being which is analogically common to God and his creatures, gives us a process by which we can transform the *via negativa* into the *via eminentiae* and . . . can achieve a real knowledge of God in this life' (E. L. Mascall, *He Who Is*, rev. ed., Longmans Green 1966, pp. 225–6). For Mascall, the 'intuition' whereby this achievement is realized is a matter of 'penetrating to the ontological depths' of 'finite beings' so as to 'know them as the creatures of God' (ibid., pp. 91, 85). Armed with this curious metaphor, Mascall elsewhere brings off the most complete misdescription of the 'fundamental thesis' of Lonergan's *Insight* that I have come across: 'knowing always consists in penetrating beneath the immediately apprehended surface of an object into its intelligible *being*. Insight is *in*-sight, seeing

into the observed object' (E. L. Mascall, *The Openness of Being*, Darton, Longman & Todd 1971, p. 84, his stresses).

41. My justification for relying so heavily, in the following pages, on David Burrell's detailed discussion of this text is, therefore, that – although his reading of these Questions confirms my own impression of what Aquinas was 'up to' – I am less concerned with the historical issue than with sketching an account of the 'way of analogy' which coheres with the general account of the critical function of theological reflection which I am offering in this essay, and which does not entail having recourse to any epistemological theory of 'intuitions' of 'being'.

42. D. B. Burrell, *Aquinas: God and Action*, Routledge & Kegan Paul 1979, p. 47.

43. Ibid., p. 48.

44. Burrell, *Aquinas*, p. 6, paraphrasing a favourite passage in Aquinas' commentary on Aristotle's *Metaphysics*: 'Philosophus [differt] a dialectico secundum potentiam' (cf. Burrell, *Aquinas*, pp. 48, 176).

45. H. P. Owen, *The Christian Knowledge of God*, Athlone Press 1969, p. 211.

46. 'Quia de Deo scire non possumus quid sit sed quid non sit, non possumus considerare de Deo quomodo sit sed potius quomodo non sit. Primo ergo considerandum est quomodo non sit, secundo quomodo a nobis cognoscatur, tertius quomodo nominetur' (*Summa Theologiae*, vol. 2; *Existence and Nature of God, Ia., 2–11*, ed. T. McDermott, Eyre & Spottiswode 1964, p. 18). In other words, the *entire* discussion of God's 'attributes' in Questions 3–11 is under the rubric of what God is *not*, the other two topics being considered in Questions 12 and 13.

47. Burrell, *Aquinas*, p. 17.

48. Ibid., p. 16.

49. Ibid., p. 13.

50. Ibid., p. 22.

51. Ibid., p. 27.

52. Ibid., p. 178.

53. Because 'being that can be understood is language', hermeneutics, according to Gadamer, is 'a universal aspect of philosophy, and not just the methodological basis of the so-called human sciences' (*Truth and Method*, pp. 432, 433). Thus, 'hermeneutics is not to be viewed as a mere subordinate discipline within the arena of the *Geisteswissenschaften*' (H.-G. Gadamer, 'On the Scope and Function of Hermeneutical Reflection', *Philosophical Hermeneutics*, University of California Press 1977, p. 19). I endorse Gadamer's insistence on the universality of 'the hermeneutic *phenomenon*' (*Truth and Method*, p. xi, my stress) and therefore acknowledge that there is a hermeneutical 'aspect' to all linguistic activity. However, by distinguishing between 'hermeneutical' and 'metaphysical' theological disciplines I intend to indicate that there are, nevertheless, distinct tasks to be undertaken not all of which are appropriately described from the methodological point of view as 'hermeneutic': cf. Bernard Lonergan's comments on 'hermeneutics' in general

and Gadamer in particular, in *Method in Theology*, Darton, Longman & Todd 1972, pp. 155, 212. The issue here is closely related to that which is central to the debate between Gadamer and Habermas (on which, cf. T. McCarthy, *The Critical Theory of Jürgen Habermas*, Hutchinson 1978, pp. 170–93).

54. Burrell, *Aquinas*, p. 7.

55. Ibid., p. 25. On Aquinas' account, to say that God is radically 'simple' is not to 'name a characteristic of God' but is 'a short-hand way of remarking that no articulated form of expression can succeed in stating anything about God' (Burrell, *Aquinas*, p. 18).

56. The debate between 'Thomists' and those highly critical of 'Thomist' views on these matters is of little interest due to the persistent failure of both parties either to submit Aquinas' texts to detailed and philosophically serious examination or sufficiently to discriminate between the logical and the substantive issues. Cf. e.g., amongst the critics, Keith Ward, *The Concept of God*, Basil Blackwell 1974, pp. 131–58.

57. Burrell, *Aquinas*, p. 55. Burrell's reading is here very close to Herbert McCabe's, according to whom 'analogy', for Aquinas, 'is not a way of getting to know about God, nor is it a theory of the structure of the universe, it is a comment on our use of certain words' (*Summa Theologiae, vol. 3; Knowing and Naming God, Ia. 12–13*, Eyre & Spottiswoode, 1964, p. 106).

58. Burrell, *Aquinas*, p. 55.

59. Ricoeur, *Metaphor*, p. 221.

60. 'No metaphor is the best possible metaphor – you can always say "I didn't really mean that". But some things we say of God even though they are imperfect cannot be improved on by denying them; their imperfection lies in our understanding of what we are trying to mean' (McCabe, *Knowing and Naming God*, p. 107).

61. There are, I appreciate, problems concerning the relationship between analogy and 'dead metaphor', but I do not think that they affect the point at issue. Cf. Ricoeur's discussion of Derrida, in *Metaphor*, pp. 284–95.

62. Burrell, *Aquinas*, p. 10.

63. Loc. cit.

64. Cf. Burrell, *Aquinas*, pp. 59–60.

65. Burrell, *Aquinas*, p. 66, commenting on Question 13, art. 5: 'Non enim possumus nominare Deum nisi ex creaturis . . . Et sic quidquid dicitur de Deo et creaturis, dicitur secundum quod est aliquis ordo creaturae ad Deum ut ad principium et causam.'

66. 'It is creative causality, therefore, that establishes between being and God the bond of participation that makes the relation by analogy ontologically possible' (Ricoeur, *Metaphor*, p. 276). Ricoeur rightly insists on the importance of the fact that, in his mature works, Aquinas pursued the enquiry *not* in terms of 'formal' causality, or 'likeness', but of *dependence in act*. Hence it is, also, that Burrell devotes the second half of his study to an elucidation of Aquinas' 'inherently analogous' (p. 116) notion of '*actus*'. For an admirably lucid summary of Aquinas' extension of the notion of causality to God, cf. McCabe's

appendix on 'Causes', with its insistence that 'God, for St Thomas, is not a causal explanation of the world . . . what we know of him does not serve to explain the world, all that we know of him is that he must exist if the world is to have an explanation' (*Knowing and Naming God*, p. 102).

67. Burrell, *Aquinas*, p. 70, commenting on Question 13, art. 6. This implication is far from obvious to Don Cupitt who, contrasting Aquinas and Kant, claims that, according to the argument of Question 13, 'we can transcend our own subjectivity and see the world as it were from God's point of view' (*The Nature of Man*, Sheldon Press 1979, p. 51). This is grossly misleading. For a more nuanced account of the similarities and differences between Kant and Aquinas on these matters, cf. Karl Rahner, 'Thomas Aquinas on Truth', *Theological Investigations* XIII, Darton, Longman & Todd 1973, pp. 13–31, esp. p. 25.

68. Burrell, *Aquinas*, p. 56.

69. Cf. Ricoeur, *Metaphor*, pp. 277–80.

70. Burrell, *Aquinas*, p. 69.

71. Ibid., p. 75.

72 Is this not true of Aristotle, Kant and Hegel? Burrell is fond of appealing to Wittgenstein's remark: '*Essence* is expressed by grammar . . . Grammar tells what kind of object anything is. (Theology as grammar.)' (*Philosophical Investigations*, I, §§ 371, 373). Cf. Burrell, *Aquinas*, pp. 17, 74, 76.

73. Renford Bambrough, 'Introduction', *Reason and Religion*, ed. S. C. Brown, Cornell University Press 1977, p. 13.

74. This *first* Question is ignored with tedious regularity by philosophers of religion commenting on the second.

75. Bambrough, 'Introduction', p. 16.

76. Burrell, *Aquinas*, p. 67. Two further comments are in order. First, Aquinas sought to moderate the even more radical agnosticism of a 'long tradition of devotion and theology' (T. Gilby, 'Introduction', *Knowing and Naming God*, p. xxxii) represented by the Pseudo-Denys (cf. Q. 13, art. 1, 1; art. 3, 2; art. 12, 1) and, in the generation preceding his own, by Alain of Lille (cf. Q. 13, art. 2, c; art. 6, c) and Maimonides (cf. Q. 13, art. 2, c; art. 5, c).

Secondly, although 'Thomist' treatments of the 'doctrine of analogy' have, in their quest for descriptions of divine attributes, supposed themselves to be far less 'agnostic' than the account of Aquinas' use of analogy offered here, it is by no means clear that they succeeded. This I take to be the drift of Campbell's comments on E. L. Mascall's *Existence and Analogy* (Longmans Green 1949; cf. C. A. Campbell, 'The Doctrine of Analogy', *On Selfhood and Godhood*, Allen & Unwin 1957, pp. 427–33). For drawing my attention to Campbell's study, and for many perceptive comments on earlier drafts of this chapter, I am greatly indebted to Dr J. A. Bradley.

77. Karl Marx, 1859 Preface to 'A Contribution to the Critique of Political Economy', *Early Writings*, Penguin Books 1975, p. 425.

78. Cf. Marx's second thesis on Feuerbach, *Early Writings*, p. 422.

79. MacKinnon, 'Lenin and Theology', *Explorations*, p. 21.

80. Wicker, *Story-Shaped World*, p. 27. I find it interesting that this 'slogan' of Wicker's should closely echo the thrust of Ricoeur's more massively learned study, which appeared in the same year.

8. Theory, Theology and Ideology

Originally published in A. R. Peacocke (ed.), *The Sciences and Theology in the Twentieth Century*, University of Notre Dame Press and Routledge & Kegan Paul, 1981 pp. 209–28.

1. K. Mannheim, *Ideology and Utopia*, Routledge & Kegan Paul 1936, p. 38. As a general indication of questions which 'problems of ideology' put to the theologian, this chapter ranges more widely than my discussion in *A Matter of Hope*, which was more concerned with Marx's thought on these matters.

2. 'How is it possible for man to continue to think and live in a time when the problems of ideology and utopia are being radically raised and thought through in all their implications?' (Mannheim, loc. cit.). I have enough trouble with concepts of 'ideology', in this chapter, without attending to Mannheim's idiosyncratic, and not always consistent, distinction between 'ideology' and 'utopia'.

3. Theologians tempted to see 'formal' sociological analysis as less challenging than Marxist criticism may be walking straight into a trap set by their own deep-rooted tendency towards idealism. In saying this, I have in mind Adorno's criticism of Mannheim: 'The sociology of knowledge expounded by Karl Mannheim ... calls everything into question and criticizes nothing': 'In its neutrality the generalizing order of Mannheim's conceptual world is kindly disposed to the real world; it employs the terminology of social criticism while removing its sting' (T. W. Adorno, 'The Sociology of Knowledge and its Consciousness', *Prisms*, Neville Spearman 1967, pp. 37, 38). According to Adorno, then, Mannheim, in issuing his reminders that no world-view, including Marxism, is immune from ideological distortion, is himself the unwitting 'ideologue' (in Marx's sense) of prevailing patterns of social dominance. In general, on the Frankfurt School's reaction to Mannheim, cf. M. Jay, *The Dialectical Imagination*, Heinemann 1973, pp. 63, 64.

4. K. Marx, 'A Contribution to the Critique of Hegel's Philosophy of Right. Introduction'. *Early Writings*, Penguin Books 1973, p. 243.

5. K. Rahner, 'Ideology and Christianity', *Theological Investigations*, VI, Darton, Longman & Todd 1969, p. 43.

6. Ibid., p. 50.

7. T. F. Torrance, *Theological Science*, Oxford University Press 1969, p. 28.

8. Cf. ibid., p. 188.

9. Loc. cit.

10. A. Fierro, *The Militant Gospel*, SCM Press 1977, p. 239; cf. p. 290.

11. Ibid., p. 412; cf. pp. 317–55.

12. 'The distinction between scientific analysis and ideology has enabled many Christians to look more favourably on Marxism', P. Hebblethwaite, *The Christian-Marxist Dialogue and Beyond*, Darton, Longman & Todd 1974,

p. 97, discussing 'the current vogue of interpreting Marxism in Latin-America according to Althusser'.

13. Which raises the interesting question of the sense in which *such* a use of the distinction is itself 'ideological': cf. A. W. Gouldner, *The Dialectic of Ideology and Technology*, Macmillan 1967, pp. 286–7. 'How are we to understand Althusserian structuralism, not in its self-evaluation as "science", but *as ideology?*', E. P. Thompson, 'The Poverty of Theory', *The Poverty of Theory and Other Essays*, Merlin Press 1978, p. 197.

14. Thompson's sustained, detailed and devastating polemic against Althusser's idealism ('The Poverty of Theory') is all the more interesting in that it is the product of an historian standing, albeit at times uncomfortably, in the Marxist tradition.

15. R. Williams, *Marxism and Literature*, Oxford University Press 1977, p. 11. Cf. B. Wicker, 'Marxist Science and Christian Theology', *New Blackfriars*, LXVIII, 1977, pp. 85–100, on category mistakes arising from the conviction 'that somehow the term "ideology", being an abstract singular, must – ultimately, in the last instance – denote a single idea, or concept' (p. 89).

16. For sketches of which, cf. K. Mannheim, *Ideology and Utopia*, pp. 63–6; M. Seliger, *The Marxist Conception of Ideology*, Cambridge University Press 1977, pp. 13–19.

17. Cf., e.g., J. Plamenatz, *Karl Marx's Philosophy of Man*, Clarendon Press 1975, pp. 86, 211; Seliger, op. cit., pp. 22, 27.

18. L. Kolakowski, *Main Currents of Marxism, I, The Founders*, Clarendon Press 1978, p. 175.

19. Marx, *Early Writings*, p. 422.

20. Christians newly awakened from centuries of mutual intolerance should stir uneasily at all this talk of Marxism now being engaged in 'the purging of eclecticism from itself and the preclusion of united fronts with other discourses at the level of theory' (F. Barker, 'The Morality of Knowledge and the Disappearance of God', *New Blackfriars*, LXVII, 1976, p. 403).

21. Cf. Raymond Williams' discussion of the 1859 Preface to *A Contribution to the Critique of Political Economy*, in *Marxism and Literature*, pp. 75–7.

22. Seliger, op. cit., p. 76.

23. Marx, *Early Writings*, p. 425.

24. Ibid., p. 426. Mannheim, commenting on this passage, seems to me justified in saying that 'the fact that our thinking is determined by our social position is not necessarily a source of error' (*Ideology and Utopia*, p. 111).

25. Williams, *Marxism and Literature*, p. 55; cf. pp. 70–71.

26. 'The entire notion of ideology, then, *as Marx used it*, was most crucially *a critique of the scientific pretensions of the new social science*' (Gouldner, *The Dialectic of Ideology*, p. 8).

27. A Giddens, *Capitalism and Modern Social Theory*, Cambridge University Press 1971, p. 209.

28. Ibid., p. 42.

29. Ibid., p. 209.

30. K. Marx and F. Engels, *The German Ideology*, tr. C. J. Arthur, Lawrence & Wishart 1974, p. 64.

31. Thompson, 'An Open Letter to Leszek Kolakowski', *The Poverty of Theory*, pp. 177–8.

32. Seliger, *The Marxist Conception of Ideology*, p. 26.

33. Thompson, op. cit., p. 119.

34. Ibid., p. 120. Notice the ironic use of geographic metaphors derived from Althusser.

35. Marx, *The German Ideology*, p. 48.

36. For Thompson, theology, together with 'astrology, some parts of bourgeois sociology and of orthodox Stalinist Marxism', is not a 'mature intellectual discipline', but 'a merely-ideological formation' ('The Poverty of Theory', p. 204). Identified with the proposal of 'an ultimate system of truth' (p. 375), it is firmly contrasted with both 'knowledge' (p. 225) and 'reason' (p. 381).

37. T. Eagleton, ' "Decentring" God', *New Blackfriars*, LVII, 1976, p. 149. Thus Jean-Joseph Goux speaks of 'le caractère profondement *théologique* du système monétaire' (*Economie ee Symbolique*, Paris, Le Seuil 1973, p. 63, my stress).

38. L. Althusser, *For Marx*, New Left Books 1977, p. 170.

39. Ibid., p. 231 (my stress). 'Although Althusser seeks to escape the polarity of ideology as "false", and science as "valid", his standpoint in fact rests upon a peculiarly ungrounded version of such a differentiation' (A. Giddens, *Central Problems in Social Theory*, Macmillan 1979, p. 181).

40. Cf. F. Barker, 'The Morality of Knowledge . . .', p. 404.

41. Barker, art. cit., p. 405.

42. Ibid., p. 410. It is not difficult to see why Lucien Goldmann's declaration that 'the phrase *Credo ut intelligam* provides a common basis for Augustinian, Pascalian and Marxist epistemology' (*The Hidden God*, Routledge & Kegan Paul 1964, p. 94) should make him unpopular in certain circles.

43. T. Parsons, *The Social System*, Glencoe, Illinois, Free Press 1951, p. 367.

44. Ibid., p. 349.

45. Williams, *Marxism and Literature*, p. 61.

46. M. B. Foster, 'Historical Materialism', *Christian Faith and Communist Faith*, ed. D. M. MacKinnon, Macmillan 1953, p. 88.

47. Cf. Giddens, *Capitalism*, pp. 208–9; Plamenatz, op. cit., pp. 211ff; Seliger, op. cit., pp. 32–3; Williams, op. cit., p. 58.

48. Mannheim, *Ideology and Utopia*, pp. 150–51.

49. Ibid., p. 165.

50. Gouldner, *The Dialectic of Ideology*, p. 14.

51. Ibid., p. 75.

52. Cf. K. Rahner, 'Experience of God Today', *Theological Investigations* XI, Darton, Longman & Todd 1964, pp. 149–65.

53. Seliger, *The Marxist Conception of Ideology*, p. 21.

54. Gouldner, *The Dialectic of Ideology*, p. 45.

55. Ibid., p. 49; cf. pp. 214–15.

56. Ibid., p. 144.

57. 'Scientific' Marxists would presumably resist this suggestion. Yet, in the course of doing just that, one of them asserts that, 'because Marxism is a scientific practice, a *praxis*, it is only in the process of changing the world that it can constitute itself as a science' (Barker, 'The Morality of Knowledge . . . ', p. 407). In which case, it may be some time before this science is 'constituted'.

58. Althusser, *For Marx*, p. 12.

59. Cf. K. Rahner, 'Thoughts on the Possibility of Belief Today', *Theological Investigations*, V, Darton, Longman & Todd 1966, p. 12.

60. Cf. Wicker, 'Marxist Science and Christian Theology', p. 95.

61. Ibid., p. 97.

62. Ethical systems that view morality, ideologically, as 'some "autonomous region" of human choice and will, arising independently of the historical process' (Thompson, 'The Poverty of Theory', p. 363) invite Marxist criticism, but do not excuse Marxist silence: 'The project of Socialism is guaranteed by *nothing* . . . but can find its own guarantees only by *reason* and through an open *choice of values*. And it is here that the silence of Marx, and of most Marx*isms*, is so loud as to be deafening' (loc. cit.).

63. F. Barker, 'Science and Ideology', *New Blackfriars*, LVIII, 1977, p. 477.

64. Ibid., p. 476.

65. Loc. cit. Marxism may 'say firmly that there is no God' (Barker, 'The Morality of Knowledge . . . ', p. 405), but firmness of assertion is no substitute for argument.

66. Thompson, 'The Peculiarities of the English', *The Poverty of Theory*, p. 79; cf. pp. 119ff., 275–6.

67. Williams, *Marxism and Literature*, p. 83.

68. Ibid., p. 86.

69. Ibid., p. 87.

70. Ibid., p. 55.

71. Gouldner, *The Dialectic of Ideology*, p. 51.

72. Cf. Ch. 7 above, 'Ideology, Metaphor and Analogy'.

73. Gouldner, op. cit., p. 49.

74. Cf. M. W. Wartofsky, *Feuerbach*, Cambridge University Press 1977, p. 448.

75. E. Bloch, 'Changing the World, Marx's *Theses on Feuerbach*', *On Karl Marx*, New York, Seabury Press 1971, p. 81.

76. D. M. MacKinnon, *Explorations in Theology 5*, SCM Press 1979, p. 165.

PART IV

9. Human Experience and the Knowledge of God

The thirteenth annual Wiseman Lecture, delivered at Oscott College on 8 October 1984.

1. Cf. Brian Hebblethwaite, 'The Experiential Verification of Religious Belief in the Theology of Austin Farrer', *For God and Clarity, New Essays in Honor of Austin Farrer*, ed. Jeffrey C. Eaton and Ann Loades, Allison Park Pennsylvania, Pickwick Publications 1983, pp. 163–4.

2. Richard Swinburne, *The Existence of God*, Clarendon Press 1979, p. 244.

3. William James, *The Varieties of Religious Experience*, Fontana 1960, pp. 428–9.

4. Ibid., p. 478.

5. Ibid., p. 62.

6. Ibid., p. 50.

7. Loc. cit.

8. Ibid., p. 69.

9. Ibid., p. 78.

10. Ibid., p. 29.

11. Cf. ibid., pp. 69, 490–91, 498.

12. Martin Buber, *I and Thou*, tr. Walter Kaufman, T. & T. Clark 1970, p. 93.

13. Friedrich von Hügel, *The Mystical Element of Religion*, I, second edition Dent 1923, p. 52.

14. Cf. F. von Hügel, 'The Idea of God', *Essays and Addresses on the Philosophy of Religion, Second Series*, Dent 1926, pp. 143–4.

15. Something of an understatement! Cf. Kasper's brief discussion of Greek mythology and philosophy in support of the contention that 'The question of . . . threeness, as much as the question of unity, is a primordial question of . . . mankind' (Walter Kasper, *The God of Jesus Christ*, SCM Press 1983, p. 236; also Paul Tillich, *Systematic Theology III*, Nisbet 1964, p. 312.

16. Cf. K. Rahner, *Theological Investigations* XI, Darton, Longman & Todd 1974, pp. 157–8; *Theological Investigations* XVIII, 1984, pp. 200–3.

10. 'Son of God': Reflections on a Metaphor

Originally published in Edward Schillebeeckx and Johannes-Baptist Metz (eds), *Jesus, Son of God? (Concilium 153)*, T. & T. Clark 1982, pp. 11–16.

1. For the debates referred to in the opening paragraph, cf. e.g. J. Hick (ed.), *The Myth of God Incarnate*, SCM Press 1977; M. Goulder (ed.), *Incarnation and Myth: The Debate Continued*, SCM Press 1979. As random illustrations of the assumptions summarized in the first paragraph of the section on 'Metaphor', cf. Don Cupitt, *Taking Leave of God*, SCM Press 1980, p. 122; Roger Trigg, *Reason and Commitment*, Cambridge University Press 1973. On the ontology of metaphor sketched in that section, cf. Cornelius Ernst, *Multiple Echo*, Darton, Longman & Todd 1979; 'Meaning and Metaphor in Theology', *New Blackfriars*, LXI, 1980, pp. 100–12. For the account of the logical status of the concept of 'God' in the section on 'God', cf. Peter Geach, *God and the Soul*, Routledge & Kegan Paul 1969, pp. 57–9, 100–16. For the sake of simplicity, in this chapter, I am taking the term 'metaphor' as a general term for the family of problems that, in a more detailed examination, would require

breaking down into questions of 'metaphor' and questions of 'analogy': cf. above, 'Ideology, Metaphor and Analogy'.

2. Ernst, *Multiple Echo*, p. 55.

3. Ernst, 'Meaning and Metaphor in Theology', p. 109.

4. Cf. K. Rahner, 'Theos in the New Testament', *Theological Investigations* I, Darton, Longman & Todd 1961, pp. 79–148.

5. On this point of logic, I must disagree with Claude Geffré, in his interesting article, ' "Father" as the proper Name of God', in Johannes-Baptist Metz and Edward Schillebeeckx (eds), *God as Father? (Concilium 143)*, T. & T. Clark 1981, pp. 43–50.

6. Cf. Martin Hengel, *The Son of God*, SCM Press 1976, p. 21.

7. Ibid., pp. 92–3.

11. Easter Meaning

Originally published in *Heythrop Journal*, XXV, 1984, pp. 3–18.

1. A. M. Farrer, 'Infallibility and Historical Revelation', *Infallibility in the Church: An Anglican-Catholic Dialogue*, Darton, Longman & Todd 1968, p. 21.

2. Ibid., p. 21.

3. Ibid., p. 22.

4. Ibid., p. 23.

5. H. A. Williams, *Some Day I'll Find You*, Mitchell Beazley 1982, p. 369.

6. Ibid., p. 369.

7. Ibid., p. 370.

8. Ibid., p. 370, my stress.

9. Ibid., p. 371.

10. J. A. Baker, review in *Journal of Theological Studies*, XXIX, 1978, p. 297.

11. Cf. M. D. Goulder, 'Jesus, the Man of Universal Destiny', *The Myth of God Incarnate*, ed. John Hick, SCM Press 1977, p. 59.

12. Cf. Maurice Wiles, 'A Survey of Issues in the *Myth* Debate' and Leslie Houlden, 'A Wider Framework', *Incarnation and Myth: the Debate Continued*, ed. M. D. Goulder, SCM Press 1979, pp. 9, 105–7.

13. G. Turner, 'He Was Raised and Has Appeared: Evidence and Faith', *New Blackfriars*, LVIII, 1977, p. 161. Turner was responding to Fergus Kerr, 'Exegesis and Easter', *New Blackfriars*, LVIII, 1977, pp. 108–21, who, in turn, was replying to Michael Dummett, 'Biblical Exegesis and the Resurrection', *New Blackfriars*, LVIII, 1977.

14. Loc. cit.

15. Cf. Dummett, art. cit., p. 64.

16. Turner, art. cit., p. 166. I am not at all sure what would count as 'seeing', in 'the ordinary sense', a dead man walking through walls.

17. In the next few paragraphs, I have used some material from Nicholas Lash, *Theology on Dover Beach*, Darton, Longman & Todd 1979, pp. 174–8.

18. I have in mind the phrase from the Easter Sequence: 'Mors et vita duello conflixere mirando.'

19. K. Barth, *Church Dogmatics*, IV/1, T. & T. Clark 1956, pp. 157–210.

20. *Church Dogmatics*, IV/2, T. & T. Clark 1958, pp. 20–154.

21. Cf. e.g. Maurice Wiles, *Faith and the Mystery of God*, SCM Press 1982, p. 59.

22. P. F. Strawson, *Logico-Linguistic Papers*, Methuen 1971, p. 196.

23. Williams, *Some Day I'll Find You*, p. 371.

24. Ibid., p. 370.

25. The historian is a specialist and, as I have already suggesed, such judgments are not, fundamentally, 'specialist' judgments at all: cf. Ch. 6 above, 'What Might Martyrdom Mean?' p. 88.

26. E. Schillebeeckx, *Jesus: An Experiment in Christology*, Collins 1979, p. 645.

27. Ibid., p. 645. Aquinas' treatment of the matter suggests that the 'experience' in question is to be understood in terms of (we might say) 'seeing the point' about something. That metaphor seems neatly to indicate the *cognitive*, interpretative element in that to which the visual imagery refers. Cf. *Summa Theologiae*, IIIa, q. 55, art.2.

28. K. Rahner, *Theological Investigations* IV, Darton, Longman & Todd 1966, p. 128.

29. Cf. Rowan Williams, *Resurrection*, Darton, Longman & Todd 1982, pp. 76–97; on the resurrection meals, cf. pp. 39–40, 108–9, 115–16. I am grateful to Dr Williams for his perceptive comments on an earlier draft of this chapter.

30. Williams, *Some Day I'll Find You*, p. 369.

31. Turner, 'He Was Raised and Has Appeared', p. 165.

32. Cf. X. Léon-Dufour, *Resurrection de Jésus et Message Pascal*, Paris, Editions du Seuil 1971; also G. O'Collins, *The Easter Jesus*, Darton, Longman & Todd 1973, p. 51.

33. We are further constrained by what we take to constitute, in different circumstances, appropriate *responses* to such experience: stoic resignation, for instance, or transformative struggle. It has ever been so. Dr Christopher Rowland has suggested to me that the move away from 'resurrection-language' in the Fourth Gospel, for example, was in part indicative of a shift towards acceptance of the political *status quo*: a shift to supposing that God, as it were, 'lifts us from' the world rather than acts (and enables us to act) to transform the world.

34. On the distinction implied here between optimism, hope and despair, cf. Ch. 13 below, 'All Shall be Well: Christian and Marxist Hope' pp. 207ff.

12. The Church's Responsibility for the Future of Humanity

A lecture given at the Seminary of the Immaculate Conception, Huntington, New York, in October 1984.

1. Wilfrid Ward, 'The War Spirit and Christianity', *Last Lectures by Wilfrid Ward*, Longmans Green 1918, p. 258. For 'Northern Ireland', Ward had 'letting Ulster arm'; and for 'radical feminists', 'the suffragettes'.

2. Ibid., p. 259.

3. Ibid., p. 262.

4. Ibid., p. 261.

5. Ibid., p. 272.

6. G. W. F. Hegel, *Phenomenology of Spirit*, tr. A. V. Miller, Clarendon Press 1977, p. 493.

7. Cf. Stewart Sutherland, *God, Jesus and Belief: The Legacy of Theism*, Blackwell 1984, p. 162.

8. Alasdair MacIntyre, *After Virtue*, Duckworth 1981, p. 204.

9. Cf. Nicholas Lash, *A Matter of Hope*, Darton, Longman & Todd 1981, p. 238.

10. Cf. Robert N. Bellah, 'Civil Religion in America', *Beyond Belief: Essays on Religion in a Post-Traditional World*, New York, Harper & Row 1970, pp. 168–86. This celebrated essay was first produced in 1966. In the light of criticisms it provoked, Bellah sought to defend himself 'against the accusation of supporting an idolatrous worship of the American nation . . . I conceive of the central tradition of American civil religion not as a form of self-worship but as the subordination of the nation to ethical principles that transcend it and in terms of which it should be judged' (p. 168).

11. Cf. *A Matter of Hope*, pp. 258–62.

12. Jonathan Edwards, *The Great Awakening. The Works of Jonathan Edwards*, IV, ed. C. C. Goen, Yale University Press 1972, p. 536.

13. M. Darrol Bryant, 'America as God's Kingdom', *Religion and Political Society*, ed. The Institute of Christian Thought, New York, Harper & Row 1974, p. 86.

14. Loc. cit.

15. Roger White, 'Notes on Analogical Predication and Speaking About God', *The Philosophical Frontiers of Christian Theology*, ed. Brian Hebblethwaite and Stewart Sutherland, Cambridge University Press 1982, p. 219.

16. Cf. Jürgen Moltmann, 'Political Theology', *The Experiment Hope*, SCM Press 1975, p. 111.

17. Cf. *A Matter of Hope*, pp. 243–9.

18. Cf. Anthony Giddens, *A Contemporary Critique of Historical Materialism, Vol. I: Power, Property and the State*, Macmillan 1981.

19. Ibid., p. 4.

20. Cf. *A Matter of Hope*, pp. 238, 252.

21. J. H. Newman, *Apologia Pro Vita Sua*, Longman Green 1864, p. 378.

22. Cf. K. Rahner, 'The Hermeneutics of Eschatological Assertions', *Theological Investigations* IV, Darton, Longman & Todd 1966, pp. 328, 334.

23. Rahner, 'On the Theology of Hope', *Theological Investigations* X, 1973, p. 258.

24. Christianity thus 'acts as the guardian of "*docta ignorantia futurae*" for the history of mankind in general', Rahner, *Theological Investigations* XIII, 1975, p. 33. Cf. 'The Question of the Future', *Theological Investigations* XII, 1974, p. 181–201.

25. Cf. Giddens, op. cit., pp. 129–35.

26. Ibid., p. 252.

27. Cf. MacIntyre, *After Virtue*, p. 146. The cynical misuse of the notion of friendship to denote relationships within political power-blocs is, of course, sheer mystification.

28. *After Virtue*, p. 237.

29. Ibid., p. 245.

30. Cf. his account of 'what they set themselves to achieve' (p. 244).

31. Cf. Richard Rorty, 'Pragmatism, Relativism, and Irrationalism', *Proceedings and Addresses of the American Philosophical Association* LIII, 1980, pp. 719–38, quoted in Richard J. Bernstein, *Beyond Objectivism and Relativism*, Blackwell 1983, p. 203.

32. Richard Rorty, *Philosophy and the Mirror of Nature*, Blackwell 1980, p. 359.

33. Bernstein, op. cit., p. 229.

34. Ibid., p. 228.

35. Dogmatic Constitution on the Church (*Lumen Gentium*), art. 26.

36. K. Rahner, *Theological Investigations* VII, Darton, Longman & Todd 1971, p. 92.

37. K. Rahner, *The Shape of the Church to Come*, SPCK 1974, p. 108. Cf. 'Basic Communities', *Theological Investigations* XIX, 1984, pp. 159–65.

38. *Lumen Gentium*, art. 1.

39. Cf. Giddens, op. cit., pp. 147, 189.

40. Ibid., p. 202.

41. Cf. Luke 24.13–35.

13. All Shall be Well: Christian and Marxist Hope

Originally published in *New Blackfriars*, LXIII, 1982, pp. 404–15.

1. Quoted from James Bentley, *Between Christ and Marx*, Verso 1982, p. 109.

2. Karl Marx, 'A Contribution to the Critique of Hegel's Philosophy of Right. Introduction', *Early Writings*, Penguin Books 1975, p. 251.

3. Cf. Bentley, op. cit., p. 110.

4. Cf. Karl Barth, *Church Dogmatics*, III/2, T. & T. Clark 1960, pp. 383–90.

5. Barth, op. cit., p. 386.

6. Cf. ibid., p. 387.

7. Ibid., p. 388.

8. Ibid., p. 389.

9. Ibid., pp. 389–90.

10. Ibid., p. 390.

11. Nicholas Lash, *A Matter of Hope*, Darton, Longman & Todd 1981. Cf. especially pp. 250–80.

12. George Steiner, *The Death of Tragedy*, Faber, second edition 1963, p. 4.

13. Ibid., p. 342.

14. Julian of Norwich, *Revelations of Divine Love*, Penguin Books 1966, p. 103. I have preferred not to take the 'motif' statement from this modern translation, where it appears, in the form taken up by the author of *Jesus Christ, Superstar*, as: 'It is all going to be all right; it is all going to be all right; everything is going to be all right' (loc. cit.).

15. Cf. above Ch. 11 'Easter Meaning'.

16. Cf. Karl Marx, 'Critique of the Gotha Programme', *Political Writings, III: The First International and After*, Penguin Books 1974, p. 213.

17. At least, I *think* that this is what Barth asked! Bentley gives it as the assertion that 'In the materialism of Marxism some part of the resurrection of the flesh lies hidden' (op. cit., p. 68). He took it from F. W. Marquardt, *Theologie und Sozialismus. Das Beispiel Karl Barths*, Munich, second edition 1972, p. 15. Marquardt took it from W. D. Marsch, ' "Gerechtigkeit im Tal des Todes". Christlicher Glaube und Politische Vernunft im Denkens Karl Barths', *Theologie Zwischen Gestern und Morgen, Interpretationen und Anfragen zum Werk Karl Barths*, ed. W. Dantine and K. Lüthi, Munich 1968, p. 181. Marsch took it from *Karl Barth. 'Der Gotze Wackelt': Zeitkritische Aufsätze, Reden und Briefe von 1930 bis 1960*, ed. K. Kupisch, Berlin 1961, pp. 120–21, where it appears as: 'Hat die Kirche eingesehen, dass im Materialismus des Marxismus etwas steckt von der Botschaft von der Auferstehung des Fleisches?'. Kupisch was reprinting an interview which first appeared in 1947 in a German evangelical periodical entitled *Unterwegs*, which (so far as I can discover) is to be found in four libraries in Germany and none in Britain.

Let this serve as a concluding cautionary parable on the perils of hermeneutics!

Index

Absolutism, 10, 66
Agnosticism, 107, 113f.
Althusser, L., 123, 124, 129, 131, 132
Analogy, 95ff., 106ff.
Anscombe, G. E. M., 108
Aquinas, Thomas, 4, 12, 97, 107ff.
Assumption of Mary, 167f., 172, 181
Authority, 46ff., 55f.; models of, 58f.
Autobiography, 10, 29, 82ff., 101ff., 117, 136f.
Autonomy, of the creature, 134; and freedom, 56ff., 203

Baker, John Austin, 170
Barr, James, 55
Barth, Karl, 4, 114, 177, 205f., 214
Bernstein, Richard, 198
Bloch, Ernst, 138
Buber, Martin, 150f.
Bultmann, Rudolf, 15, 78, 83, 168
Burrill, D. B., 109ff., 114
Butler, Bishop, 62, 65, 74

Calvary, 9, 15, 135, 180, 195, 213f.
Catholicity, 25, 30, 32
Christian practice, as interpretative action, 42ff., 90f.; and social policy, 188
Church, congregational and catholic, 199f.; as sacrament, 5f., 8, 11f., 23f., 31, 48, 191, 200
Collingwood, R. G., 63

Creation, and production, 142ff., 153ff., 164f., 210; and redemption, 23, 67f.

Descartes, René, 144
Despair, 65f., 74, 184f., 195, 198, 207f., 212
Dualism, of matter and spirit, 71ff., 130, 142ff., 192, 204, 206
Dunne, John, 83f.
Dummett, Michael, 173
Durkheim, E., 163

Eagleton, Terry, 128
Ernst, Cornelius, 161
Eschatology, and anthropology, 23, 205f.; see also Hope
Eucharist, 45f., 181, 199ff.

Faith, and iconoclasm, 11f.; and knowledge, 97, 123f., 132; as quest, 11, 60f.; unity of, 19ff., 26ff.; see also Theological reflection
Farrer, Austin, 143, 167f.
Feuerbach, L., 97, 125f., 134, 163
Fierro, Alfredo, 123f.
Flemington, W. F., 89f.
Foster, Michael, 95
Fundamentalism, 42, 59

Gadamer, H., 91, 100, 104, 198
Gallie, W. B., 63
Geach, P. T., 108

Gethsemane, 9, 15, 74, 135, 195, 215
Giddens, Anthony, 193, 196
God, and analogy, 106ff.; death of, 214, 215; dependence on, 152; as Father, 14f., 53, 162, 164, 215; and incarnation, 169f.; knowledge of, 8f., 132; mystery of, 15, 26f., 38, 45f., 51, 53, 64, 71, 100, 106, 131, 143, 152, 164, 170; not a particular entity, 14, 72f.; 148f.; not a proper name, 159, 162f.; and religious experience, 147ff.; as spirit, 72, 74; as Trinity, 156
Gouldner, A. W., 131, 132, 137
Grace, 11, 14; and freedom, 204; as God's self-gift, 27f., 212f.; history of, 6, 66f.; as mystery, 6, 17

Habermas, Jürgen, 57, 198
Hebblethwaite, Brian, 143
Hegel, G. W. F., 187, 192
Heidegger, Martin, 64
Hengel, Martin, 165
History, evolutionary views, 194; meaning of, 64, philosophy of, 63f.; theology of 62ff.
Holy Spirit, 15, 53, 155
Hope, 16, 23, 26, 27f., 55, 97, 151, 161, 166, 184, 191, 197f., 202ff., 209ff.; and the interim, 195f, 199; and middle distance, 66f.; and nescience, 194ff.; unity in, 28; *see also* Despair, Optimism
Human nature, 26, 205ff.; as narrative, 23, 72f.; as symbolic action, 5

Idealism, 19, 91, 124, 130; and realism, 50f., 95ff.
Ideology, 16, 96, 98, 102, 105, 118, 120ff.
Idolatry, 9, 10f., 135; and absolutization, 10, 26, 116; and social messianism, 189ff.

Illusion, 10f., 15, 17, 52, 114, 119, 137
Interpretation, 10, 25, 37ff.; and application, 38, 75; as discovery, 41, 73, 96ff.; and exegesis, 75ff.; performance as, 40ff., 85, 90; poles of, 42, 89ff.; and translation, 39, 77ff.; and truth, 40, 76, 87ff.; and use, 40, 85

James, William, 143f., 145ff.
Jesus Christ, 5, 16, 27, 29, 38f., 44, 51, 58, 163, 195ff.; event of, 58, 170, 177f.; following of, 46, 53, 60, 74, 91, 213; memory of, 69ff.; obedience of, 60f., 180, 196; passion of, 9, 15, 61, 80, 87f., 91, 102f., 191, 201; presence of, 70f., 201; and Prometheus, 203f., 211, 213; 'Son of God', 158ff.; unsurpassable significance of, 52f., 156; *see also* Resurrection
Julian of Norwich, Lady, 209, 211ff.

Kähler, Martin, 49f.,
Kant, I., 56, 96, 107, 109, 153
Kasper, Walter, 74
Kelsey, David, 78
Kermode, Frank, 73
Kingdom of God, 6, 24ff., 53
Küng, Hans, 47, 49

Language, of action, 5, 48f.; conditioning and determination of, 134f.; immobility of, 54f., 57
Léon-Dufour, X., 183
Liberalism, 21ff., 48f.
Lindars, Barnabas, 80
Lochman, Jan, 203
Lonergan, Bernard, 20, 108, 174

MacIntyre, Alasdair, 188, 197
MacKinnon, Donald, 95f., 98, 102, 107
Mailer, Norman, 99f.
Mankind, redemption of, 9, 12;

unity of, 8, 22ff.; *see also* Human nature

Mannheim, Karl, 120f., 126, 131

Marx, Karl (Marxism), 56, 91, 95, 115, 121, 124, 125ff., 192, 202ff.; critique of religion, 133ff.

Meaning, of Christianity, 7f.; definitive, 44; not embodied in texts, 84ff., and metaphor, 159f.; past and present, 39, 55, 75ff.; and truth, 87ff., 167ff., 182; *see also* Interpretation

Memory, 25, 32, 67, 193; conditions of, 70f.

Metaphor, and analogy, 95ff., 106; and literal description, 110f., 160f.

Metz, J. B., 4, 6

Narrative, 124, identity and difference, 30, 44f., 183; and making sense, 98f., 102, 160; and metaphysics, 99ff., 117f.; and narratability, 73ff.; *see also* Autobiography, Human nature

Newman, J. H., 62, 64, 99, 115, 195

Nietzsche, Friedrich, 64

Nihilism, 9f.

Nineham, Dennis, 76, 82f., 86

O'Neill, John, 87

Optimism, 65f., 73f., 184, 194f., 198, 208f.

Owen, H. P., 108

Parsons, Talcott, 130

Power, 22, 190, 191ff.

Rahner, Karl, 29, 68, 122, 180, 196, 200

Rationalism, 56, 100; as adolescence, 60; and fideism, 114f.

Religious experience, 143ff.

Resurrection, 161, 169–84, 196, 212ff.; and the empty tomb, 174, 182; evidence for, 173, 179ff.; and Marxist materialism, 214

Revelation, 49ff., 97

Ricoeur, Paul, 56, 106

Robbe-Gillet, Alain, 99f.

Rorty, Richard, 187f.

Salvation, history of, 67ff.

Scripture, as constitution, 43f.; interpretation of, 7, 39f.; performance of, 42ff.; reading of, 30

Schillebeeckx, Edward, 180

Schleiermacher, F. D. E., 122

Seliger, M., 126, 127, 132

Silence, and suffering, 105, 155f.

Steiner, George, 207

Stendahl, Krister, 76ff., 82, 86

Swinburne, Richard, 144, 151

Theological pluralism, 18ff.

Theological reflection, and faith, 7, 31ff., 89; and religious practice, 101, 103, 115, 137

Theology, academic, 4, 7f.; as common responsibility, 4ff., 12; and grammar, 109, 113, 116; as mediating interpretation, 31f.; and self-criticism, 16, 137, 190; systematic and exegesis, 75, 79f.

Thompson, E. P., 127, 128

Torrance, T. F., 122

Tradition, 18ff., 53ff.

Tragedy (the tragic), 15, 27, 95, 103, 105, 155, 202, 207f., 213f.

Trinity, doctrine of, 53, 156

Truth, as construction, 9ff., 96ff.; as discovery, 9ff., 96ff.; and freedom, 11, 61; grounds of, 10, 138; and meaning, 87ff., 167ff., 182; and verification, 104, 114ff.

Turner, Geoffrey, 173f., 181, 182

Unity, of creed, 28ff.; of faith, 19ff, 26ff.; of mankind, 8, 22ff.

Vatican II, 6, 23, 199

Von Hügel, Friedrich, 151f.

Ward, Wilfrid, 186f., 189
Wicker, Brian, 98, 99f., 134
Wiles, Maurice, 49f.
Williams, Harry, 167ff., 172, 179,
  181

Williams, Raymond, 84f., 90, 124
Wittgenstein, L., 64
Word, incarnation of, 15, 53, 156,
  178, 188; and resurrection,
  170f., 177